The Hill on the Net

Congress Enters the Information Age

The Hill on the Net

Congress Enters the Information Age

───────────── ★ ─────────────

Chris Casey

Technology and Communications Committee
Senate Democratic Policy Committee, Washington, D.C.

AP PROFESSIONAL

Boston   San Diego   New York
London   Sydney   Tokyo   Toronto

AP PROFESSIONAL
1300 Boylston Street, Chestnut Hill, MA 02167
World Wide Web site at http://www.apnet.com

An Imprint of ACADEMIC PRESS, INC.
A Division of HARCOURT BRACE & COMPANY

United Kingdom Edition published by
ACADEMIC PRESS LIMITED
24–28 Oval Road, London NW1 7DX

Casey, Chris.
  The Hill on the Net: Congress Enters the Information Age / Chris Casey.
          p.   cm.
      Includes bibliographical references and index.
      ISBN 0-12-162870-1
      1. United States. Congress—Computer network resources. I. Title.
      JK1108.C37   1996
      328.73'00285'467—dc20   96-3547
                                                       CIP

Senior Editor—Jenifer Niles
Production Manager—Karen Pratt
Production Editor —Barbara Northcott
Editorial Assistant—Jacqui Young
Cover Design—MicroArts Corporation
Composition—Parker-Fields Ltd.

Printed in the United States of America
96   97   98   99   IP   9   8   7   6   5   4   3   2   1

Contents

━━━━━━━━━━━━ ★ ━━━━━━━━━━━━

Acknowledgments

Senator Edward Kennedy, Jonathan Gourd, Eric Loeb, John Mallery, Jock Gill, Senator Bill Frist, Senator Pat Leahy, Representative Charlie Rose, Representative Vern Ehlers, Mike Bartell, Jack Belcher, Peter Loge, Judy Russell, Steve Corman, Jeff Hecker, Marlo Meuli, Paul Mann, Jack Merrit, Gary Ruskin, Jamie Love, Grace York

Foreword

S ome folks seem to think that, rather than this being the end of the 20th Century, it's the end of the 19th Century—an' some o' them young whipper-snappers have been runnin' 'round town in them gas-buggie thangies, an' they're *scarin' the horses!* (to say nothing of some of the town's elders).

Now you, dear reader, must decide: Are you going to learn how to drive and become proficient at using the rapidly evolving technology of the Information Age, that—for better and worse—*will* have as much impact in the next several decades as the automobile had beginning a century earlier, or are you going to cozy up to your loyal old hay-burner and grimly watch as the world moves beyond you—much too fast for comfort?

Even more important in some ways: If you are a community or political leader, are you going to learn enough to continue to lead? Or will you make increasingly embarrassing decisions based on ignorance?

Or worse still, will you foolishly attempt to halt the future, as local officials attempted in some communities at the end of the last century—enacting local ordinances that required someone to walk 50 paces ahead of any horseless carriage, ringing a bell and swinging a lantern? Just think how ignorant those officials looked only a few years later, when automobiles had become the norm—and those "leaders" quietly rescinded their naive ordinances, *hoping* that the press and their constituents wouldn't notice their lack of vision.

In many ways, the gas buggy's prelude to the 20th Century compares to how today's developing computer networks will impact the 21st Century.

It's already begun. It has so many advantages that it won't be suppressed—no more than horseless carriages were suppressed by those frightened, rear-facing village "leaders." There are 30- to 60-million people already using the networks worldwide, with about two-thirds on them in the United States. And that number has been growing by 5% to 10% per *month* for most of the 1990s, just as did the introduction of automobiles, radio and telephones beginning around the end of the last century—and their later counterpart, television, beginning in the 1950s.

Like the transportation revolution of the last century, and the later impacts of television, pervasive computer networking *will* change the fabric of society. Just as automobiles created suburbs where people could live far distant from their work, the computer nets are beginning to complete that transition—allowing more and more people to tele-commute from shared community tele-work centers, or even from home. (The latter can facilitate childcare and enhance family cohesion—and also destroy it.)

But networking's greatest impact, by far, is that it is allowing individuals a far more powerful voice in their community affairs than has ever been possible before—which is a focus of this book.

And like automobiles—and also, many would say, television—unfettered global personal communications has its dangers, sometimes real but often imagined.

There are millions more killed by automobiles than were ever killed by horses and their carriages, and vehicular air pollution is much more pervasive and dangerous than horse droppings ever could have been. And thanks to television, it is almost impossible for a homely politician or one with a poor speaking voice to get elected to state or federal office—regardless of their *important* qualifications.

Union leaders justifiably fear that telecommuting will expand managements' use of computer-timed piecework and far-distant, lower-wage employees, and that dispersed workers will make them more difficult to organize (although reasonable union access to employees via the company's electronic mail and online union bulletin boards can significantly empower outreach and organizing efforts).

And there are those who fear the "dangers" of allowing citizens to conduct personal communications or electronically distribute information, images, and opinion that are anything other than completely appropriate for the youngest of children—regardless of the fact that most of such conversations and exchanges are completely protected when they use soundwave speech or ink-based press.

Like those poor, ignorant village leaders, there has been a rash of current-day "leaders" howling for government to become the thought police throughout modern global communications. Disturbingly, some of the most ardent demands for government control of voiceless speech and inkless press are coming from the United States Congress and White House, just as they have come from Communist China and religious zealots in the Middle East.

The other great fear—that has much more justification—is that government will utilize the power of computers to conduct massive covert surveillance of citizens and businesses. In 1994, Congress and President Clinton enacted a half-billion-dollar national wiretap bill, and in 1995, the Federal Bureau of Investigation used it to demand that all phone companies install enough wiretap circuits to permit simultaneous surveillance of at least one call per 400, nationwide—with no independent oversight of its predictable abuses—saying that the Attorney General has determined that such massive surveillance capabilities would be "essential" for use by late 1998.

Counterbalancing these fears, like the personal transportation options opened by automobiles a century ago, the computer nets empower individuals at state, national and even international levels, in ways never previously possible—via robust, timely, free and low cost personal and mass communications. And globally-available, free and low cost, easy-to-use encryption software can enhance personal privacy protection for files and communications in ways never before possible (although various governments including the Clinton administration are seeking to prohibit its use—thus limiting robust privacy only to criminals).

Please note that there are two absolute prerequisites for a free society:

- Citizens must have timely access to adequate information on which to base sound decisions about their communities— local, state, national and global.

- The body politic must be able to communicate with itself—in a timely and economical manner that is, thus, effective.

The computer nets are rapidly fulfilling both of those prerequisites.

The global nets and local computer bulletin board systems (BBSs) have already been used to effect political change.

- *All* substantive political movements in France now routinely use that nation's Minitel computer system for organizing and coordinating effective action.

- A temporary BBS set up by several irritated citizens has been credited with being instrumental in unseating former House Speaker Tom Foley in 1994.

- Other grassroots activists used computer networking in efforts that indirectly led to the downfall of the entrenched President Pro Tempore of the California Senate in 1994.

- In late 1995, Oregon chose its first Democratic Senator in almost 30 years—elected by a tiny swing vote in favor of a candidate whose grassroots supporters made *massive* use of the computer nets, while his opponent ran a textbook-perfect traditional campaign, but eschewed online activism.

This is only the beginning. The immediate future—the next ten years—will see an empowering of grassroots activists as has never before been possible. Networked citizens *will* change the way state and federal politics operates—at *least* as much as automobiles have changed society and television has changed politics. And online activists will impact local politics as communities implement the growing number of local civic-nets.

Those who learn how to "drive" these cantankerous, powerful, frightening, exciting, infuriating, economical, pervasive intellectual and organizational tools—globally networked personal computers—will gain pervasive power.

Sooner or later, more and more Members of Congress and their staff will also learn how to routinely drive the information highways, potholes and all. The others, who simply can't or won't accept enhanced public discourse and information access, will be retired— one way or another.

The question is—are you going to join the millions of others who are learning how to empower themselves and regain control of their lives, or are you going to wander out to the barn and doze off next to Old Paint?

Jim Warren, Open Government Advocate and Columnist
jwarren@well.com (geographic:Woodside, California)
January 1996

Introduction

I joined the staff of Senator Edward M. Kennedy's Washington, DC office as systems administrator in the Spring of 1992. Although handy with a Macintosh computer, I brought no formal computer training to the job. While familiar with computer bulletin board systems, I had never heard of the Internet. My understanding of how Congress works was the sort gained in High School and College courses. And I certainly never imagined that my experience would lead me to write a book.

On the job, as a result of my efforts to help Senator Kennedy communicate with his online constituents, I learned a great deal more about the workings of all of these things; computers, Congress, and the Internet. I benefited greatly from circumstances; bosses that encouraged my efforts, a great deal of assistance from many like-minded individuals who encouraged and supported me, and the good fortune to begin my service in Congress at the dawning of the Information Age. My own reputation became inflated, boosted by positive press coverage of Kennedy's presence on the Net. But the truth is there are plenty of people who know more about Congress than I do, and many more than that who are more knowledgeable of the Internet. I have learned a little bit about each, and have worked to develop and share my understanding of the current benefits and future promise of a Congress that is on the Internet. That is why I wrote this book.

This book you are about to read, browse, buy, or return to the shelf is part history, part how-to, and part hypothesis about the U.S. Congress' developing and future use of the Internet. It will tell you something about the efforts that Congress has or hasn't made during the past few years to get on the Internet, and about the unique problems and possibilities that doing so presents to the world's most powerful legislative body. It will assist you in your exploration and use of congressional Internet resources, and offer you suggestions about how to best utilize the Net in order to learn about and communicate with members of Congress and the candidates who hope the Net can help make them members. It will also do some speculating as to how Congress's use of the Internet is likely to develop in the near future.

This book is not a directory of congressional resources on the Net. Certainly some information on how to find Congress on the Internet is included, but no attempt is made to be an Internet phone book for the legislative branch of the U.S. government. Other books exist that attempt to do that, but sadly they often fall victim to the fact that the Net changes faster than books are published, dooming them to be out of date as soon as they hit the bookstores. My focus will instead be on the efforts of the House of Representatives and the Senate, their members and their committees, and not on congressional support agencies, such as the General Accounting Office or the recently closed Office of Technology Assessment, which also post information on the Internet.

Although this book offers a history of Congress on the Internet, it is a personal history written by a participant who was present for much, but not all of it. I have not set out to write a comprehensive history that covers every single event of note, or every legislative branch agency's efforts to get wired. This book describes events as I saw them as a participant and as they have been described to me by people who were participants when I was not. Because my own experience has been working for Democrats in the Senate, you can expect this book to reflect the point of view that this position offered to me. I have tried to present a balanced description of events, and any perceived tilt in my coverage is more likely to reflect the state of the Net in Congress at the time of this writing rather than my own political leanings. It just happens that at this moment Democrats cling to the only majority they have left, the one in cyberspace.

Tourists who wander through the hallways of the Capitol, and gaze up at the paintings in the Dome and Brumidi's fresco in the Rotunda, cannot help but feel a powerful sense of our nation's history and pride in our democratic institutions. As a congressional staffer, I am fortunate to enjoy that sense every day, and I am proud to be among the many hard-working and dedicated public servants who work in Congress. At points in this book I am critical of Congress and its efforts to get on the Internet. This criticism is shared to explain to readers that the many bureaucratic and political hurdles that confound efforts to put Congress on the Net are the unavoidable nature of the institution. Any criticism I offer is intended to be constructive, with the hope that they can contribute to improved online access to Congress.

Finally, generalizations can often be made about the way members of the House of Representatives or the Senate work and behave; however, for every rule there is an exception and any generalizations made in this book do not necessarily apply to all of the 535 individuals who make up the U.S. Congress. Also, the descriptions of Internet sites in this book reflect their state at the time this book was written. Many of them will probably have changed by the time you read this. Please, let this book tell you something about their beginnings, and then go online yourself and take a look at what they've developed into today.

Chris Casey
chris@casey.com
Montclair, Virginia
February 1996

If a Nation expects to be ignorant and free in a state of civilization,

it expects what never was and never will be...

if we are to guard against ignorance and remain free,

it is the responsibility of every American to be informed.

Thomas Jefferson

Prologue

March 3, 1843

Samuel Morse has demonstrated his telegraph for Congress by stretching a line between two committee rooms in the Capitol building. Now, he awaits word on whether the Senate will vote to support the development of his invention. His demonstration within the Capitol had shown that the telegraph did indeed work, but to prove its practical use as a means of long-distance communications, a much larger demonstration would be required.

That evening, the Senate passed a bill appropriating $30,000 for Morse to construct a telegraph line between Washington, DC, and Baltimore, Maryland. More than a year after that vote, the first inter-city telegraph message was sent. From a room in the Senate side of the Capitol building, Morse tapped out his message to Baltimore, a line from the bible, "What hath God wrought!" The reply revealed a more practical concern: "What is the news from Washington?"

September 11, 1991

Almost 150 years later, the Internet had become an established communications medium that was growing at tremendous rates. The binary code of computers that carries text, sound, video, and computer programs across the Net, strings of zeros and ones, is reminiscent of the dots and dashes that carried information from Washington, DC, on Morse's telegraph. Spanning the globe, the Net carried amounts of data that Morse could never in his wildest dreams have imagined.

Recognizing the importance of further research and development of high-speed data networking, the Senate voted to create a new national program as part of the High Performance Computing Act of 1991. The National Research and Education Network (NREN) sponsored by Senator Albert Gore, Jr., of Tennessee would help "catalyze the development of a general purpose high speed communications infrastructure for the nation," better known today as the Information Superhighway.

But this time Congress wasn't itself leading the way. The Internet had already been around for twenty-two years, but in 1991 the Senate couldn't even get an e-mail message to the House.

ONE

★

Why Wire Washington?

> *In the financial marketplace "Intellectual capital is becoming relatively more important than physical capital...the new source of wealth is not material, it is information knowledge...." There is a corollary in politics: For the electorate, information and knowledge are now key and the new source of political power lies in the widespread dissemination through telecommunications.*
>
> The Electronic Republic

Why should the Senate be able to send an e-mail message to the House, the White House, or anywhere else? And why should the public have any expectation of finding Congress on the Internet? After all, in 1989 the Congress celebrated its bicentennial, the Capitol building turned 200 in 1993, and Congress had managed for all those years without the Internet.

The reason Congress needs to get on the Internet is because members of Congress are the representatives of the citizens who send them to Washington. They are sent to the nation's capital to act on their constituents' behalf, and they have a duty to report back to and inform their constituents about the legislative efforts they are undertaking. If those constituents adopt a new communications technology by the millions and the growth in the use of this technology develops into nothing short of an information revolution, then Congress should likewise embrace it. But sometimes Congress doesn't catch on too quickly.

In a story that appeared in March 1993, the *Los Angeles Times* reported that "more than 12 million Americans regularly log on to one of the nation's 60,000 bulletin boards, which have doubled in number in the last 18 months alone." Between 1987 and July 1994, the number of U.S. e-mail addresses increased by more than twenty-six million.[1] The growth of computer bulletin boards and e-mail addresses is indicative of the growth in the numbers of people with access to personal computers. In his 1995 book *Being Digital*, Nicholas Negroponte wrote:

> *[In] exponential fashion, computers are moving into our daily lives; 35 percent of American families and 50 percent of American teenagers have a personal computer at home; 30 million people are estimated to be on the Internet; 65 percent of new computers sold worldwide in 1994 were for the home; and 90 percent of those to be sold this year are expected to have modems or CD-ROM drives....The use of one computer program, a browser for the Internet called Mosaic, grew 11 percent per week between February and December 1993. The population of the Internet itself is now increasing at 10 percent per month. If this rate of growth were to continue (quite impossibly), the total number of Internet users would exceed the population of the world by 2003.*

In February 1996, America Online (AOL) announced that it had more than five million subscribers, a ten-fold increase in just two years. In an AOL press release, company CEO Steve Case described their growing

---

[1] *Fortune Magazine*, July 11, 1994, page 62 (source: EMMS).

population. "If you think of AOL as an electronic community, AOL is now among the largest 'cities' in the world. As we reach this important milestone of 5 million members, we recognize that more people live in the AOL community than in many large cities across the globe. And more people now subscribe to AOL than to The Wall Street Journal, USA Today, and The New York Times combined."

The Case of Television

Television had already proved itself as a medium capable of having a powerful impact on the political process and public perception of Congress. Television coverage of Senate hearings helped turn Senator Estes Kefauver into a presidential hopeful, and helped bring an end to Senator Joseph McCarthy's anti-communist witch hunts.

The House of Representatives first permitted coverage of the House floor by the Cable Satellite Public Affairs Network (C-SPAN) in 1979 during the speakership of Tip O'Neill of Massachusetts. In his memoir *Man of the House*, the Speaker described the concerns related to permitting cameras into the House chamber, and how these cameras have since impacted perceptions of the institution.

> *People get used to new situations very quickly, but when television first came into the House, many of the members were skeptical. In the past, even committee hearings were off limits to radio and television. Sam Rayburn used to say that microphones and cameras would detract from the dignity of the House, and long after his death that view continued to prevail.*

Another reason most members were wary of allowing TV cameras into the House was that we were disgusted with how the major networks covered the Republican and Democratic national conventions. If a guy was reading a newspaper, they'd always show a close-up of him. If a delegate was picking his nose or scratching his ass, that's what you'd see. If somebody had a bald head, you could be sure of getting a close-up view of the shiny spot. No wonder so many of us were skittish. After all, why should the greatest legislative body in the world allow itself to be demeaned and humiliated before millions of people?

But what if we allowed TV cameras on the floor of the House that were controlled by us instead of the networks? And what if those cameras showed only the person who was actually at the microphone and nobody else? That struck me as a reasonable compromise, and that's exactly what we did in setting up the cable network known as C-Span.

Today, of course, it's hard to imagine Congress without it and the results of our broadcasting experiment have exceeded my wildest hopes. One benefit is that Americans who watch C-Span are much better informed on the issues. Another is that in a nation where an embarrassingly high percentage of voters just don't bother to go to the polls, it's heartening to know that over 90 percent of C-Span viewers voted in the 1984 elections.

Television has also led to a tremendous improvement in the image of the House. Before we allowed the cameras in, 90 percent of the press stories about Congress had to do with the Senate. That, of course, has been a problem ever since our system of govern-

*ment started. With only a hundred members to keep
track of, the Senate has always been easier for the
media to cover and for the public to follow. After
all, most people can name their two senators, but
how many can run down the list of their state's
members of Congress? For this reason alone the
Senate has always seemed more glamorous than the
House.[2]*

It would take seven years for the "more glamorous" Senate to follow
the House onto C-SPAN. Of the reasons each chamber had for permitting television coverage, Roger Davidson and Walter Oleszek
wrote, "The House panel that examined the matter concluded that TV
coverage would help members and staff carry out their duties, provide
a more accurate record of proceedings, and contribute to public
understanding of the House. When the Senate followed suit after
protracted debate, the unstated reason was the perceived need to catch
up to the House in media attention."[3]

During the debate on allowing television coverage then Democratic
Leader Robert Byrd, one of the Senate's longest serving members,
offered a historical perspective on the Senate's need to utilize new
communications technologies. Well known for his reverence for the
institution and for history, Byrd is author of several volumes covering
the history of the Senate. But in the television age, Byrd recognized
that even the Senate, an institution that still keeps boxes of snuff in
the chamber filled for tradition's sake, must not let itself be left
behind in the past.

*Mr. BYRD. Mr. President, in 1944 the first resolution
calling for the broadcasting of Senate floor proceedings was introduced. Forty-two years have inter-
vened. We have spent almost half a century debating*

---

[2] Tip O'Neill, *Man of the House*, Random House, New York, 1987.

[3] Roger H. Davidson and Walter J. Oleszek, *Congress And Its Members, 3rd ed.*,
CQ Press, Washington, DC, 1990, p. 424

whether or not to permit our floor proceedings to be televised. Senator Hubert Humphrey told us: "A 20th Century Congress cannot be content with employing 18th or 19th Century technology." It is 1986. We are leaving the 20th Century and approaching the 21st Century. Yet we still have not found a way to go beyond the technology of the 19th century in communicating with the American public. If we do not act quickly to embrace the communications technology of the 20th century, we may find that in the 21st century, the Senate will have lost its relevance.

There are at least three compelling arguments for supporting the televising of Senate floor proceedings. There is a democratic argument, there is an institutional argument, and there is an educational argument....

Let us give the American people a more informed basis on which to judge what the Senate is and what the Senate does.

We are doing the people's business here. We do not need to fear their scrutiny. The Senate is a body of able and intelligent people. When we have given the public a chance to observe us closely, they have responded favorably. Let us look at some historic episodes to verify this.

The highest public opinion rating for the Congress in recent memory was registered in 1974. In that year, the Nation had a chance to observe the House Judiciary Committee conducting impeachment hearings. The American people saw a group of serious, thoughtful, and reasonable men and women doing their job, and they were impressed with what they saw. The opinion polls reflected that fact.

The year before, 1973, the Nation gathered daily around its television sets to watch the Senate Watergate Committee conduct its hearings under the leadership of Senator Sam Ervin. A survey conducted by Broadcasting Magazine showed that 85 percent of all U.S. households had tuned in to some portion of the Watergate hearings. Senator Ervin was not a product of the television age. He did not style his hair. He did not surround himself with media advisers. Yet, he became a folk hero. He may not have had the polish of a news anchor. But he had wisdom and character. And the American people saw that and responded favorably to it...

To give this debate some historical perspective, I remind Senators—and it has been said on this floor several times that in 1789, and indeed for the first five years of its existence, the U.S. Senate met behind closed doors. That policy was the target of as much criticism then as our failure to open our Chamber to television is today. In fact, the 18th century opponents to opening the doors of the Senate Chamber to the public have much in common with those in the 20th Century who oppose opening the Senate Chamber to television. They feared that, with the public in attendance, Senators would pander to the galleries with rhetorical speeches long on style but short in substance. There would be so many speeches, they warned, that the Senate would no longer be able to carry out its responsibilities in an efficient manner. Sometimes we feel that is the case around here, but it is not because we allowed the public to sit in the visitors' galleries. And, in response to the 20th century opponents, I do not believe that televising our proceedings to a national audience will have that effect either...

Mr. President, the coming of television to the U.S. Senate is not an occurrence to be feared—it is an opportunity to be seized. Let us not run from the public. Let us meet them where they already are—out yonder on the airwaves. The age of electronic communication is no longer the wave of the future. It is the reality of the present. Let us embrace this moment and become part of it.

The Senate has done this in the past. When we opened our doors to the public and the press in the 18th century, no more than three reporters were in attendance. However, in the early years of the 19th century their numbers grew steadily, and in 1857 the Congress responded by establishing Press Galleries in the Capitol. In the last quarter of the 19th century, the spread of the telegraph communications began. Newspapers across the country were suddenly able to receive instantaneous wire-service reports of events in Congress. This heightened the American people's interest in congressional news. Again, the American people responded favorably to this new and timely access and so did the Congress. By 1919, both Chambers had adopted the policy of holding open committee hearings on important legislative proposals.

In the 1920's, advances in radio technology again transformed mass communications. In the following two decades, news magazines and political periodicals began to appear on the scene. Now there were even more journalists on Capitol Hill, and the appetite for congressional news on the part of the American public continued to grow. By 1944, in response to the growing demand, the Congress had established the galleries for radio correspondents and for the periodical press. Between the years of

1945 and 1979, television brought the proceedings of various Senate committees into the homes of millions of American viewers. Interest in the legislative branch grew as a result of this exposure and now, in the 1980's, we are again being asked to respond to that interest.

The historic pattern has repeated itself. New technology enhances the communication process. It brings greater access to the Congress. The American people respond with greater interest. Now let us do what our predecessors have done throughout the history of the Congress. Let us respond favorably. Let us embrace contemporary technology and the opportunities it provides to enhance our democracy and prepare our future generations for their participation in that democracy.[4]

Less than ten years after Byrd made these remarks in support of permitting televised coverage of Senate proceedings, the historic pattern of new technology and its use by Congress would repeat. This time the technology was computer networking, *and the public was out yonder on the net.*

Although the gap would not be as large as with television, a similar experience was taking shape regarding computer networking in the House and Senate. When Congress considered getting wired to the Internet, it would be in very unfamiliar territory, unlike television, which as candidates many of them had mastered. But the pace of rapidly changing technology would not allow for forty-two years of debate as with television. Although running behind the academic and business community, Congress needed to get online soon and follow the argument Senator Byrd had made in favor of television to embrace

---

[4] Robert Byrd, Congressional Record, 99th Congress, 2d. Session, February 6, 1986, pages S1107-S1111 (daily edition).

contemporary technology or risk losing its relevance. In his book *House and Senate*, Ross K. Baker described many of the differences between the two chambers of Congress and the members that serve in them: "Not only are the Houses different, they are also distant, mutually suspicious, and inordinately prideful and sensitive."[5] His statement holds true in the contrast between the willingness and different approaches the House and Senate have taken in their attempts to open a virtual visitors gallery in cyberspace.

[5] Ross K. Baker, House and Senate, W. W. Norton & Company, New York, 1989, p. 12.

TWO

★

The Beginning

At first, I found myself exploring computer bulletin board systems at work to fill the time. Being a systems administrator is something like being a fireman. In a crisis everybody wants you, there is no one more important. But between fires you sit around the station and wait. Between printer jams and network crashes, I killed time at my desk dialing into computer bulletin board systems.

11

It was 1992, and I had been hired by Senator Edward Kennedy's office as the systems administrator, a position I came to with no formal computer background or training. After earning a B.A. in political science from the University of California at Santa Barbara, a member of the class of '87, I picked up and moved East to make my mark on Washington, DC. Among the few items that found space in my blue Honda Accord for the cross-country journey that brought me to the nation's capital was my Macintosh computer. My Mac was one of the originals. It was only three years old, not ancient yet. Its familiar shape and yellowish case that looked something like faded newspapers housed a whopping 128k of RAM. It had no hard drive. The operating system, applications, and data were all contained on 3.5" disks and performed only after seemingly endless swapping of them in the disk drive. That Mac had been a loyal servant throughout my college years, and I considered myself handy with it, but would not have described myself as a computer geek or anything like that.

I had been to Washington only once before when my sister and I had accompanied my mother there on a business trip. I was hooked. Long after Mom and Sis had tired of the tourist trek during that unusually warm February, I would still be out on the Mall, marching from monument to monument, from one museum to another. Plenty of people go to California and become star struck. I came from there to Washington and became politics struck.

Of all the sights in Washington, none had more impact on me than the Capitol building. L'Enfant got it right when, in laying out the plans for the city of Washington, he called Jenkins Hill "a pedestal waiting for a monument." Jenkins Hill became Capitol Hill and that is how the place is known around the world, except to those who work there. In Washington, it's simply the Hill.

After a brief internship in my congressman's office, an almost obligatory step for newcomers to DC, I held two real jobs before I again found work on the Hill. The first, as a document researcher, exposed me to the vast amount of information available in Washington and taught me something about how to find it. The second, as an account coordinator with a public affairs firm, taught me about the task facing almost everybody in Washington: getting their message out. The second job also introduced me to the tasks of a systems administrator, a role I inherited for the office's small network of Macs.

By 1988 I had retired my faithful but outdated 128k Mac for the power of a Mac Plus. Ignoring the fact that in order to buy it I had to finance the purchase and go into debt, I was able to convince my wife, Jennifer, that 1 megabyte of RAM and a 40-megabyte hard drive offered enough computing power for anybody.

In January 1992, while Washington was celebrating the Redskins' victory over the Buffalo Bills in Super Bowl XXVII, I was given two weeks notice that I was to join the ranks of the unemployed, the victim of a recessionary cutback. I had been interested in returning to the Hill since my brief time there five years earlier. Faced with the need to earn a paycheck quickly to deal with the fiscal realities of a mortgage and my newborn daughter, I took my job search to the Hill and pitched every skill I could muster—typing speed, research skills, writing, and proficiency with Macintosh computers.

I was very fortunate in my search. I managed to find a part-time position in the office of a member of the House of Representatives, troubleshooting some problems they were having on their Mac network. I spent several weeks trying to figure out what was causing their frequent computer crashes. They were using an integrated correspondence management system and constituent database to record, respond to, and track every single communication they had with a constituent. The database also maintained their library of "robo" letters, canned responses that are constantly updated to keep an arsenal of replies on current issues ready for any possible constituent query.

Sending a letter to Congress is an important and fundamental cornerstone of representative democracy, an essential means of communication between lawmakers and the public. The vast amount of mail sent to Members of Congress by individuals who utilize our system by informing their Congressperson what they think challenges the member's ability to carry on a correspondence with scores of individuals personally.

Managing mail with a correspondence management program is an obvious thing to do and there are a number of packages designed specifically to meet the needs of members of Congress and other elected officials at all levels. All members of Congress receive letters on the same issues and concerns over and over again, day after day, week after week. Letters expressing the same position on the same issue are not likely to each receive an individually drafted reply. It's more likely the office will maintain a library of robo letters, replies that have been drafted and approved by the member or senior staff, and use these robos to ensure that all letters going out of the office on a particular issue are consistent with each other.

The robo library can be integrated with a constituent database that contains information about the constituent's previous letter writing history and personal information such as names and birthdays of their spouse and children. A correspondence program can be a powerful tool for any member seeking to maintain a personal touch with their constituents back home. Suppose a constituent writes a letter supporting gun control. Before sending off the "Pro-Gun Control" robo (a "Con-Gun Control" robo will likely also exist, expressing the member's views, but written with regard to the writer's position), a quick look at the constituent history may reveal that this individual wrote a letter on the same issue only weeks before. Sending the standard robo again would be a mistake, but a slightly modified version might thank the sender for following up, and provide an update on where the issue currently stands, and a birthday greeting for a family member. The impersonal robo is now a personal update thanks to the database.

The software being used in the office of Congressman Jay Rhodes of Arizona was designed specifically for use in the House of Representatives, and only for Macintosh computers, a small niche market to be sure. The problem was that the constituent database and the integrated word processing for writing robos were not working well together, much to the frustration of the congressman's staff. I tried to locate any possible hardware or software conflicts that might be causing the problem, but without much luck. I was unable to do much more than offer some general recommendations that could provide some protection against the inevitable crashes. But the experience did give me an opportunity to get a foot in the door on the Hill and I carried on my search for more permanent work.

Two months later my application in response to an ad for a systems administrator for an all-Mac network in the office of a "New England Senate Democrat" led to an interview in the office of Senator Edward M. Kennedy. Unsure myself if I had the skills necessary for the position, I somehow managed to land the job. I later learned that the applicants I had beat out for the position all had much stronger technical credentials than I did. They were programmer types who offered the ability to write custom applications or take a computer apart and put it back together. But during my interview I had demonstrated an understanding of what the office hoped to get out of their computers, and that prevailed over the technical expertise of my competitors.

Senate offices were still in the process of making the transition from mini-computers (not at all mini by current standards) and the dumb terminals which relied on them. Honeywell, Prime, and Data General provided the three available mini-computers approved for use in the Senate. The transition from mini-computers to Local Area Networks (LAN) in the Senate had been delayed by at least a year in the Senate as a result of the Rules Committee insistence that a pilot test compare minis and terminals against desktop computers and LANs for cost effectiveness in deployment to the state offices (Senators typically maintain one to six offices in their states). Putting terminals in state offices and linking them all the way back to Washington to do word processing wasn't "a real logical thing to do... probably not even worth a pilot," according to a former director of the Senate Computer Center. But as I would come to learn, technology advances slowly in the Senate, and logic isn't always a factor taken under consideration.

The Honeywell mini that had served Kennedy's office had already been removed prior to my arrival, much to my relief. A rare all-Macintosh network had been installed to replace it, a few token IBM Compatibles around as a safety net in case going with Macs proved to be a mistake. Some Senate offices had at most a couple orphan Macintosh computers, often used by the Press Secretary to desktop publish attractive newsletters and press releases. But only a few offices were predominantly served by Macs. I learned later that Kennedy chose to go with Macs rather than the more prevalent DOS-based computers because of a friend's recommendation. The Senator's Chief-of-Staff, who at that time was not a computer user herself, heard that Macs were easier to use, and so that's the way they went. That advice proved fortuitous for me in providing an office in which my Mac experience could flourish.

So there I was, happy to again have a paycheck and health insurance and to be working in an interesting place, but concerned that I'd set myself on a career path I hadn't sought. I had not studied political science in college to come to Washington and unjam printers! That's not to say I didn't take my work seriously. Initially I wondered if I could do the job I had been given. I was plagued by doubts that my abilities would not measure up to the task. But I learned quickly that it wasn't necessary to have all the answers for any problem on the tip of my tongue, so long as I was at work figuring them out, and many of these problems proved to be pretty routine anyway.

My first call for help came immediately, a printing problem. On my way to the troubled printer I mentally poured over every LaserWriter problem and fix I could think of. Red light. Printer jam. I opened it and saw nothing until a closer look revealed a tiny piece of paper folded up like a miniature accordion. I pulled it out, closed the printer, and figured, "I can do this."

Next call—someone's Mac can't find the network. Again I pondered the problem on my way to the challenged computer. Hardware? Software? No. Ethernet plug kicked out of the jack. I put it back in; the Mac's back on the network. I'm getting good at this.

When faced with something I couldn't deal with, I was on the case working to figure it out. RTFM (Read The F***ing Manual), wait on hold for vendor tech support, or, as a last resort, call the Senate Computer Center (SCC). It was not that there were not good, able people in the SCC who did a commendable job supporting the thousands of computers in the Senate. But I had come to discover that Macintosh computers were generally not well supported within the Senate, a consequence of the overwhelming majority that DOS-based computers hold over Macs in Senate offices. I often found that I knew more about Macs than those the SCC would send to assist me when I called for help. I eventually stopped calling for anything short of a hardware failure I could not fix myself, or a problem with any of the few DOS machines in our office (which still remain completely foreign to me).

I became accustomed to the job quickly, and was able to keep this small Mac network working better than it had been before. I now found I had some time on my hands between fires. I spent that time online.

Bulletin Board Systems

Fate smiled on me early in my work in Senator Kennedy's office. There was an unused analog phone line just sitting there by the rack on which our network's file server lived. Senate offices are allotted three analog lines (the phones on the desks are digital) for fax machines and an e-mail gateway. Why we had an unused one I wasn't sure, but it did not stay unused for long. Among my first purchases for the office was a network modem, accessible to every Mac on our network. We were now well equipped to put that phone line to use. I had recommended the modem very strongly for its ability to provide remote access to our LAN, and for this purpose it did an excellent job. But I really wanted it for dialing out, because I was familiar with computer bulletin board systems and knew that they would provide a useful resource for information on fixing computer problems I would encounter, and for the software available on them.

The Senate's newly installed Senate Data Communications Network (SDCN) allowed us access to a number of Senate-provided and commercial services, such as wire stories, Congressional Quarterly's Washington Alert, DataTimes, and The Hotline. But SDCN did not allow for dialing out to any phone number not approved by the Senate Rules Committee and built into the system by the Senate Computer Center.

Our modem freed us of this constraint and allowed me to go wherever I wanted online. Initially I spent my time on the bulletin board system (BBS) operated by Washington Apple Pi, the Washington area Apple users group. But about this time I discovered FirstClass, a communications package developed by SoftArc that allowed bulletin board operators to present a graphical point-and-click interface to their users. The Mac's intuitive interface had long before convinced me it was the computer for me, but I had found that bringing a Mac online often meant leaving that friendly interface behind. FirstClass succeeded in bringing the Mac's ease of use to online communications. There was a BBS in DC that I began spending some time on named Foggy Bottom, but I soon took my travels up to Massachusetts' systems to better justify to myself the time spent online.

Technology is a major industry in Massachusetts, and in education, manufacturing, healthcare, and other fields it is of critical importance to the economy of the state. Massachusetts ranks near the top of the list for states ranked on the number of personal computers in use per capita. So it was no surprise when I discovered that Massachusetts offered a wealth of online treasures to be explored. A large number of user groups, school, commercially and privately operated bulletin boards existed for the benefit of Massachusetts' well-wired population, and out-of-state visitors, such as myself, as well. From these systems I downloaded software, found answers to my computer-related questions, and read postings on a vast array of non computer-related topics ranging from cycling, to gardening, to politics.

It was while reading these conferences that the proverbial light bulb went on in my head. Why wasn't Senator Kennedy reaching these online constituents on their own systems? I had only managed to explore a handful of the hundreds of BBS systems in Massachusetts, but I had seen plenty of evidence that their conferences related to politics were as active as any of the computer-related areas. How easy it would be for our office to begin reaching these virtual communities! How obvious a thing to do!

At least putting the Senator online seemed obvious, and yet I could not locate another office in the Senate that had done anything like it. I did find a couple of House committees that posted press releases to an online news service, PR ON-LINE, and the Senate Indian Affairs committee had posted some information to a regional system, but I could not locate any individual member of Congress who was regularly posting information from his or her office to any computer network.

For members of Congress, getting the message out to constituents is both a matter of duty and survival. Reporting back to constituents about work carried out in Washington on their behalf is an essential function of the job. For all Members, keeping their names, their words, and their faces in the press and in the voters consciousness is essential to retaining that job. This is why the press secretary on a congressional staff holds a position of great importance and influence. Every effort is made to craft the words and actions of the member for the greatest possible advantage in the media.

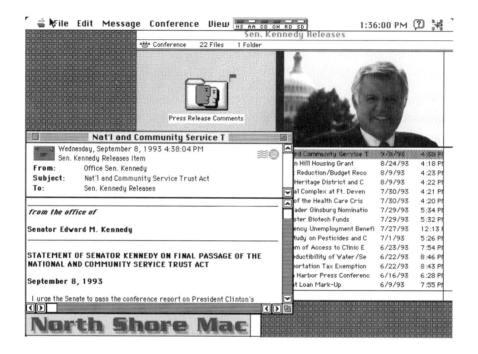

North Shore Mac

After making a couple of e-mail inquiries to the systems operators (sysops) of a few of the bulletin boards that I had been frequenting, Jonathan Gourd, sysop of North Shore Mac, replied. A computer hobbyist since 1973, when his junior high school gained access to a time-sharing system on a DEC TSS-8, Jonathan began his first BBS, The Sounding Board, in 1989. Not attracting the Mac audience that his 286-PC based board sought, Jonathan began looking for a Macintosh-based system with a graphical user interface. After examining the available products, he was quickly hooked on the FirstClass software, which he purchased and put on the only Mac he owned, an accelerated SE with five megabytes of RAM. Finding a name that offered some sense of locality and of the users he sought to attract, he launched North Shore Mac in 1992. The Mac SE, four hard drives, and the single phone line that together created this online community fit snugly on a workbench in the cellar of Jonathan's home in Beverly, Massachusetts, right next to the washing machine.

Jonathan describes himself as a registered independent who is "basically apolitical," but he was interested in the possibility of utilizing his BBS in a way that could have a positive impact on his online community. And his wife, a strong Kennedy supporter, encouraged him to reply to my inquiry and really get something started.

Jonathan and I agreed to meet on my visit to Boston the next month, February 1993, and over dinner we worked out the mechanics of how a Kennedy conference on Jonathan's system could work. The basic idea was that Jonathan would create two conferences on North Shore Mac, one for our office to post material into, and a subconference in which users could discuss and debate the items they read. Unsure of what it would entail, I was still too timid to invite electronic mail to be sent directly to the Senator. Our office promised visitors that any comments made in the discussion conference would be monitored by the Senator's staff, and that any question or comment for which they expected a reply would still require a snail mail letter to the Senator's office.

Upon my return to Washington, I logged onto North Shore Mac to send Jonathan a thank you note. To my surprise, I found a conference had already been created named "Ted Kennedy PR." My thank-you note let Jonathan know I hadn't quite received a go ahead yet, and he restricted access to the as yet very empty conference. I was learning what Jonathan didn't know yet, that our first steps towards the Net would come much more slowly than either of us would have liked.

The challenge I faced in pitching the idea in my own office was that of overcoming a lack of understanding. Computer bulletin boards were a vague concept at best, and more often a complete unknown to my bosses. Jonathan and I had estimated that a conference shared with a couple of other bulletin boards had a good chance of reaching something between 2,500 and 4,500 regular visitors. Three months and several case-making memos later, I eventually got the go-ahead to begin posting Senator Kennedy's press releases to North Shore Mac.

The Senator was an immediate and enthusiastic supporter of my efforts to help him reach out to his online constituents. Considering that he was a man who had served as a member of the Senate longer than I had been alive, and that he did not use a computer himself, I was a bit surprised. After a year on his staff, I had virtually no direct interaction with the Senator (what good is a computer guy to someone who doesn't use a computer?) and little confidence that he even knew who I was. I had every reason to expect my plan to be shot down, that I'd be told he'd never done anything like this before and didn't see any need to start now. Instead, Senator Kennedy's reaction was something more akin to "If you can find a way for me to reach constituents using computer networks, do it."

Another member of our staff had previously described to me what she thought was one of Senator Kennedy's greatest strengths as a Senator, his ability to quickly grasp the essence of a subject or an issue and get straight to its heart. I often describe friends or colleagues who understand my interest in the Internet and my drive to develop useful means for accessing government information as someone who "gets it." Senator Kennedy got it. He didn't have to be an Internet surfer or even a computer user to get it, he just did. He understood the importance of technology to his state of Massachusetts, the large role technology plays in business, manufacturing and education, and the potentially huge numbers of constituents in the state that were already online and would be happy to communicate with their Senator in this new medium. He got it.

Of course, a little good press didn't hurt. *MacWEEK* magazine was the first publication to report on Senator Kennedy's online efforts, but it was the *Boston Globe* story that appeared on September 15, 1993, that really caught his attention. On page three the Globe reported, "SEN. EDWARD M. KENNEDY IS 61, but he hasn't lost the drive to be ahead of the curve when it comes to politics." I couldn't have written it better myself.

It wasn't too long before other bulletin board systems across Massachusetts started linking up with North Shore Mac and participating in the Senator Kennedy Releases conference. The Boston Computer Society and the Boston branch of the Berkeley Macintosh Users Group (BMUG) both picked the conference up, as did about six other systems, including one run by students on campus at Lincoln-Sudbury High School.

Our posted guidelines made it clear that we would not be responding to online inquiries and offered the office's postal address for anybody who expected a reply. The reason I'd set the conference up this way was specifically to avoid being drawn into long running threads, debating and defending the wide variety of materials being posted into the press release conference. I was not a spokesperson for the Senator. I was not conversant with every issue that we covered in our posted material, and I had not been authorized to (nor would I have always been able to) argue any details. It had taken a great deal of effort to get the office to agree to post materials at all, and I didn't want to blow it by finding myself caught in any online debates in which I could quickly get in over my head. I just read these messages over and passed items of interest onto appropriate members of our staff for their own information.

Early on some debate began over what the ground rules should be in the Press Release Comments conference. Some individuals felt that the conference should be simply a bulletin board on which to post a message to Senator Kennedy, aware that others could read their public message. Others felt it should also provide an area for discussion and debate about the press releases that we were posting, and about each others' comments. Shortly after one woman commented that health care should be provided to all Americans just "like public education," another reader replied to her remark and said, "God save us all if the quality of our health care ever falls to that of our public schools." While this comment was not exactly harsh and could by no means be considered a personal attack on the sender, it transformed the comments conference from a public mailbox for Senator Kennedy into a forum of debate among readers.

The woman who posted the original message followed up with this message:

> *I think this folder is for citizens to leave a message for the senator's office. I don't think this is the place for you to reply to my message. If you want to further discuss this, leave me a message, or don't, but don't stifle my communication with my senator.*

Despite the attempts of a moderator from one of the bulletin boards carrying the Kennedy conference to keep things on an "even keel" and suggest that comments should be directed only toward the Senator, and not to the comments of others, her critic replied:

> *I am under the impression that this folder is for the discussion of the press releases posted by the Senator's office, and that his office would monitor the discussion. I apologize for misunderstanding if this is not the case. I do not, however, accept your claim that I stifled your communication with the Senator in any way. (I did not delete your message, for instance, or forge one from you.)*
>
> *If you are so insecure in your beliefs that simple criticism of them constitutes "stifling" them, I suggest you invest some well-spent time contemplating*

them or reevaluating them altogether. Senator Ken-
nedy is my senator too, and if I disagree with
something posted here, I am going to let him know.
That is my "communication with my senator" and,
I believe, my right as well.

I stayed out of the debate, reading every message, but not responding or participating. I did not want the Comments conference to have any rules for its use devised by our office. While the Senator Kennedy Releases conference was available only for postings from the Senator, the Press Release Comments was the users' forum and I wanted it to suit their needs. It wasn't my position to offer any advice or direction, but for these netizens to decide for themselves how to employ this new avenue of communication with their Senator. The conference did evolve along the latter track, as an open forum for debate with many comments developing into threads of discussion on a topic.

Not responding to simple and straightforward questions such as "How did the Senator vote on a particular bill?" was frustrating and difficult for myself and the users. The lack of any reply was very awkward, and it wasn't too long before some of the comments in the Press Release Comments conference expressed doubt as to whether anyone from the Senator's office was actually reading the messages. Even though I was fulfilling our promise that these messages would be seen by the Senator's staff, I needed to become active and participate in the Press Release Comments conference.

I did not take this seemingly obvious step of interacting online lightly. As one of about thirty on Senator Kennedy's personal staff, my job was simply to keep the computers running, the printers printing, and the network up. It was not to start taking questions fielded from the Net and meant for the Senator and respond to them from my seat in the mailroom. But as it became apparent that my experiment with putting Kennedy online could not be one-way, I carefully began to participate in the Comments conference myself.

After one constituent had posted a question looking for information about gender-equity legislation pending before the Congress, I revealed myself as the man behind the curtain and posted a reply to the conference. I explained that while I would try to be as responsive as possible, that I could not always ensure a satisfactory answer. Having offered that disclaimer, I obtained a list of bills for the gentleman interested in gender-equity legislation, much to his delight. And I offered the occasional straightforward answer to easy questions. "Where does Senator Kennedy stand on NAFTA?" "He voted in support of it. His statement made on the Senate floor is available in the Press Release Conference." I answered the easy ones and stayed out of any debates, referring people to the Senator's posted statements and releases whenever possible.

I was very pleased with how frequently we demonstrated the ability to make useful information available to the online public. In September 1993, President Clinton addressed a joint session of Congress to introduce his proposal to reform the nation's health care system. As chairman of the primary committee in the Senate that would consider the legislation, The Labor and Human Resources Committee, Senator Kennedy recognized the need to inform the public on this complicated issue. The same night that Clinton went before Congress, I posted a summary of the legislation prepared by the committee to the Kennedy conference. Dozens of people downloaded the summary, some as much as five months later like the woman who wrote in the Comments conference, "I was very happy to finally read an intelligent description of the substantive elements of the plan. So far, most of what has shown up in the mass media boils down to a journalist's narration of some third party's reaction." For me, this example proved how in many circumstances our posted materials could provide individuals with information that they might not be able to find elsewhere, and how the medium could extend the life span and usefulness of that information.

I read all of the comments and passed them on to other staff in our office who dealt in the issue areas being discussed. The Press Release Comments conference was shared among several systems just as the

Senator Kennedy Releases conference was, so that users of different systems all participated in the same dialog together. This also allowed me to monitor the comments without individually signing on to each separate board that carried the Senator's materials. But I did have to go to each system separately in order to look at the message histories that would tell me which files were being read or downloaded.

One of the BBSs that carried the Senator's conference was called Quantum, and it was maintained by students at Lincoln-Sudbury High School in Sudbury, Massachusetts. Once, while connected to Quantum, I was invited to participate in a live chat by some students curious to find out who the stranger on their system was. I was in a chat with about three students, all sophomores as I recall. "Who are you?" they asked me. "My name is Chris, I'm calling from Washington, DC," I responded. "Really?!, What do you do there?" "I work for Senator Kennedy." A young man named Nick wasn't buying that line, "LIAR!" he typed. I tried to offer some means to prove myself, suggested he read my user profile on the system, or contact Kennedy's office, but he refused to believe me. While I think a certain amount of skepticism is a good thing for anybody to bring with them when they venture online, it always bothered me that this kid wasn't willing to believe that someone from his Senator's office could be interested in what was taking place on their small bulletin board system. If you're reading this, Nick, I hope you're finally convinced.

Later, with assistance from MIT, the same releases we posted to the bulletin board systems were distributed to two Usenet news groups. The news groups we were posting to, "ne.politics" and "talk.politics.misc," were both preexisting forums that did not experience any of the struggles deciding how to handle the new messages they were finding from Senator Kennedy. As with the Comments conference on the bulletin boards, I had promised only that we'd be monitoring the news groups for any comments (which I did with the dial-up Internet account I had established). For those who sent replies to our Usenet posts directly via e-mail rather than as a follow-up posting, an auto-acknowledgment was sent to confirm that their message had been received, but made it clear that no further reply would be forthcoming and, if one was needed, would require a letter or phone call to our office.

Our first two messages in response to Usenet posts couldn't have been much more different. One offered us some assistance as we worked to see if our Usenet posts were going through:

> *Hello, office of Senator Kennedy. Since you seem to be unclear whether or not your post made it to usenet, I'll let you know that it, and your previous post with the correct subject line (the subject line that actually described the content of the post) did make it to talk.politics.misc.*
>
> *If you need to test whether or not your posts can make it out to usenet, you can post a test message to alt.test (assuming you're getting it), or misc.test. If you desire any other help, I'm sure many people on the net will be happy to assist you.*

The second simply offered a quote:

> *What do you say about a generation that has been taught that rain is poison and sex is death? If making love might be fatal and if a cool spring rain on any summer afternoon can turn a crystal blue lake into a puddle of black poison scum right in front of your eyes, there is not much left except TV and relentless masturbation.*
>
> Hunter S. Thompson
Generation of Swine

And perhaps maybe the net.

Other messages would vary from thoughtful, to rude, to bizarre. Anonymous remailers that deliver e-mail while protecting the sender's identity were used to send us information about the alleged wrongdoings of Republicans. Other messages included lengthy analyses or critiques of the material we were posting, dozens of messages ran along the lines of "Is this really Ted Kennedy's e-mail address? Neat!" Another less impressed individual wrote, "Shaddup ya great bag o wind!"

The White House, the House, and MIT

In January 1991, while unemployed prior to starting in Kennedy's office, I was knocking on doors in New Hampshire passing out Clinton campaign videos to anyone who would take one (obviously I did good work). A year later I attended Bill Clinton's inauguration as the 42nd president of the United States and took some small pleasure from knowing that any campaign volunteer can share in his candidate's victory.

During the first month of the Clinton administration, word that both the President and Vice-President had e-mail addresses was starting to get around. I had picked up the name of Jeff Eller from a news clip about e-mail access to the White House and gave him a call. He told me that the person I needed to speak with was Jock Gill. Jock was agreeable to discussing our shared interest in access to government over the Internet and we arranged a meeting in his office in the Old Executive Office Building.

I quickly learned two things that would prove tremendously fortunate for me. Jock was from Massachusetts, and the White House was being assisted with their Internet efforts by the Artificial Intelligence Laboratory at the Massachusetts Institute of Technology. As a citizen of the Commonwealth, Jock was excited to find Senator Kennedy interested in the Net and was full of encouragement for our effort. He even sent me on a path to contact others who might be of assistance to me.

In early 1993, I read an article in *ROLL CALL* (one of two newspapers that chronicle the workings of Congress) titled "The New High-Tech House," which described a number of new innovations that could be expected in the House within the year. Among the technologies that were expected to move beyond the pilot stage to widespread availability in the House were office-to-office e-mail, wide-area network access to district offices, improved legislative searching through the House-developed Integrated Systems and Information Services (ISIS) system, and access to "a nationwide communication network called INTERNET."

That article, and just about any other article you might have read about technology in Congress, credited Congressman Charlie Rose of North Carolina as "the mastermind behind the influx of new technology...himself a high-tech junkie." First elected to Congress in 1972, Rose's personal interest in technology as a user remains a unique trait for a member of Congress. As chairman of the House Administration Committee, Rose governed virtually every aspect of the day-to-day operations of the House of Representatives, and he took special interest in the House's computer and information resources support arm, House Information Systems (HIS).

That roll call article was also the first of many that began to reveal to me a trend that offered a clue to the differences between the House and the Senate. Such stories would typically describe some new innovation or service available in the House, and if any mention was made of the Senate at all, it was usually a Rules Committee spokesperson offering some explanation as to why the Senate wasn't yet at the same stage.

The founding fathers designed the House of Representatives to be more directly responsive to the citizenry than the Senate. The brief two-year terms of representatives were intended to ensure that the House should demonstrate, as James Madison put it in *The Federalist* papers, "an immediate dependence on, and an intimate sympathy with, the people."[1] In contrast, the Senate's longer terms and appointment by state legislatures were intended, according to Madison, "to consist in its proceedings with more coolness, with more system, and with more wisdom, than the popular branch."[2] Interestingly, and perhaps simply out of habit, the House is typically several steps ahead of the Senate in implementing new technology. House members are often quicker to adopt the new technologies that can help them perform their jobs and to improve public perception of the institution. The Senate, on the other hand, takes pride in its status as the "world's greatest deliberative" body, and as an institution it is very slow to change.

Interested in learning what the House was doing, I contacted Jack Belcher, who had been mentioned in articles I had read about the development of Internet connectivity in the House of Representatives. Jack, who was manager of information systems at House Information Systems, invited me to pay him a visit. When I met with Jack, and with Doreen Albiston, electronic mail administrator for HIS, I learned very quickly something that I hadn't previously realized. They were both very interested in learning from me what the state of Internet access was in the Senate. This was something I had assumed they would know more about than I did. Certainly the Senate Computer Center and House Information Systems were sister services that worked hand-in-hand, weren't they?

I explained what I knew of Senate Internet services (that there were none) and asked to learn more about what the House was doing. Jack described the steps they were taking to implement Internet e-mail

---

[1] James Madison, *The Federalist*, No. 52.

[2] Richard Baker, *The Senate of the United States: A Bicentennial History,* Krieger Publishing, Malabar, Florida, 1988, p.6.

access, and he also explained how they had hooked up a Senate committee to the House e-mail system in order to allow them to reach their House counterparts.

I asked Jack if they had hooked any personal offices in the Senate up to their system as they had with the Senate committee.

No.
Would they?
Sure.

A brief letter from Senator Kennedy to Congressman Rose, the chairman of the House Administration Committee which oversees HIS, sealed the deal. And before I knew it I could be reached at *ccasey@hr.house.gov*. Jack and Doreen did more than just offer to hook me up, they told me to feel free to spread the word among my Senate colleagues. Several other Senate offices had signed up for House e-mail before the Senate caught on and began offering Internet e-mail as a service to its members.

Unlike the Senate, which approved and supported a single e-mail application for use by Senate offices, the House supported nine separate e-mail programs. But what The House had gained in variety and choice hampered them with the difficulty of sending office-to-office e-mail across different platforms. This required a central mail facility, a store-and-forward system that could accept outbound messages from different e-mail packages, convert them to the recipient's required format, and ship them. This ability meant that messages could also be sent outside the House to the Internet. House staff were first able to send Internet e-mail sometime in the summer of 1992. Despite assurances from the Senate Computer Center that the Senate was just as far along as the House in development of Internet e-mail, the fact was that the only Internet e-mail addresses in Senate offices came courtesy of the House.

Several months later, after Internet e-mail had become available in the Senate, I learned that *Open Computing* magazine had printed a list of celebrity e-mail addresses and included Senator Kennedy. The magazine's source was a new book, *E-mail Addresses of the Rich and Famous*, which listed Ted Kennedy's e-mail address as "*ccasey@ hr.house.gov.*" My House e-mail address was getting famous.

Finally able to get an e-mail message out to the Internet, I sent a note to John Mallery, a Ph.D. candidate in MIT's Artificial Intelligence Laboratory. Jock Gill had suggested I contact John as he would be interested in knowing about Senator Kennedy's recent efforts to reach bulletin board systems in Massachusetts. "Why aren't you posting to the Internet?," John asked. "Because we can't get to the Internet from the Senate" was my reply. John offered to assist us and introduced me to another graduate student, Eric Loeb.

Eric was a Ph.D. candidate in MIT's Psychology Department working toward a degree in cognitive neuroscience. Despite the half-dozen attempts he has made to explain it to me, I still don't know what cognitive neuroscience is. To the untrained eye, Eric's poking at frogs after lobotomizing them seems little different from an adolescent playing "Dr. Frankenstein," rather than the breakthrough research that Eric said it was. Eric had conceived of and, together with John, implemented the Presidential Campaign Information Service at MIT in 1992 (more on this later) and later assisted with the pilot project to put the White House on the Net. Later, Eric was also instrumental in putting the City of Cambridge on the Net. I asked Eric once what cognitive neuroscience, dicing frogs, and politics on the Internet had in common for him, and you could probably see the hair on my head move as his answer passed over it. Something about building the nation's brain. Many of my conversations with people at MIT went like that, almost as if you were speaking English to someone and all of a sudden they switched to Chinese—I was hopelessly lost. I did catch enough to understand that MIT had begun pioneering a new field of political science, and they were willing to help Senator Kennedy. I understood enough to accept.

Eric set up a system that allowed me to e-mail a press release, speech, or other statement of the Senator's up to MIT, where it would automatically be posted to two Usenet news groups and archived for access via file transfer protocol (ftp). While these were routine actions to millions of regular Internet users, within Senate offices these services were unavailable. By helping Senator Kennedy reach the Internet, Eric had broken the first hole in the wall that separated the Senate from the Net.

I followed the same procedures in Usenet as I had in our bulletin board Comments conference. I read the comments made in the *ne.politics* news group in reply to the Senator's statements, and quite frequently our postings acted something like conversation starters that resulted in long running threads in which the participants of *ne.politics* would discuss whatever issue had been raised by the Senator's posting. But I was a lurker who followed these threads and shared them with our staff, and did not myself jump into the debate. As I had on the bulletin boards, I eventually needed to jump into discussion threads in the news groups, to answer an easy question now and then and demonstrate that Kennedy's office was actually reading the comments that resulted from our postings.

E-mail messages sent in reply to the Senator's Usenet postings would make it back to me, but only after triggering an auto-acknowledgment message confirming receipt of the message and informing the sender that only snail mail correspondence would actually receive an individual reply.

Beginning with Jock Gill at the White House, and then expanding to new acquaintances made in the House of Representatives and MIT, I was now part of a growing circle of like-minded individuals who seek to make government more accessible via the Internet. I was present at the formative meeting of a group called Americans Communicating Electronically (ACE), whose membership consists largely of federal government employees from a wide range of departments and agencies. The members of ACE share a vision of utilizing the Internet for improving access to government information and services. Attendance at ACE meetings grew rapidly, from a handful of people around a table initially, and only a few meetings later, to a group large enough to fill an auditorium. From these meetings I gained insight into the Internet outreach efforts underway in other agencies, and left emboldened to push my own office and the rest of the Senate to take the next big step, e-mail.

THREE

★

"HE'S PROBABLY SORRY HE SIGNED UP FOR INTERNET E-MAIL."

Reprinted with permission of *Government Computer News* magazine, July 11, 1994,
© by Cahners Publishing Company

Electronic Mail

Electronic mail is being embraced by millions of people around the world as a routine form of communication. Combining the immediacy of a telephone call with the composed text of correspondence and the patience of a letter, e-mail arrives and waits to be read at the recipient's convenience. It was the first Internet service available in the Senate. I was very happy to have my House-provided e-mail address for the months while I used it, but explaining why I was reached in the Senate via "house.gov" had become tiresome and a bit embarrassing. Once Internet e-mail became available in the Senate I no longer needed to rely on a friendly neighbor to pick up

My Sig

Not long after I gained the ability to send and receive Internet e-mail from the Hill, I set out to create an appropriate signature to attach to my messages. The early versions were pretty plain, but I got more ambitious after seeing many impressive examples of ASCII art in other signatures. No artist myself, I still undertook to create an image that reflected the origin of my e-mail, and the ASCII Capitol Building shown here was the result. At the risk of creating a signature that was too big, I attached the Jefferson quote anyway because I find it particularly appropriate to the subject of developing electronic access to government, and because I am a fan of Tom's.

Apparently my effort succeeded because I am frequently complimented on my sig and it has been mentioned in a couple of books about the Internet. I suppose now I should be concerned that my sig gets more attention than the messages I write!

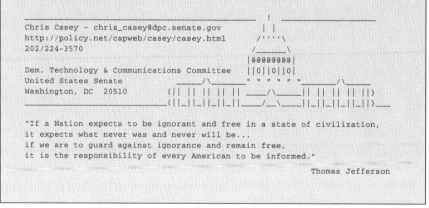

```
_____    !  _____
Chris Casey - chris_casey@dpc.senate.gov       | |
http://policy.net/capweb/casey/casey.html     /'''''\
202/224-3570                                  /_____\
                                             |@@@@@@@@|
Dem. Technology & Communications Committee   ||0||0||0|
United States Senate            _____/_____" " " " "_____/_____
Washington, DC  20510           {|| || || || ||_____/\_____|| || || || ||}
_____{||_||_||_||_||____/_____||_||_||_||_||}___

"If a Nation expects to be ignorant and free in a state of civilization,
it expects what never was and never will be...
if we are to guard against ignorance and remain free,
it is the responsibility of every American to be informed."
                                              Thomas Jefferson
```

my mail. I now had a mailbox of my own, and it was nice to be addressed at "senate.gov."

Long before we had Internet e-mail in the Senate, I had worked hard to increase our office's connectivity to other offices within the Senate. The Senate's standard e-mail package was Lotus's ccMail, and virtually every Senate office that had a LAN used it. E-mail connectivity between one office and another, or with a state office, required that a simple dial-up connection be established. To do this you had to know the phone number of the gateway modem for the office you wished to reach. I believed that it was in our office's interest to be able to reach each and every other office in the Senate via electronic mail. Even if we were to use some of these connections infrequently—or never—as a Boy Scout, I had been taught to "be prepared." If Senator Kennedy or someone on our staff was faced with a pressing need to e-mail something to Senator Helms's office right away (not that they ever did), I did not want to have to say, "Well, um, we could do that if only we had exchanged gateway phone numbers with them, but we haven't."

Many offices shared this philosophy, but there were plenty of others that were very reluctant or completely opposed to the idea of sending e-mail beyond the walls of their own office. The prospect of utilizing Internet e-mail to reach the rest of the world—and being reached by the world in return—completely terrified some of them. At one Senate Computer Center briefing on Internet e-mail, a shocked Democratic system administrator asked, "Do you mean Republicans will be able to send us e-mail?!?" In Kennedy's office I encouraged staff to share their e-mail addresses just as they would their phone numbers, to put them on their business cards, and to offer them readily.

The usefulness of even e-mail-only Internet access was immediately apparent. I subscribed to the MIT server that had been established for the presidential campaigns, and that had continued its service by distributing all White House press releases and publications. The first widespread use of the Net discovered by staff in Senator Kennedy's office was the new-found ability to read these documents using the computers on their desks. The White House documents became popular reading with staff at all levels in our office. I later described to the Senate Press Gallery's systems administrator how we were obtaining these releases. Disappointed that he couldn't yet do the same, I arranged to forward the White House releases to the Press Gallery as well. Other electronic mailing lists (listservers) proved similarly useful to staff. The member of our staff responsible for Senator Kennedy's work on the Armed Services Committee received releases from NATO directly via e-mail. There was little question that he was getting timely and useful information, even if some of it was in French.

Ready access to White House publications was one of the best arguments that I could make to an office considering using e-mail. When Jock Gill, the White House Internet evangelist, came to the Senate to speak to a meeting of Democratic press secretaries, he spoke in his usual impassioned manner regarding the promise of improved service to citizens that an electronic government could provide. The press secretaries in general, and their leader from Majority Leader Mitchell's office in particular, were unimpressed and repeatedly pressed Jock for more concrete examples of how the Net could make them more effective *TODAY*. From the back of the room, I spoke up and described how in Kennedy's office the entire staff had immediate access to all White House publications. Staff at all levels in our office read these releases regularly. The press secretaries at the meeting quickly recognized the benefit of such access and became a more receptive audience for Jock, who called me later and thanked me for my timely intervention.

Many congressional staff approached the use of e-mail timidly, and when it came to setting up a public e-mail address for their bosses, they were even more afraid. Although e-mail offered the promise of instant one-to-one communications between constituents and their elected representatives in Congress, no one was certain if this was doable, or even desirable. And yet the surge of interest in the Net left little time for considering such questions. As public e-mail began to seem inevitable, many waited to see who would go first, and how they would manage.

The House and the Senate have taken very different approaches towards handling e-mail for members. The House announced an Internet e-mail pilot program in June 1993, holding up their announcement by one day to allow the White House to announce the President and Vice President's e-mail addresses first. Seven Representatives were to be Congress's Mercury astronauts in cyberspace, and the Hill anxiously waited to see what fate was in store for them. The seven brave Representatives to establish e-mail addresses were Jay Dickey (AR-07), Sam Gejdenson (CT-02), Newt Gingrich (GA-06), George Miller (CA-07), Charlie Rose (NC-07) Pete Stark (CA-13), and Melvin Watt (NC-12). The instructions for sending e-mail to any of these members included a cumbersome procedure by which individuals wishing to send e-mail to their Representative were asked to send a postcard requesting the privilege and to include their own e-mail and postal addresses. Only after it had been established that the sender was a constituent were they then registered and permitted to send that Representative an e-mail message. Messages from individuals not registered could be filtered out and deleted unread at the office's request. Of course, those seven members with e-mail addresses could not prevent nonconstituents from learning them, but using this registration process provided a means to weed them out. Using these public mailboxes set up by HIS, House offices are protected from any potential floods of e-mail. Messages to individual members make it only as far as the HIS mailbox, and not all the way to the office's LAN.

The use of this elaborate registration requirement for sending e-mail to members of the House was quickly abandoned by most offices after proving unwieldy. The whole idea of asking someone to first send you a post card in order to be allowed to later send e-mail struck many on the Net as a bizarre anachronism. But it was a system developed by members and staff who were accustomed to seeing their mail rooms buried under the weight of mass-mailing campaigns and their fax machines running day and night receiving the public's input, and had every expectation that public e-mail would invite an unmanageable new influx of the same. Although the practice of pre-registering e-mail users never took hold, the concerns that led to its development proved accurate, and offices would turn to doing their filtering at the receiving end.

The press generated many positive stories about the House and White House announcements, and the silence from the Senate did not go unnoticed in the press or within the Senate itself.

But things worked differently in the Senate. Although the House and the White House had developed the tools to allow for some automation of the management of electronic mail, particularly the use of auto-acknowledgment messages, the Senate Computer Center did not follow suit. Under pressure to deliver long-promised access to Internet e-mail, little thought was given to how an office might handle it. Those Senate offices interested in inviting e-mail from the public were on their own to find solutions for dealing with what would be an unknown number of messages, delivered directly to their offices and filling up their file servers.

The Senate made no effort to coordinate and announce the Senate's use of the Internet as the House had done. House Information Systems reported to Congressman Rose, and he was no stranger to promoting the use of technology in the House. HIS officials could frequently be found quoted in stories reporting the House's efforts. Senate Computer Center officials report to a political appointee, the Senate Sergeant at Arms, who in turn reports to the Rules Committee. Unlike the House, the Senate showed no interest in speaking about or promoting Senate Internet services, and the Sergeant at Arms would not permit computer center staff to discuss their efforts with the press. Any word about use of the Internet within the Senate would only come directly from the individual offices using it.

The lack of an orchestrated unveiling of e-mail services by the Senate makes it difficult to determine exactly who was the first Senator to establish an e-mail address, but I believe it was Senator Chuck Robb of Virginia. Following some of the early press we'd received for our office's presence on the Internet, Senator Kennedy did some boasting about it with some of his colleagues. These occasions would usually come full circle after the other Senator would ask their own systems administrator more about the Internet, and that sys admin would contact me. Among the Senators who quickly pursued their own Internet efforts after hearing about Senator Kennedy's were Senator Jeff Bingaman of New Mexico and Senator Chuck Robb of Virginia. Like Senator Kennedy, both were facing difficult reelection challenges in 1994, a factor that certainly must have come to mind as they sought to further develop their capability to reach constituents (like Kennedy, both were reelected).

Senator Robb's systems administrator, Matthew McGowan, had established a forum in partnership with the Washington-area freenet, CapAccess, in October 1994, without any fanfare. No press release to stir up a positive press hit. The Robb forum was created, ready to be discovered and perused by visitors to CapAccess. Those who looked close enough would find an e-mail address and an invitation to send a message to Senator Robb. Nothing to it.

When I first explored the forum myself, I was surprised to find the e-mail address, disappointed that we hadn't done it first, but still pleased to know someone else was testing these unknown waters of constituent e-mail. At that time in Senator Kennedy's office we were still only accepting online comments about our postings, and encouraging users to use postal mail (snail mail) if they expected a reply. We did not yet have a direct e-mail address for Senator Kennedy. How much e-mail would Robb get? Would they get overloaded? Could the office network be brought to a halt under the sheer volume of e-mail, and might someone maliciously attempt to do just that? These questions haunted any Hill sys admin thinking about e-mail.

Matt's replies to these questions were reassuring. There was nothing unmanageable about the amount of e-mail Senator Robb was receiving. Certainly the numbers would increase as more people discovered the address and word spread that the Senator could be reached via e-mail. But Robb's quiet entrance onto the Net did not bring any immediate hordes of e-mailers.

© 1995 Joe Troise, Network World

To most people such concerns might seem extreme, but on the Hill they are genuine. To understand, you must understand exactly how big a role mail plays in any congressional office.

Reading and responding to constituent mail is one of the most fundamental and important tasks in any congressional office. And rightfully so. Writing a letter to your congressperson is an act of representative democracy at its purest. If a citizen (constituent/voter) has a concern about a legislative issue, a problem with a government agency, or any kind of opinion to express, her or she can write a letter to their elected Representative or Senator in Congress. Such mail is an essential tool for members who wish to know the concerns of their constituents. Knowing also that with their votes these constituents will demonstrate their approval or disapproval of the work being done in Washington on their behalf, any member of Congress ignores the mail at his or her peril.

Because of the importance that members of Congress place on the mail, and the tallies that result in pro and con input from constituents on any issue, it is routine for interest groups and lobbies to generate huge amounts of mail to Congress. Lobbyists brag about their ability to generate vast amounts of mail quickly to pile up in a member of Congress's office as a powerful (if artificial) display and indicator of the public's mood. Postcard campaigns, telegrams and mailgrams, computer-generated form letters, these are among the tools available to those who wish to influence Congress.

These tactics don't stop with the postcards. Often some material prop is included to help emphasize the point being made. When lumber prices were rising, hundreds wrote their messages on pieces of 2x4, placed postage on the wood, and mailed them into Senator Kennedy and other members of Congress. "Do you know how much this piece of wood costs?" some of them asked. Our mailroom looked like a scrap pile in a lumber yard! On another occasion, when the FDA was considering new regulations on vitamins, hundreds of people mailed in their empty vitamin bottles to show their opposition.

Generating such onslaughts of mail is also a very big business, and millions of dollars are spent to generate piles of letters in Congress' mailrooms each year. The mechanics of generating such "astroturf" mailings (an artificial display of grassroots support for an issue) were put on display in the summer of 1995 when one such effort went awry. Seeking to turn up the heat in its lobbying efforts regarding the consideration of telecommunications reform legislation, the Competitive Long Distance Coalition hired a lobbying firm, which hired another firm to generate a flood of mail to Congress through a "grassroots" campaign. The problem was that as many as half of the letters were sent without the signer's approval, and others were sent by children who were too young to vote and by individuals who were deceased. Many members of Congress were disturbed at the revelation that children and dead men were sending them letters generated by deep-pocketed lobbies, but no criminal investigation was pursued when it was found that no laws had been broken.

Members of Congress and their staffs recognize the difference between a letter from an individual constituent and an interest group-generated postcard or mailgram. This factor is taken into consideration by all members when reviewing their mail.

It's not hard to imagine how e-mail could be used in a similar manner. No organized campaign or powerful lobby is required. Any individual clever or malicious enough could single-handedly generate a deluge of e-mail by programming a computer to send a message to a member of Congress (or every member for that matter) over and over and over again! Unlike the deluges of snail mail that simply accumulate in boxes in the mailroom, an e-mail deluge is eating up space on the file server and potentially bogging down the office's LAN.

The tens of thousands of individuals who exercised their new-found power to send e-mail to the President found a computer-generated reply in their in-boxes. When setting up e-mail, most congressional offices followed the White House example of sending an automated e-mail acknowledgment followed by a snail mail reply to those messages that included a postal address, and often only to their own constituents.

While auto-acknowledgments and snail mail replies may seem a disappointing manner with which to handle electronic mail, there are a number of good reasons why it is a logical first step in the implementation of electronic mail to Congress. The auto-acknowledgment lets the sender know that the message was received, and the included postal address lets the member of Congress know if the person writing is a constituent or not. An e-mail address alone does not always offer such geographic clues. A message arriving for Senator Kennedy from the domain *harvard.edu* can pretty safely be assumed to be originating in Massachusetts, but what about e-mail from *aol.com*? It could be from anywhere. Members of Congress are sent to Washington as the representatives of the citizens of their state or district. They want to know they are hearing from constituents of theirs, and a postal address can accomplish this.

An auto-acknowledgment also helps smooth the transition toward accepting constituent e-mail as a routine occurrence for congressional staff. No new staff position is required. No hapless electronic legislative correspondent has to know about every issue and send out e-mail replies as fast as they arrive. By requesting a postal address, members of Congress not only know if they're hearing from a constituent, but their staff ends up with a message containing a constituent concern with a postal address at which to reply. Hill staffers know what to do with this, they're good at it. From this point onward, the e-mail can be treated as if it had come in an envelope with a stamp on it.

This approach also helps to avoid any equity issues that e-mail can raise. The use of e-mail is growing tremendously, but access to it is far from universal. While every member of Congress may be interested in utilizing e-mail to allow the public a more convenient means for reaching them, they do not want to create any impression that their high-tech constituents will now somehow have better access or receive a more timely reply than others. During this transitory period, as offices are just beginning to learn how to deal with electronic mail, the auto-acknowledgment/snail mail reply approach is a useful first step.

Another unexpected result of this approach also deals with equity. Not too long after the establishment of Senator Kennedy's e-mail address someone did decide to become a one-man mass e-mail campaign. Apparently he felt that if sending his feelings on a particular piece of legislation to the Senator once was a good thing, then it must somehow be better to send his message over and over again. Perhaps he thought he was stuffing some sort of electronic ballot box. While the auto-acknowledgment doesn't do anything to prevent a mailing like this, it does go a long way toward discouraging it. The Senator's e-mail gave back as good as it got. For every message sent, an acknowledgment was likewise sent. If a deluge is sent, a deluge is returned. Mutual assured destruction comes to e-mail. A low-tech but effective defense.

The message below is typical of auto-responders in use by members of Congress. Senator Warner's reply is notable for promising a response to any message that includes an address, and not only to his constituents in Virginia.

```
Subject:      Re: Senate Internet Stats
Sent:         12/02  12:49 AM
Received:     12/02  1:04 AM
From:         Senator@warner.senate.gov
To:           Chris Casey, casey@cais.com
```

Dear Friend:
Thank you for sending an e-mail message to my office.
Please accept this response as acknowledgment to your
message and I will note your comments. If you have included
an address I will respond through the U.S. postal system as
soon as possible.
I look forward to hearing from you on other issues of
importance to you and your friends.
With kind regards, I am,

Sincerely,
John Warner
United States Senator

Warner has demonstrated a strong interest in improving the use of technology in the Senate, and as the new chairman of the Senate Rules Committee he is in a position to do so. I wrote to Warner in this capacity (he's also one of my own Senators) seeking Senate e-mail statistics for use in this book which were subsequently provided.

The best auto-acknowledgments are straightforward notes, confirming that the sender's message has been received and acknowledging that a postal reply will be forthcoming for those who included a postal address. Adding directions on how to locate additional information from the office in a gopher directory (gopher is a text-based, menu-driven means for retrieving and posting information on the Internet) or on a home page can often help senders answer their own questions from material already on the Net. The acknowledgment need not be static. Updated regularly, an acknowledgment might include Congress's legislative schedule, that particular member's legislative efforts or schedule, or other timely information.

When given a straightforward explanation as to why staff and resource limitations prevented our office from replying to e-mail via e-mail, we found in Senator Kennedy's office that people were generally understanding of the unique challenges we were facing with our efforts to make the Senator and his office available on the Net, and did not begrudge us the first step we were taking by employing auto-acknowledgments.

More than one congressional office has tried to offer some excuse or explanation in their auto-acknowledgment messages explaining why they are unable to reply via e-mail. Often such excuses were either poorly thought out or just plain wrong. Representative Norman Mineta represented a high-tech district right in the heart of California's Silicon Valley for 20 years before retiring in October 1994. In the spring of his final year on the Hill, he claimed in his e-mail auto-acknowledgment that "At present there is concern about hackers intercepting and changing e-mail messages or even possibly changing the e-mail I.D. and sending out messages with my address. To ensure the security of our correspondence, I will be responding to you by mail." His high-tech constituents knew better and called him on it, pointing out that freely available encryption technology is available that could eliminate concerns about spoofing. Jim Warren, a well-known activist for electronic access to government, wrote about Mineta's excuse in his electronic newsletter GovAccess, "This smells much more like this 'Representative' is simply using the vile-cracker-horror myth as an excuse for not responding to modern communications—e-mail—in a timely, modern manner."

Other members used the blame game, with one acknowledgment in the Senate falsely claiming that "Senate Rules prohibit my replying via e-mail," and a similar excuse on the House side stating that House security rules barred anything but an auto-acknowledgment. Valid reasons exist for members of Congress to use an auto-acknowledgment when establishing public e-mail access to their offices. It is an effective first step toward the development of a fully integrated constituent e-mail system within an office. But be on the lookout for those offices that want to reap the positive high-tech image that having an e-mail address offers them, but at the same time offer up excuses for not replying via e-mail, rather than an honest explanation as to why they are not yet ready to. They can't have it both ways.

The same tools that allow an office to setup an auto-acknowledgment are likewise employed to help sort and manage incoming e-mail in other ways. In Senator Kennedy's office we learned to sift out constituent messages by having the computer scan the text of incoming e-mail for text strings that indicate a constituent postal address is included. In an attempt to find messages from Kennedy's constituents, messages that included the strings "Massachusetts" or "Mass." or "MA" were presumed to contain a mailing address in the state and were pulled from the in-box and sent to a printer to more quickly join the regular mail for a reply. One office in the Senate took this approach a step farther, sending every single incoming message directly to a printer. The office's system administrator called me in a panic, "We're going through reams of paper!" he told me. "What am I going to do?" I suggested he try to leave as much of his electronic mail electronic and try printing only those messages that they needed to print.

As public access to e-mail increases, and more constituent communications and individual replies from Members of Congress are carried over the Net, real cost savings could result. Contrary to popular perception, Congressional offices do not operate with unlimited budgets. Office supplies such as paper and toner for fax machines are purchased from a limited office account for such items. A supply cost is associated with fax machines that run all day, or e-mail messages sent straight to a printer. Even snail mail brings the associated expense of replies sent out under the Congressional franking privilege (the ability of members to send mail under their signature, rather than regular postage). The amount of franked mail an office can send is also a budgeted amount with real limits. E-mail does not currently have any "per-message" costs associated with it as snail mail does. If left electronic as they wend their way through a Congressional office, e-mail messages won't use a grain of toner or a page of paper.

Another option that offices employ is intended to keep people who follow-up the auto-acknowledgment message from getting the same acknowledgment a second time. Frequently individuals learn from the acknowledgment that lacking a postal address in their message they should expect no further reply, and they send their postal address in a second message. Others receive the acknowledgment and take it to be a direct individual reply from the Congressman they wrote to. Amazed at the personal and rapid attention that their e-mail has received, some of these individuals will follow-up with a note of thanks and praise for the quick reply. In either case there is no point to sending the same auto-acknowledgment again, and by simply excluding messages that contain "re:" in the subject line from receiving it, constituent in-boxes and illusions can be protected.

Many people take a member of Congress's e-mail address as an invitation to send very frequent, often daily, messages to impart another nugget of wisdom on their elected representatives. We had a couple of such regulars, a right-to-bear-arms advocate and a pro-lifer, who would send several missives to Senator Kennedy each week, usually tirades against his holding a position on the issue opposed to their own. By using what's known on the Net as a "bozo filter," such messages can easily be found by the sender's name, sorted out from the rest of the incoming e-mail, and set aside to be counted and given all the attention they deserve.

A number of offices have taken the next step in handling electronic mail from constituents by replying to e-mail with e-mail, including the offices of Senator Barbara Boxer of California and Kennedy's. They have done so not due to any enhanced technical ability to route and respond to e-mail, but because of a determination to stay at the forefront in using technology to best meet the needs of their constituents. While auto-acknowledgment messages are still sent for each incoming message, e-mail from constituents is sorted manually and the appropriate response is delivered via e-mail. As more offices accommodate themselves to handling e-mail, it is likely that many will follow this example.

Senators Kennedy and Boxer have also led the way in another use of e-mail on the Hill, the creation of custom e-mail addresses for particular purposes. Senator Boxer first set up a custom address for responses to the health care survey (more on this later) that she put on the Internet, *health_survey@boxer.senate.gov*, and she has since set up a special address at which children are invited to contact her office, *kids@boxer.senate.gov*. During the debate over proposed cuts to financial aid programs for college students in early 1995, the e-mail address *studentaid@kennedy.senate.gov* was created specifically for input from students who wished to express their concern and describe the impact that such cuts would have on their education. During the debate on the Senate floor, Senator Kennedy held up a stack of hundreds of messages he'd received via electronic mail from students across the country to demonstrate the widespread consequences that the cuts would have on students across the country. We could have more easily put them all on a disk for the Senator to hold up during the debate, but a stack of paper is still a more impressive display of a volume of evidence than a 3.5-inch computer diskette!

Congressional E-Mail Addresses

Once e-mail became available on the Hill, it was a simple matter for a congressional office to create new addresses for members, and a number of different approaches are used. Domain names in the Senate were unique to individual offices or committees and followed the formula of "@*senator's lastname.senate.gov*" or "@*committee name. senate.gov*". For Senate staff, your Internet address was simply your existing e-mail address with blanks filled in by an underscore in front of the office's domain name. In my case, I was *chris_casey@kennedy.senate.gov*. A number of offices created long addresses along the same lines of the existing staff model, either *firstname_lastname@lastname.senate.gov* or *senator_lastname@lastname.senate.gov*. When creating an address for Senator Kennedy, I figured that the domain name "*@kennedy.senate.gov*" pretty much said it all and that a lengthy user name in front was unnecessary. We opted for the shorter "*senator@kennedy.senate.gov*." Some other Senators use even shorter and more informal addresses such as *bob@kerrey.senate.gov* and *max@baucus.senate.gov*.

In the House of Representatives, every Internet e-mail address has the same domain name, *@hr.house.gov*. The extra "hr" is required to route incoming messages to the House's central e-mail directory. One result of identical domain names in the House is that e-mail addresses for House members have shown much more variety than in the Senate, partly because there are so many more Representatives than there are Senators making name recognition harder to come by. Many follow a simple approach using the Representative's name. Others use the district name in the address, which conveys a stronger identification with the district itself rather than with the individual who represents it. Examples include *fla15@hr.house.gov* (Dave Weldon, Florida) and *ninthnet@hr.house.gov* (Rick Boucher, Virginia). The opposite approach has been used by some members who've created often all-too-cute names associated directly with the Representative such as annagram@hr.house.gov (Anna Eschoo, CA) and *talk2bob @hr.house.gov* (Robert Goodlatte, VA). Some sound more like addresses for advice columnists than for members of Congress; consider *askhelen@hr.house.gov* (Helen Chenoweth, Idaho) or *dearsue @hr.house.gov* (Sue Kelly, New York).

Once the first few members of Congress had established a public address, people would frequently simply change the name to another member's to see if a message might get through. For the handful of members who actually used e-mail within their offices, some found that the public and press had stumbled onto their e-mail addresses and into inboxes. They often found it necessary to create separate public and private e-mail addresses.

Snail mail to Congress often gets to the correct destination even when improperly addressed. The House and Senate both have their own zip codes, but even letters with terribly inaccurate addresses on their envelopes regularly get through, especially in the Senate (after all, there are only 100 of them). Misaddressed e-mail, however, is another story.

Assumptions that every member of Congress followed a single formula for their e-mail address sometimes led to confusion and frustration among writers. One week in December 1994, I found myself receiving a barrage of messages addressed to *administrator@kennedy.senate.gov* complaining that their e-mail messages to Senator Kennedy were not getting through. After replying to several of these with an apology and a correct address, I noticed a pattern. Every single one of these complaints had originated from an America Online (AOL) user.

I logged onto AOL and went to the political section, Capital Connection. Sure enough, there was a recently created section for congressional e-mail addresses. The list of Senators with e-mail had incorrectly assumed that all Senate addresses followed the same formula. For some this formula worked, but for others messages sent to the given address were doomed to bounce. After bringing this problem to AOL's attention, they quickly corrected their list. For my part, I added several possible variations as aliases for Senator Kennedy's e-mail in order to try and catch more misaddressed messages in the future.

This home page, maintained by an opponent of Fetal Tissue Research, invites individuals to send a note of opposition to every member of the Senate with one click. A duplicate page sends spams to members of the House of Representatives.

Definition: Spam (or Spamming)

An inappropriate attempt to use a mailing list, or USENET or other networked communications facility as if it was a broadcast medium (which it is not) by sending the same message to a large number of people who didn't ask for it. The term probably comes from a famous Monty Python skit which featured the word "spam" repeated over and over. The term may also have come from someone's low opinion of the food product with the same name, which is generally perceived as a generic content-free waste of resources. (Spam is a registered trademark of Hormel Corporation, for its processed meat product.)

EX: Mary spammed 50 USENET groups by posting the same message to each.[1]

Spamming Congress

As more members of Congress establish e-mail addresses, they are finding themselves on the receiving end of constituent spammings. Citizens who are taking advantage of their new-found ability to send e-mail to their representatives in Congress are frequently taking the opportunity to copy the message to every other member of Congress who has an e-mail address. Often they copy the President, Vice President, and any other e-mail address for a public official or media outlet they can locate. A number of sites on the Web, such as the one illustrated above, encourage the spamming of Congress by providing a one-click path to the electronic in-box of every member of Congress with an e-mail address. While these individuals may feel they're performing some sort of righteous act of electronic activism, the reality is that they are doing harm to the usefulness of electronic mail as a means of constituent communication.

Every member of Congress deals with legislation that impacts a public far beyond his or her own state or district. Committee chairmen in the House and Senate wield tremendous influence over legislation that falls within their domain. Members of the party leadership, caucus chairs, and members with varied professional backgrounds or

---

[1]Matisse Enzer & Internet Literacy Consultants, A Glossary of Internet Terms, http://www.matisse.net/files/glossary.html

personal interests likewise hold sway over the bills of interest to them. When Congress was considering health care reform in 1994, it was entirely appropriate for people from outside of Massachusetts to share their views on the issue with Senator Kennedy because of his long history of working on the issue and his position as chairman of the Labor and Human Resources Committee, which considered the legislation. There are plenty of reasons why individuals might send e-mail to a Representative or Senator who is not their own.

But there is no good reason why anyone should, as a matter of routine, copy his or her message to *every single member of Congress!*

Imagine that a person from each of fifty states decides they want to share an opinion with Congress and sends a letter to his or her own Representative and two Senators. One hundred and fifty letters arrive on Capitol Hill, delivered to the members of Congress that are directly responsible to that individual. Now suppose that every member of Congress has an e-mail address, and that those same fifty individuals decide to send their messages via e-mail. While they're at it, they figure they can have a greater impact by copying their message to every other member of Congress in addition to their own. All 532 of them. Then 26,750 messages arrive on Capitol Hill, and that's only one person from each state. If a single person from each of 435 congressional districts sends e-mail to every member of Congress, then 232,725 e-mail messages will arrive in Congress. And each Representative will have to wade through 535 messages to find one from a constituent, while Senators will perhaps find a few more needles in that haystack.

In April 1994, by sending an advertisement to more than 5,500 Usenet news groups without any regard for the groups' topic of discussion, the now infamous "green card lawyers" spammed Usenet and were vilified across the Internet. One of the most basic rules of good Internet behavior (netiquette) is to post messages only to news groups appropriate to the subject of the message. Similarly, carelessly copying an e-mail message to a large number of people without any regard for whether they'll actually want it is frowned on in proper Net society. Filling someone's e-mail with endless messages with the intent to over burden their system is not just bad manners, but an act of Net terrorism. Spamming and mail bombing, repeatedly sending messages to an individual with the intent of overwhelming their ability to manage the deluge, are certainly considered poor netiquette. Why then is netiquette so often cast aside and the proper manners of e-mail ignored when writing to members of Congress? If Congress is expected to embrace the Internet, and enter the information age as both information provider and responsive participant, then Congress ought to be welcomed with the normal rules of netiquette applying.

But mountains of e-mail in a congressional office aren't always the result of efforts by mad mail bombers. The Net is particularly well suited for allowing like-minded individuals across the country and around the world to send a unified message on an issue of concern to them to any or all members of Congress with an e-mail address. The electronic version of the postcard campaign duplicates its snail mail counterpart, but does it on the net.

Our first real experience with an large-scale, organized e-mail campaign came in early 1995 when within a couple of days we received more than 500 e-mail messages that expressed opposition to the proposed "Communications Decency Act." According to the bill's sponsor, Senator James Exon of Nebraska, the bill would help to "keep the information superhighway from looking like a red light district." But to millions of Internet users, the bill threatened to have a chilling or even fatal effect on privacy and free speech on the Internet. Internet users mobilized and initiated a number of online efforts to defeat the bill including an Internet petition and an electronic mail campaign that reached every online member of Congress. The messages were identical, all addressed to Senator Larry Pressler, chairman of the Senate Commerce Committee under whose purview the telecommunications reform bill fell, and they were typically copied to dozens of other offices as well. Just about every one of these messages included a snail mail address for the sender.

It is very likely that most of these messages went unanswered. Offices that have a policy of not responding to mail that originates outside of their state or district would likely have deleted the messages outright upon seeing that they weren't addressed directly to them, or that they included a postal address outside of their own responsibility. But this effort led Senator Kennedy's office to take the seemingly obvious step of replying to all of the messages at once. We did reply to non-Massachusetts mail in Kennedy's office and by my own procedures (any message with an included postal address was printed and received a reply) I ought to have printed out these 500+ messages. They would have been added to the regular postal mail for sorting, coded with the number that indicated the appropriate reply, keyed into the correspondence management system, printed, auto-penned with a signature, folded, stuffed, franked, and mailed!

Even though I had initiated the snail mail reply to e-mail messages procedures we were following, I always knew that this was only a first step, and now we were presented with the opportunity to try and do better.

I was one of the staffers in Kennedy's office dealing with the issues raised by Senator Exon's Communications Decency Act. I had written a number of memos for the Senator describing both sides of the issue and recommending that he oppose the bill. Senator Kennedy agreed with my arguments, and I drafted a letter outlining his position to send in reply to all of the mail we had received on the issue. Typically, the e-mail we received mirrored the subject areas that the postal mail did and the e-mail made up only a tiny percentage of the total messages received on any particular subject. But this issue was unique in that the amount of electronic messages received far outpaced the snail mail messages. We had more than 500 individuals send e-mail opposing the Exon bill and fewer than ten messages sent either by postal mail or fax. Only a single letter arrived in support of Exon, no messages in support of Exon arrived over the Net.

Once Senator Kennedy's response had been drafted, I could have either sent the reply via franked letter or e-mail. In this case the choice was obvious. In the couple of minutes it took my PC to send Senator Kennedy's e-mail reply to the hundreds of people across the country who had E-mailed their concerns to the Senator, we saved a tremendous amount time, resources, and expense that would have been used had we replied the old way.

Considering the fact that the Senator's reply showed him to be in agreement with the senders' position on the issue, it was not surprising that this technology-savvy audience was pleased to not only get a reply, but to get it via e-mail. The follow-up messages we received were complementary and demonstrated the satisfaction felt at having their concerns directly addressed:

> *Of the many replies from senators I have received to my e-mail note, yours was by far the most informative. Most were just standard form letters, as if they either had no comment or had no interest in replying to me.*

> *Thank you for your thoughtful and reassuring reply to my message expressing concern about Senator Exon's Act. I should also add that yours is the first reply I have received which directly addressed the substance of our concerns. As a non US citizen I am sorry to have trespassed on your time, but some issues transcend national boundaries, and what you do in the US affects us all.*

One offered a somewhat backhanded compliment with an accurate assumption of how the message had been handled.

> *It's interesting to note that I sent my message concerning the "Communications Decency Act" to approximately 12 members of Congress and received a reply from all of them. However, your reply was*

the only one of any substance. All the rest were of the general form "Isn't the Internet a wonderful thing? I'm so glad you sent me your opinion. Bla bla bla..." I have the suspicion I got back form letters that someone put together to cover e-mail. I don't mean to imply that YOU read what I sent, you probably didn't. But at least it shows you have a staff capable of supplying a form letter that's an appropriate response to the letter you received. Hey, I'm not complaining. In fact, providing an appropriate response appears to be quite an accomplishment for a member of the Senate, so you did good.

In addition to the large amounts of issue-oriented e-mail that arrive in Congress, a member's own notoriety combined with political events can also bring torrents of e-mail upon an unprepared office. Following the recapture of both the House and the Senate by the Republicans in November 1994, Speaker-elect Newt Gingrich's office began receiving about 3,000 e-mail messages a week. Unable to keep up with the influx, Gingrich's staff first asked House Information Systems staff how to delete the messages, but then instead requested that the messages be printed. Thousands of messages were printed out onto three large flat loads.

Although his staff told reporters pursuing the story of the e-mail backlog that the messages had been archived, others report that the still unread e-mail, together with unopened snail mail, was all shredded in a marathon session in a small room at HIS. By one account, so many letters were shredded the staff wore masks to filter the amount of dust being circulated.

Nevertheless, this story should not discourage individuals from contacting members of Congress via electronic mail. Deleting unread constituent e-mail is by no means routine on Capitol Hill. Printing e-mail first in order to shred it is rarer still.

Locating Your Congressman's E-Mail Address

Since late 1993, Internet e-mail has been available to just about every office in both the House and Senate. In some cases there are offices that, for either technical reasons, or for having special circumstances or security concerns such as the intelligence committees, that cannot or will not connect to the Net. But for most member offices and committees, setting up a public e-mail address is not a technical hurdle.

The chances that your Senator or Representative has a public e-mail address are steadily improving. From the original seven members of the House of Representatives who launched the House's pilot constituent e-mail program in June 1993, the number of Representatives with e-mail addresses had grown to 175 by mid-February 1996. Although only about five Senators had e-mail addresses by the June 1994, just over a year later the Congress's first online majority was established when in August 1995 more than fifty were receiving e-mail. Soon after, that number had reached almost seventy.

The House of Representatives has established an autoresponder that delivers a complete listing of Representatives who have an e-mail address. This listing will be automatically sent in reply to any e-mail message addressed to *congress@hr.house.gov*.

The Senate was much more coy when it came to actually telling anybody what their e-mail addresses were. A basic server for the transfer of files over the Internet, an ftp server, was in place in the Senate by late 1993. By February 1994 an easier to use gopher server had been added (one of the rare circumstances in which the Senate beat the House to something!). But among those files available on the Senate servers, there was no listing of e-mail addresses for members of the Senate. As more offices began posting files to the server, they often would share an e-mail address among their postings. But for any Net browser looking for Senate e-mail addresses, the best you could do on the Senate server was to plunge into the growing number of directories on an e-mail treasure hunt. After almost two years of hearing from people who were looking for such a file, in early 1995 the Senate finally created a listing of e-mail addresses for Senators and made it available on the Senate server.

The best single source for a complete listing of e-mail addresses for members of Congress and congressional committees is without question the one maintained by Grace York, coordinator of the Documents Center at the University of Michigan Library. Since September 1994, Grace has done the legwork of exploring both the Senate and House gophers and other sources to locate e-mail addresses (and URLs) for members of Congress and compile them into a single listing. A copy of Grace's list can be found in the appendix of this book. But the most up-to-date version is on the Net at *gopher://una.hh.lib.umich.edu/0/socsci/poliscilaw/uslegi/conemail*.

If all else fails, then go low tech and either write or call the office of your Senator or Representative and tell them that you are a constituent that requests that they establish an e-mail address and a presence on the Internet. Few things carry more weight with members of Congress than a number of constituents asking that something be done, and a handful of phone calls and letters will go a long way toward dragging a reluctant member online. Don't let them tell you it's not possible, because for most members of Congress getting on the Internet is a matter of choice and not a technical hurdle. Your input can help them to make that choice.

Number of Representatives with public e-mail addresses

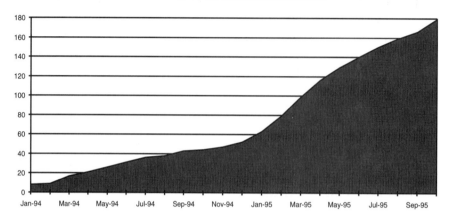

Some members have begun to feel the effect of not having set up an e-mail address. When America Online, the largest of the commercial online services, invited their subscribers to send a budget message to President Bill Clinton, Speaker of the House Newt Gingrich, and Senate Majority Leader Bob Dole, they ran into a small problem. Although both the President and the Speaker had established e-mail addresses more than two years earlier, the majority leader of the Senate did not yet have one. Knowing that Senator Dole's campaign for president, unlike his Senate office, was on the Internet, AOL figured they could just direct Senator Dole's messages to his campaign e-mail address. But the messages never arrived at the Dole campaign. They went instead to an address belonging to one of several sites on the Internet that parodied Dole's campaign, and the message sent out in reply by the spoofers was certainly not what the real campaign, or the Senator's office, would likely have sent for themselves:

> *"Thank you for your suggestions regarding the Federal Budget. As an important senator, and a candidate for President, it is important that I appear to care about your opinion."*

AOL formally apologized to Dole's campaign for the misdirected mail. There was no indication about whether the event would encourage Dole's Senate office to begin accepting e-mail. But Senator Arlen Specter, another GOP Presidential candidate got the message. He set up an e-mail address the next week.

Being a member of Congress with an e-mail address is no longer groundbreaking or unique. It won't be too long until a member of Congress having an e-mail address will be no more unique than having a telephone number. Holdouts will eventually recognize this trend and join their wired colleagues, or they will hang on until retirement or defeat at the polls replaces them with someone who does.

Sending Electronic Mail
to Congress

Sending e-mail to Congress can be a very effective means for quickly and conveniently communicating with your elected representatives. A few basic steps can be taken to greatly enhance the likelihood that your message will be received, and your concern addressed:

- *Be brief:* Don't write a book. Make your point clearly and succinctly. Don't include any file attachments. Some offices delete any messages with attachments or messages that exceed a particular file size. If you can't say it in less than 20k, in the body of the message, and without any attachments, then consider writing a letter.

U.S. Senate Internet e-mail

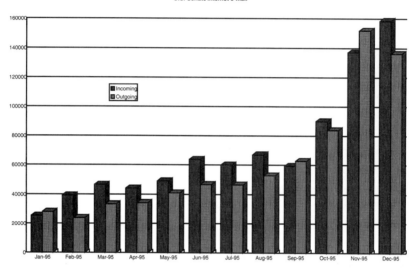

- *Include a name and postal address:* Members of Congress want to know who they are hearing from, and they particularly want to know if you are a constituent of theirs. Including a real name and return address will provide the information they need to best handle your inquiry.

- *Address your message to a single recipient:* The likelihood of a reply increases if the recipient feels the message was sent to them directly, rather than feeling that they were just one of many on a long list of copies. Don't look for anything more than an auto-reply from members of Congress who find themselves halfway down a long list of cc's to a message that begins "Dear Member of Congress" or "Dear Mr. President."

If you vote NO I will remember you

- *Do some research:* Whether writing a member of Congress a letter or an e-mail message, you will always do well to be specific about the issue you are writing about. In Senator Kennedy's mailroom we kept a postcard sent by an angry constituent taped on the wall. It said only "If you vote no, I will remember you." If you have access to the Internet, then use it to explore and see if the member of Congress you are writing to posts any information to the Senate or House servers. You may find that he or she has posted information that will answer your question, or give you more information to use when writing your letter.

- *Write once:* Although it is easy to do, there is no point in sending the same electronic message to any member of Congress over and over again. If you think the pile of e-mail you're sending is somehow having a greater impact that a single message, you're wrong. It's much more likely that you're taking the quickest route toward adding your name to a "bozo filter" that will sift out any messages you send in the future and delete them unread and unmissed. Electronically harassing a members of Congress or staff is the wrong way to bring them around to your point of view.

- *Write sparingly:* While any citizen should be encouraged to send e-mail to their representatives in Congress whenever they feel like it, you will increase the likelihood of your messages being handled and replied to promptly if you do not send off a daily message to Congress. In Senator Kennedy's office, we had a number of regulars who wrote almost daily because they seemed to think a daily reminder message to the Senator of their strongly held views might in time wear him down and bring him around to their way of thinking. They were wrong. If you're looking for an e-mail pen pal, don't look to your Congressman.

- *Be realistic:* For some reason there is a tendency for people to be more willing to believe things read on the Net while being more suspect of information gained by other media. The same holds true for e-mail. Many seem to expect that an e-mail address is always going to be a direct path to the recipient, who is sitting in front of a computer staring at the monitor just waiting for it to arrive. You should not be disappointed to know that the odds of your message actually being read by the member you are writing to are very poor. It is much more realistic to expect that a systems administrator, mail manager, staff case-worker, or legislative correspondent will likely be the ones who read and respond to your e-mail message, just as they handle the postal mail, phone calls, faxes and drop in visitors.

Of course, circumstances vary office by office, and some members of Congress may receive a manageable volume of mail that allows them to give it all their personal attention, but generally you can expect a reply that's been drafted by a staffer and passed through the office's system to ensure that it reflects the member's position or views. Members generally see a representative sampling of their mail and receive correspondence reports that break down the numbers and subjects of the mail they're receiving. Just as you shouldn't expect that your e-mail to the president is making any bells ring on a PC in the Oval Office, neither should you expect the same from the Hill.

Electronic mail is rapidly becoming a routine and accepted way for the public to communicate with their representatives in Congress. In the near future every member of Congress will have an e-mail address, and individuals with an understanding of how e-mail is handled on the Hill will be well prepared to make the most out of this new-found access to Congress and better equipped to participate as citizens in the legislative process.

Representative Charlie Rose - Democrat, North Carolina, 7th District

Currently serving his twelfth term as Representative of North Carolina's 7th Congressional District, Charlie Rose is well know on Capitol Hill for his interest in computers. But unlike most members of Congress of his age and experience, many of whom don't use a computer at all, Rose is a hands-on user and it shows. I met briefly with Congressman Rose in November 1995, but our time was cut short when more pressing business came up. The Congressman entered his office where I was speaking with his chief of staff and where two technicians had been working all afternoon trying to get the Congressman's new recordable CD-ROM drive connected without success. After giving me as much time as politeness required, he immediately took his seat in front of his computer and took command of the effort to finish this hardware installation.

Until the 1994 elections brought the Republicans to power in the House of Representatives, Rose chaired the House

Administration Committee which had oversight authority over House Information Systems (HIS) and all computer support in the House. From this position Rose was able to personally oversee the development and use of new technologies within the House, and his own experience helped chart the course. The development of an integrated e-mail capability with Internet access was initiated in the House following a call Rose made to an HIS staffer after he had encountered difficulties transferring a file between his Washington and North Carolina offices via a direct modem connection.

Rose's personal interest in technology is equaled by his support for developing free public access to government information. He often pushed the issue of public access to congressional information forward by instructing HIS to make some of the same information it made available within the House for member offices, such as the *Congressional Record* and the text of legislation, available to the public free of charge on the Internet.

Surprisingly, although he was among the first Representatives to establish a public e-mail address and to establish a gopher site (his was at Fayetteville Tech in North Carolina), Rose has yet to unveil a Web home page and his gopher is largely inactive. The Congressman attributes this to the great amount of time required to develop and maintain a good site, something he says he and his staff don't have. His chief of staff adds that developing access to official public documents should be a higher priority than the use of the Net by individual members of Congress as a public relations tool.

But Rose is a regular explorer of the Net himself, and he's bound to find the time to put himself there eventually. Perhaps as soon as he gets that CD-ROM drive hooked up.

FOUR

An early look at the Senate gopher. By this time Kennedy had been joined by Senators Stevens (AK), Robb (VA), Leahy (VT), Nunn (GA), and Bingaman (NM).

Tools of the Trade

Usenet

Although Senator Kennedy's initial efforts to reach the Internet included posting to two appropriate Usenet news groups, there is, in general, very little activity in Usenet coming from the Hill.

One reason Usenet has not really seen much participation by members of Congress is that they are not ready or willing to participate in the type of running dialogues that characterize the discussion threads found in a Usenet news group. It's easy to explain to a members of Congress why they should be posting information to a gopher directory or on a home page for others to find and read, but e-mail accessibility is often only grudgingly accepted by offices because they understand they must always at least appear to be willing to receive feedback (although a few members do post information to the Internet without also offering an e-mail address). Although some offices may see Usenet news groups as another place where they can post information, it is less likely that they will devote the time and attention necessary to carry on a conversation in Usenet. Reaction to Kennedy's posts in *ne.politics* was generally very positive, but often reflected disappointment that the office did not follow-up and participate in the discussions that his postings initiated.

Another reason that Congress is likely to tread lightly into Usenet is the potential for embarrassing or inappropriate postings that could reflect poorly on the member. One such incident was described by Dinty Moore in his book, *The Emperor's Virtual Clothes*, when the author described his experience in the news group *alt.hi.are.you.cute*.

> *The purpose, as best I can discern, is for people to tell one another whether they are cute or not. Of course, participants in this group are talking by computer, so it is easy enough to lie. Nor does it seem to matter. Just say that you are cute, and you will be welcomed with open (electronic) arms.*

> *Perhaps the reason I am so fond of this group is that the evening I discovered it someone sent a message from an address that ended with "house.gov". What this means in Internet idiom is that the individual on the other end was posting from a government account, specifically one connected to the House of Representatives. The important federal message asked, "Are there any cute girls out there?"*

I was hoping to catch my local congressman cheating on his wife, or maybe even Newt Gingrich trolling for babes, so I quickly sent the house.gov person an electronic mail reply, asking, "Why is a House staffer (or are you a representative) posting to alt.hi.are.you.cute? Sounds fishy. Fess up or I will tell Bob Dole."

This apparently spooked the poor guy because I got a lengthy message back thirty minutes later explaining House policy on Internet use and making very clear that any and all alt.hi.are.you.cute activity happened very late at night, after business hours. For all the fellow knew, I might have been Bob Woodward at The Washington Post. I could feel the fear coming off the screen.

"I realize that America thinks Congress wastes their money," he wrote, "but let me assure you that I am in no way abusing the privilege of serving you." He admitted to being a legislative analyst for the Republican leadership and eventually asked me, "How cute do you consider yourself?"

Cute enough to know when my tax dollars are being wasted.[1]

Bob Dole need not worry about any similarly embarrassing episodes in the Senate, because Senate staff don't have access to Usenet. None at all. Except for Senate Computer Center staff. They've maintained a news host (a server for distributing news groups) since 1993 and are "evaluating" the service, but until the Rules Committee specifically proclaims that the Senate needs it and that staff can have access

---

[1] ©1995 by Dinty W. Moore. From The Emperor's Virtual Clothes: Truth About The Internet Culture. Reprinted by permission of Algonquin Books of Chapel Hill, a division of Workman Publishing Company

to it, there will be no Usenet in the Senate. Not to *alt.hi.are.you.cute,* and not to *alt.politics.usa.congress.*

The domain names that would come attached to Senate Usenet posts would more directly identify the originating office than those from the House would. For example, a message posted to a news group from Senator Kennedy's office would have *"username@kennedy. senate.gov"* attached to it, whereas the same posting from Representative Kennedy's office (either one of them) would appear only as *"username@hr.house.gov."* Imagine if a bored intern or staffer in a Senate office were found leaving trails of postings with their bosses names all over various news groups. Whether it's *alt.hi.are.you.cute, alt.fetish.feet,* or *alt.binaries.pictures.erotica,* Usenet news groups are a minefield in which an indiscreet staff member could easily embarrass their boss. Such a cyber-scandal will inevitably hit the Hill some day; nevertheless, the attempt to postpone that day is one reason for Congress's cautious approach to Usenet today.

On closer examination, such fears of Usenet are far outweighed by the potential gain in access to a tremendous new source of information on virtually every topic under the sun from which any congressional staffer could benefit. Given the enormous number of issues that every member of Congress deals with daily, the value of Usenet as a source of information and a place for discussing congressional actions on any subject should be obvious.

The Senate could at least maintain a news server that restricted access to news groups of questionable value, but I would argue that no such restrictions should exist. It should be up to individual offices to establish their own policies on what is appropriate and inappropriate use of news groups. If a Senate phone were used to dial 1-800-DANCE-PARTY, that would be an obviously inappropriate use of that equipment. But with members of Congress having demonstrated their willingness to pass legislation restricting the Internet, wouldn't it make sense if they and their staffs at least had full access to the Net so they could gain some firsthand experience with it?

As more members of Congress take steps to communicate with constituents via Usenet, they are bound to be faced with the dilemma of choosing an appropriate news group in which to participate. Some will certainly be doomed to face the wrath of the Net when by inexperience they err and post to an inappropriate news group or commit some other blunder. Not every state or region has a political discussion group such as *ne.politics* (New England Politics) has provided for Senator Kennedy. And if every member of Congress were to post to a general political news group such as *talk.politics.misc* (as Kennedy and the White House have) the group could quickly degenerate from an arena for political discussion into an ocean of congressional spin.

I have long thought that a possible solution to this potential dilemma would be the creation of a new hierarchy of news groups for each state that would provide an easy-to-find, appropriate Usenet forum for members of Congress and their staffs to post information and participate in discussions with constituents. A group such as *alt.politics.congresss.ma* would provide an obvious place in which members of the Massachusetts congressional delegation could post information of interest to their constituents. Such a solution really won't become necessary until many more members of Congress are contributing to news groups than currently are, and it remains unclear if they ever will. But the creation of news groups for their purposes could help to pave the way for many more to follow.

Listservers

Electronic mailing lists, also known as listservers, offer individuals the ability to subscribe to discussions covering a wide variety of topics as well as to other various electronic newsletters and publications, and have them delivered via electronic mail. For many Internet users whose have e-mail-only access to the Internet, or who prefer using e-mail to perusing the Net for information, a listserver can provide a useful means of obtaining information of their choosing and having it delivered to them.

The White House began its distribution of White House publications by way of an elaborate program that permitted individuals to subscribe to all White House documents, or to only those of a particular type or subject category. Thousands have subscribed to receive White House documents directly via e-mail. But listservers remain surprisingly underutilized by Congress.

A listserver was part of the new Internet services that then-Representative Sam Coppersmith of Arizona announced in January 1994. In cooperation with Arizona State University (ASU), Coppersmith's office established the *COPRSMTH* mailing list to distribute the congressman's press releases, the House schedule, and other related information from his office. During the first quarter of that year use of the *COPRSMTH* mailing list grew to 80 subscribers, while the Coppersmith gopher directory had been visited by an estimated 1,000 to 3,500 individuals. Comparing these numbers and the value of a member of Congress using listservers. Steven Corman, director of the Public Communication Technology Project at ASU, reported his findings on the use of Rep. Coppersmith's listserver:

These findings suggest that e-mail based distribution lists may not be worth the effort for political representatives. Users may simply gravitate toward self-activated, information-on-demand services like Gopher when they can. Still, e-mail based technologies like COPRSMTH should not be dismissed without further research: they are likely to serve an important class of new or inexperienced users who need a "low-tech" entry point for learning about and exploring network information technology. An explicit goal of the NII [National Information Infra-structure] is to extend access to such users, and research aimed directly at them should explore the value of e-mail based technologies[2]

As constituent services director to Representative Coppersmith, Peter Loge oversaw the congressman's Internet services. When I left Senator Kennedy's office in early 1995, Peter filled the position and quickly established a listserver for Kennedy. Reflecting the Coppersmith experience, the numbers reached by the Kennedy listserver (it had about 150 subscribers in December 1995) do not compare to the many hundreds and thousands who find his posted information via gopher and the Web. Nevertheless, the need to develop the widest possible variety of means for communicating with Congress to suit individuals of many skill and access levels, together with the relative ease of maintaining such a list, argue in favor of a member of Congress establishing a listserver.

FTP/Gopher

In September 1993, *Government Computer News* ran a story about the pilot e-mail program in the House and Senator Kennedy's bulletin board/Internet outreach. The Senate Sergeant at Arms refused to permit the Computer Center to comment for the story, and the Senate came off looking very badly under a bold subheading that read "Delay in Senate." Some of the facts about the Senate in the story were not exactly accurate, and someone reading the article might have gotten the impression that the Senate didn't even have e-mail access to the

---

[2]Steven Corman, "Use and Users of a Congressman's Network Information Services," *Internet Research*, Vol. 4, No. 4, Winter 1994, pp.36-51

Internet, which by that time it did. But since no official in the Senate was willing to speak with the reporter who wrote the story, they had invited an inaccurate story. A computer center staffer later told me that this story had led the Senate's Sergeant at Arms to order the Senate Computer Center to get an Internet site up in two weeks.

When the Senate did establish an ftp server, Senator Kennedy was the first Senator to post files to it. Senator Stevens of Alaska was the second, and for a few weeks these two Teds were the lone members of the Senate on the Internet. We continued taking advantage of MIT's assistance with posting to Usenet and to the ftp archive, and also to the network of Massachusetts bulletin boards, and now we were on a gopher server as well.

When Senator Barbara Boxer of California took her first venture into cyberspace, she rejected the cautious approach favored by the other Senators who had preceded her. Senator Boxer dove in head first.

In her newly established directory on the Senate gopher server, Senator Boxer posted a single file. It wasn't a biography, a list of office addresses, or information on how to buy a flag flown over the Capitol building. Senator Boxer posted an "Internet Health Care Questionnaire" along with the following message:

> Dear California Internet User:
>
> The Senate is going to act this year on an issue that touches the lives of every American—health care reform.
>
> In order to better gauge the health care needs of Californians, I have prepared a series of questions for Internet users to answer. Your answers will help me to better represent you during the health care reform debate.
>
> This questionnaire also represents my first venture onto the Internet. I am excited to be participating in a communications network that has enriched the lives of so many Californians. If this questionnaire elicits a positive response from 'Net users, then you'll be hearing from me again on public policy issues.

You can respond to the attached questionnaire at my temporary Internet address, *health_survey@boxer.senate.gov*. Please put the phrase "health care" (without quotes) in the subject line.

Due to limited staff resources, our Internet address will be open for this survey from June 3 to June 13. Should we wish to respond to you in the future, we would like to have your California Postal Address. We will post survey results on the U.S. Senate gopher bulletin board in Washington, DC, or *ftp.senate.gov.*

Please forward this survey on to other Internet users who you know who may interested in this survey. Please feel free to post it in a place where other people may see it.

Thank you for taking the time to share your concerns with respect to health care reform. I hope that this will be the first of many such exchanges.

The questionnaire itself included nine questions regarding health care reform. Responses were given on a numerical scale, a five meaning the respondent felt the statement to be "very important" down to a one which meant "not at all important." The questionnaire also asked if the user had ever been without health care and invited him or her to offer a personal story of an experience with the health care system that Senator Boxer might share with her Senate Colleagues.

For those in the Senate who were closely following the Internet efforts of other offices—some waiting for their own fears to prove justified, and others just glad to see someone else trying this first—Senator Boxer seemed to be courting disaster. Inviting e-mail from California?! California, the most populous state in the nation and home to more Internet users than any other state! And on health care reform, the most hotly debated issue of the day! Mike Bartell, former director of the Senate Computer Center, described expectations for Boxer's survey with a single word, "suicide," self-inflicted death by e-mail.

Senator Boxer's staff was not unaware of the fact that they were exploring uncharted waters with their questionnaire. They knew that in order to tally results and make any sense of the untold number of responses they would receive, they would have to set a cutoff date. The special e-mail address established for replies would be available only for a ten-day period, after which the address would be deactivated.

Despite all of the dire predictions, Senator Boxer's questionnaire drew a respectable but certainly manageable 1,248 responses. The answers were collated and the results sent back to all of the respondents and posted to Boxer's gopher directory. Senator Boxer had demonstrated that an office can do more than just broadcast on the Internet. She proved that an office can do more than just accept feedback from constituents via electronic mail—she proved that it can be actively solicited. The Boxer survey also proved that a Senator need not fear the Net.

Representative Sam Coppersmith of Arizona established a gopher directory (together with previously mentioned listserver) through which interested netizens could obtain information about his activities in Congress. Coppersmith was able to provide these services, well in advance of their availability within the House itself, thanks to the assistance of the Public Communication Technology Project at Arizona State University (ASU). The first Democrat elected to represent this largely Republican district since 1950, Coppersmith was the first (and initially the only) member of the Arizona congressional delegation to accept ASU's offer to assist his office with an effort to develop an Internet-based information resource.

Coppersmith's efforts were well received within his district, which is home to a growing number of high-tech companies, and they brought him a good deal of positive press. "Will these technologies be adapted and adopted as a part of representative democracy?" Coppersmith asked himself in an April 1994 story in the *Phoenix Gazette*. "I think the answer is clearly yes. Will it fundamentally change the nature of democracy? I'm not sure." Despite the aggressive manner with which his office embraced the use of technology, Coppersmith (who left the House in a failed pursuit of a Senate seat in 1994) still describes himself as "a bit of a skeptic about the widespread public applications" of an Internet-accessible Congress.

Project Director Steven Corman published a study on the usage of the Coppersmith gopher directory and listserver during the first quarter of 1994. The study included both an analysis of usage data on the gopher directory and a survey of individuals who used Coppersmith's gopher and/or listserver. Interestingly, the study found that survey respondents placed the highest value on "information that is timely and/or not readily available through other channels" such as issue statements and the House schedule. But actual usage found that the most frequently accessed files were those that contained general information such as a map of the district, and information about Coppersmith's Internet services, how to contact his offices, and his biography. Whatever the reason for this discrepancy, it seems clear that both basic information about a congressional office as well as timely content about the individual members' positions on issues and legislative activities should be fundamental elements of any member of Congress's Internet offerings.

When the House of Representatives established its own gopher server, it initially did not permit member offices to maintain a local directory on the House's server due to concerns that it would not be appropriate for House resources to be used to provide a forum for the political issues that were certain to end up there. Representatives who wanted to establish a gopher directory were encouraged to follow Coppersmith's example and find a site, most often a university, in their own district that would establish and maintain one for them. The House gopher would link to these off-site member gophers, but it would not create a directory for Members unable to make their own arrangements. Only several months later, after the House Administration Committee held a hearing on use of the Internet did the committee's Internet Task Force recommend that members be permitted to post files on the House server and create rules governing what could be posted. A look at directory names on the House gopher today still reveals those that are hosted off-site by the inclusion of the name of the university hosting the site, a dead giveaway that you're looking at the gopher directory of one of the House's early adopters of the Net.

What You Will Find

While many members of Congress have been skeptical about establishing an electronic mail address and have approached e-mail with caution, they are generally much quicker to grasp the benefits of the ability to spread their own press releases, statements, and other information via the Internet. By posting material to the Net, a member of Congress can bypass traditional media and enhance their ability to deliver material directly to constituents. Netizens who are interested in learning more about a particular member of Congress can get a great deal of informative, if not unbiased, information directly from the congressional office itself. Reading the press releases that a member of Congress posts to the Net can offer telling insights into the issues and legislation that member hopes the media and public will notice. Reading the speeches and other statements of a member of Congress will tell you much more than you would get from the sound bite coverage (if any at all) that print or broadcast media gives to these types of events.

In addition to reading the issue-related materials that an office will post, practical constituent concerns are addressed and answered online. A great amount of a member office's time is devoted to the seemingly mundane but very important tasks of helping visiting constituents make tour arrangements while in Washington, DC, arranging for the sale of commemorative American flags to be flown over the Capitol as keepsakes or gifts, taking applications from high school and college students interested in an internship in Congress, and from constituents' who seek a nomination to study at a military service academy. These are the services that can have a long-standing positive impact on a constituent, and the congressman who neglects them may as well be throwing votes away. Placing information about how to take advantage of such services on the Net establishes a 24-hour-a-day info booth and service center on the Net for a congressman, a simple and practical thing for them to do.

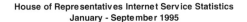

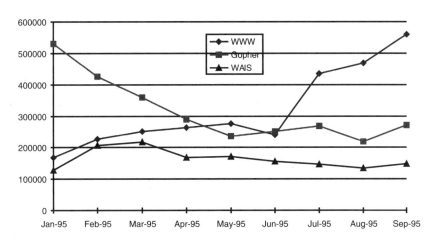

One of the first things you ought to find in your congressman's ftp or gopher directory is information on how to contact their Washington and state or district offices and, in particular, their e-mail address. Some offices that see the advantages of posting to the Net do so without offering an e-mail address to allow Net visitors to offer them immediate feedback and comment on the material they've found. I advise offices not to plan on posting material until they are ready to accept e-mail from the public. Members of Congress should not treat the Net as a television set that allows them the ability to broadcast their point of view to millions. If they aren't ready to accept feedback online, they aren't ready to be on the Net.

As Congress's utilization of the World Wide Web becomes more sophisticated, so will their ability to invite constituent feedback using fill-in forms. The ability to create forms to collect data on the Web will offer new opportunities for members who seek to survey constituent opinions on the net, accept e-mail with pre-defined subject categories, and allow for advanced search features that will help individuals find the information they are looking for.

Representative Pat Schroeder and Senator Barbara Boxer respond to questions in an online forum.

Electronic Town Halls and Press Conferences

During the 1992 presidential campaign, billionaire independent candidate Ross Perot spoke about his promise to hold regular electronic town meetings as president. The prospect has caught the imagination of many citizens of cyberspace, eager to see the Net give them the opportunity to directly question their elected officials. Real-time online communications can permit members of the public the opportunity to, for a brief time, supplant the members of the media who they are accustomed to having ask all the questions. They can ask for themselves in a virtual exchange that might not be possible in real life.

Using Internet Relay Chat (IRC), Web Chat, the discussion forums that can be found on all of the major commercial systems, or even a small local bulletin board system, a member of Congress can engage netizens in real-time discussion and debate.

Vice President Al Gore tested these waters from the White House in January 1994 when he participated in a town hall forum on CompuServe. He also discovered some of the pitfalls unique to the medium when his discussion with one young man was interrupted when the boy's father picked up another telephone extension in the house, briefly garbling the on-screen discussion.

The first hurdle that has to be overcome when trying to arrange an online chat for a member of Congress is often just explaining the concept to them. For someone who has been online for even a brief amount of time, it is very likely that he or she has discovered or at least heard of real-time chats. But for the uninitiated, the very concept can be difficult to grasp.

This difficulty was put on display during an ambitious experiment held in the Senate when a virtual component was added to a hearing. Before each Senator on the committee sat a laptop computer on which discussion with the virtual witnesses was displayed. One befuddled Senator confessed that he simply did not get it. "Where are these people," he asked. "Am I supposed to just talk to the screen?"

Once the understanding hurdle is overcome, another hurdle arises. Should the congressman do their own typing? Typing skills vary greatly among members of Congress, just as they do among the general population. Some type well, some hunt and peck, and others don't type at all. For members who are comfortable with their own typing skills, or even if they are a little unsure, they will usually be willing to grab the keyboard and give it their best shot. Especially when they consider that any photo of them in their chat will be all the more impressive if they're seen at the computer, and when they learn that virtual audiences are very forgiving of typos and bring no expectations of error-free typing to such events. But for those who don't type well enough to keep things moving, or just don't type at all, there's nothing wrong with having a typist take the keyboard for them. An effort to type for themselves is more likely to slow the give and take of the discussion to a crawl, and distract from the real purpose of communicating. People who communicate with members of Congress online are usually much more interested in their responses to questions than in their typing skills.

Other difficulties also exist. The same loss of visual cues, body language, and voice inflection that have made smileys or emoticons common in e-mail messages, occurs in a real-time chat. And even with a skillful typist, the text-based interaction of an online forum moves more slowly than if the same words were spoken. Usually scheduled to last about 45 minutes to an hour, ten to twenty questions are about the average number that can be responded to in an online forum of this length.

But the loss of visual contact can also be seen by the guest as one obvious advantage of an online forum. In a real-life press conference or town meeting, a politician or any speaker stands alone and exposed. They have only their own knowledge to rely on, and their preparation to carry them through. They either know their stuff or they don't, but they are alone out there and expected to have some answers. But safely hidden from view behind a computer screen, a virtual speaker can be surrounded by staff who are able to come up with the finer details necessary to respond to a complicated question or to help craft a reply to a tricky one.

If during a virtual town meeting however, a member of Congress isn't doing the typing, and relies on staff for answers to questions, can you help but wonder if the member's presence is required at all? Couldn't such an event be easily faked? Perhaps it could, but I am not aware of any instance in which one has been. Perhaps sometime in the near future a scandal will arise when a busy member of Congress, forever on a tight schedule, is asked to explain being seen among the guests at some public event, while at the same time he was supposedly entertaining questions from hundreds of virtual guests in cyberspace. "That was my virtual self," will be the likely reply.

So far, members who've been challenged to prove their identities have managed in a couple of ways. When Senator Patrick Leahy was asked "How do we know this is really you" in the first of what became regular town meetings he holds via Internet Relay Chat, he responded, "Because I wouldn't let anyone else in my office have this much fun." His staff then snapped a Polaroid of him at the computer, digitized the photo with a scanner, and added it to his home page together with a transcript of the event. Senator Tom Harkin was nearing the end of his first virtual town meeting when a pending vote forced him to bring the event to an early end. With a little time to spare before going to the Senate floor to vote, the Senator took some time on the way out of the virtual auditorium to thank individuals for coming and take a few final questions. One whose screen name identified her as "Hillary" challenged, "You're not really the senator." Harkin replied, "If Hillary doesn't believe me, she can turn on her television and watch me vote. That is if she has C-SPAN. It's the Shelby Amendment."

FIVE

★

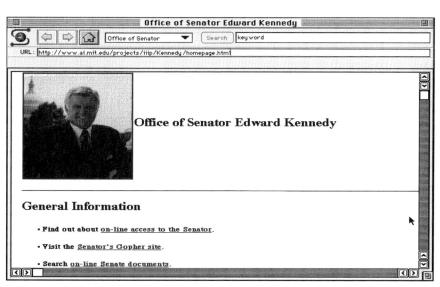

The Kennedy home page version 1.0, the first legislative branch resource on the World Wide Web.

The World Wide Web

In early 1994, I replaced the single dial-up Internet access in Sen. Kennedy's office with a PPP (point-to-point protocol) account from a Washington-area service provider. Use of either a PPP or a SLIP (serial line internet protocol) account permits you to gain full Internet access over a modem and phone line, which allows access to some features of the Net not available via the more limited access of a dial-in account. The Senate still provided only ftp/telnet access to the Internet, but I had read about the World Wide Web and wanted to see for myself what it was about. Like so many others, I found the Web to be wonderfully easy to use and spent many hours exploring many sites. It wasn't long until I wanted to know how Senator Kennedy's Internet outreach could be applied to the Web. I sent a message to my friend Eric at MIT and asked him what it would take to build a home page for Senator Kennedy. Eric had likewise only recently begun exploring the Web, and was just beginning to teach himself Hypertext Markup Language (HTML), the language for creating a home page on the Web, but he was quickly able to put together a rudimentary home page for Senator Kennedy. I placed a GIF image of the Senator in his gopher directory (another first for Ted, the first image file on the Senate's server), and Eric built it into a page with a few basic links. But even this very plain page was a breakthrough by its very existence, and I showed it off to a large crowd when MacWorld Expo came to the Washington Convention Center that same month. With additional help from John Mallery, the Kennedy home page rapidly developed into a first-of-its-kind Internet resource for a member of Congress. It was much more advanced than the still underused gophers, which were then the only available means on the Hill for members to reach the Net. Only four Senators had even begun to utilize the Senate's gopher server: Kennedy, Stevens, Robb, and Leahy.

The existing means by which members were distributing information on the Internet did not fully utilize the Net's ability to link to other resources. There were few connections from member's gopher directories to other gophers on the Net. Among the few member directories that did exist, one could expect to find the usual stuff, press releases, statements, information about constituent services, flag requests, internships, and Washington tour information.

The Web allows a great deal more.

A home page on the Web could still contain links to the same kind of material from a member's office as an ftp or gopher directory might. Many of the links from the original Kennedy home page and the pages of other members of Congress simply linked back to the directories and plain text files they were already posting on the Senate and House gophers. The same bios, press releases, etc. that could be put on the Net using ftp and gopher. It's useful information, but it's usually plain text. The Web, however, offered the opportunity to create a whole new view of a member of Congress on the Internet. All of the features that made Mosaic and other graphical Web browsers so appealing—the inline images, hypertext links, interactivity and multimedia—had brought a whole new meaning to "surfing the net." For myself and millions of others, Mosaic brought the same ease of use to the Internet that I had found FirstClass brought to bulletin boards, and Macs brought to desktop computing. The Web caused a wave on the Net so big that even Congress couldn't help but catch it, even if slowly and sometimes reluctantly.

The home page that Eric, John, and I had developed for Senator Kennedy took advantage of the basic features the Web allowed, and became the model that other members of Congress followed. More than just linking to the plain text files our office was already posting, the Kennedy home page provided the means to carry out some of the other fundamental roles performed by every member of Congress. As the elected representative of their state or district, every member of Congress performs the role of liaison between their constituents and the government. Similarly, members are advocates for their states and districts, and as they promote their states' qualities, they fight to protect their interests. Each of these roles is well suited to the nature of the Web.

As a function of being a liaison to the government, the Kennedy home page provided links to other federal and state government resources on the Net. Links to FedWorld, an online index to electronic government information, and other indices provided browsers with quick access to these resources. When the White House unveiled a home page several months after Kennedy, the Kennedy page linked to it directly, but it also took advantage of the subject codes that are assigned to all White House publications. A preconfigured search link allows visitors to the Kennedy page to retrieve the forty most recent White House releases that have been specifically flagged as Massachusetts related, allowing the Senator to help retrieve from another government site information of particular interest to visitors of his own site.

As a representative of the Commonwealth of Massachusetts, the Kennedy home page contained links to numerous Internet resources across the state such as businesses and universities. From Kennedy's home page a visitor might find themselves exploring one of the many online communities across Massachusetts, searching for a job or a place to live, or checking out the menu of a Boston restaurant.

Unlike the dead ends that a member of Congress's ftp and gopher directories can be, the Web allows a member of Congress to build paths for Net browsers to follow, constituents and nonconstituents alike, and help them to better fulfill these basic functions of their office.

CapWeb

For the first couple of months, we made few changes to Senator Kennedy's home page. John and Eric would add an occasional new link or tweak the appearance slightly. When I had a change I wanted made, I would send Eric an e-mail and ask him to make the change. But I wanted to be able to administer the home page directly, and also to construct for myself the coolest calling card of the Net, a personal home page. With some pointers from my MIT mentors, and a copy of *The Beginner's Guide to HTML*, I was able to construct a simple Chris Casey home page. Along with a short blurb about myself and small collection of links to other sites, my page included a photo of my daughter Katie and I together in a rocker with my PowerBook. With a little help from dad, three-year-old Katie had sent her Christmas wish list to Santa Claus via e-mail, and landed in the *Washington Post* accompanying an article about Santa's new reach on the Net. Once I'd put myself on the Web, I was looking for a new challenge.

A friend pointed me toward some Canadian pages on the Web called Open Government that I found to be of tremendous interest. The pages were a guide to Canada's parliamentary and judicial system, built in a manner that you could search by party or province and locate detailed information about individual members of Canada's Parliament as well as their Supreme Court justices. I was amazed. That this information was available did not mean that each of these individual members was personally contributing anything to the content as we were on the Kennedy home page. It was simply a guide, a hypertext directory to government.

In Washington, publishing congressional directories is a very big business. The Government Printing Office produces a simple pictorial directory of members and the more exhaustive congressional Directory, and many independent publishers compete over the market for compact, detailed guidebooks about Congress. What does a particular member look like? Where is his (or her) office and what's the telephone number? What committees does he sit on? What district does he represent? Few people in Washington who deal with Congress in any capacity haven't owned or used one of these books at one time or another.

And yet no equivalent directory existed on the Net. The Canadian example showed how it could be done, but no one had yet created one for the U.S. Congress. Stuck in traffic on my way home from work in August 1994, I asked myself how long it would take for Congress to put such a directory on the Net. Based on my own experience as a congressional staffer for two-and-a-half years, I answered my own question quickly: probably never. At the time the only legislative branch presence on the World Wide Web at all was Senator Kennedy's office and the Library of Congress (LOC). Both the House and Senate had gopher servers up, but on them you would only find information about those individual members who were using them, still a very small number at the time. I knew of no existing efforts by the House or the Senate to develop a home page for either institution, and I could not imagine who might undertake to create any higher level page for the whole legislative branch. But something else occurred to me in that traffic jam going home. Such an Internet guide to Congress didn't necessarily have to be "official," it didn't even have to be "authorized." Just as independent publishers create their pocket guides to Congress, who was to say that I couldn't create a Net guide?

I imagined a hypertext version of the guides to Congress that could be found in so many lobbyists' briefcases in Washington. Unlike the existing gopher servers that the Senate and House maintained, this guide would contain basic information about *every* member of Congress, not just those few that had found their own way to the net. It would include all of the basic information about a member of Congress found in printed directories: a phone number, address, e-mail address (if available), committee assignments, and even a photo. If that member did have an Internet resource of their own—an e-mail address, a gopher directory, or whatever—this guide would simply add a link to it, helping netizens to find their way to that resource. The guide would also include links to other legislative branch resources on the Internet. In addition to the Library of Congress, other congressional agencies were likewise working to make information resources available on the Internet. The Government Printing Office, the General Accounting Office, and the Office of Technology Assessment were among those agencies that either already had or were developing Internet resources. Finally, this guide would include links to other relevant sites, a hypertext version of the Constitution at Cornell, a bill searching tool in New Jersey, anything related to the legislative branch of government, the members who serve there, and the issues that rage there. I began working that night, mapping out the basic structure of this Web site and started spinning some HTML to build it. Very quickly I realized the magnitude of the task I had undertaken.

There are twenty committees in the Senate and twenty more in the House of Representatives. Additionally there are four joint committees. The 535 members of Congress and five delegates, representing fifty states, four territories, and the District of Columbia, each serve on anywhere from one to five or even more committees. The organization of Congress is a Web of its own. Creating a hypertext guide to reflect it would be a straightforward but time-consuming effort.

The following day, I shared my idea for this Web guide to Congress that I was already calling "CapWeb" with a friend, colleague, and fellow Internet enthusiast in the Senate, Jeff Hecker. Jeff was the systems administrator in the office of the majority leader, Senator Mitchell of Maine. But unlike many sys admins such as myself, who were perhaps just handy enough with a PC to get their jobs done, Jeff actually knew something about computers, about UNIX, and about the Internet. Soft spoken when met face to face, Jeff is devastatingly effective when discussing the state of the Senate via e-mail, and he was famous for the sarcastic wit he employed in his many fair but frank e-mail messages to the powers that be in the Senate Computer Center and other Senate bureaucrats who were so often put on the defensive when faced by someone that they couldn't baffle with techno-babble.

Unlike the support that I had found in Senator Kennedy's office for my online adventures, Senator Mitchell's office showed much less enthusiasm for the Internet and was quick to accept the excuses/ explanations proffered by the Senate Computer Center, Rules Committee, Sergeant at Arms, or whomever as to the retarded status of the development of the Internet within the Senate. Nevertheless, Jeff's was one of the more frequent voices arguing in favor of the Internet. Mitchell's own office network was UNIX-based, a rarity in the Senate and not among the few network operating systems that the Senate Computer Center supported. Within his own office Jeff was often able to develop his own solutions to various problems and needs, wanting and needing no assistance from the Senate. But he was still not able to connect his office to the Internet until the Senate would allow access, leading to his frequent offering of unsolicited advice and assistance, which usually fell on deaf ears. His own interest in the Internet and in seeing congressional information made available on-line, combined with Jeff's own "just do it" attitude, made him an enthusiastic partner in CapWeb. We divided up the Congress and started spending our evenings writing HTML.

After having built a basic structure of home pages for both houses of Congress and every committee, we needed a place on the Net where we could further develop and test it, and where we could invite some comments on its usefulness. I again turned to my friends at MIT, who were willing to provide CapWeb a temporary home while we developed it. During its time on the Artificial Intelligence Laboratory's server, we kept CapWeb under access restrictions in order to prevent the premature unveiling on the Net of an unfinished work, and to lessen any impact its presence might have on the AI server.

A personal effort, and not part of our work in the Senate, Jeff and I developed CapWeb on our own time in the evenings and weekends at home. As we built the pages, we invited individuals from the White House, the House, the Senate and the Library of Congress, among others, to visit CapWeb and share some feedback with us, adding them to the access list to allow them to reach the still restricted pages. We also took a couple of opportunities to demonstrate CapWeb to small groups.

Less than a month after we had begun working on CapWeb, the Senate Computer Center hosted another one of its Internet seminars, events at which they invited Senate staff to come and take a watch a demonstration of Internet resources. Access to most of the demonstrated features, such as the Web, remained unavailable to staff. We took the opportunity to show some of our colleagues what we'd been working on. At this point only the Senate half of CapWeb was near completion. With November's election just six weeks away we didn't think we should go to the trouble to enter what might soon be obsolete data (which turned out to be a very good decision considering the large turnover in the 1994 elections and the Republicans' gaining of a majority in both chambers).

Knowing that upon seeing our creation the initial reaction from the Rules Committee and Senate Computer Center (SCC) staff was likely to be, "You can't do that!" we took some satisfaction from the fact that it was already begun and on the Net outside of the reach of any Senate spoilers. Despite their frequent habit of letting any opportunity to do something groundbreaking or even interesting with technology slip away due to their own paralytic approach, the Rules Committee and SCC staffs still did not enjoy seeing the House or anyone else do something first. But someone else almost always did.

We did consider the fact that perhaps CapWeb should develop into an "official" resource. The thought of having our work help establish a presence on the Web for the House and Senate both was appealing to us. Assuming that eventually both chambers would develop their own home pages, the need for some higher level Web site that encompassed the entire legislative branch remained apparent. The only Web server on the Hill at the time was the one at the Library of Congress, and that seemed an appropriate neutral site for housing CapWeb. Neither the House or Senate yet had Web servers, and it was unlikely that either chamber would have accepted the other playing host to *the* Web guide to Congress. The Library of Congress, however, could play a neutral role between both chambers. It was the only logical place where an "official" CapWeb might be moved. We tried the idea on some people at the Library, but it didn't get anywhere, so we found a home on the Net where we could put CapWeb and continue to maintain it as a personal, unofficial, and unauthorized effort. But within a few months, the Library would find itself pushed into the limelight as the preeminent source of congressional information on the Internet. CapWeb would precede them by a couple of days, making it's public debut on the Net on New Year's Day, 1995.

In the months that followed an increasing number of congressional Internet resources were launched, and CapWeb has succeeded in providing a starting point from which they could all be found. On September 21st, CapWeb earned one of the Web's highest honors when it was selected as "Cool Site of the Day." A large number of Web sites link to CapWeb, including other politically oriented sites, state and local governments, and the home pages maintained by members of Congress. A line from CapWeb's disclaimer is often repeated on these other sites to describe CapWeb:

> *CapWeb is not an "official" product of the U.S. Congress, any legislative branch agency, or any other government agency. It is a product of a couple of impatient Capitol Hill staffers who felt it was an effort worth undertaking and don't mind writing some HTML late at night. CapWeb is designed to be an effective means of providing information about Congress and links to related Internet resources via the World Wide Web.*

The guestbook that Jeff created for CapWeb allows visitors to leave comments and browse those left by others. It quickly filled up with entries originating from all across the country and around the world. Teachers have let us know how they use CapWeb as a resource in their government courses, and students of American government in foreign countries have thanked us for providing a tool that aides their studies. Others have suggested new sites that CapWeb should link to, or pointed out errors that need correction, but invariably they have been positive comments from individuals who are interested in accessing Congress online and are thankful for the assistance CapWeb gives them.

Jeff and I continue to maintain CapWeb, working on it on our own time as a public service. Although it can be time consuming and has brought us no financial rewards, knowing that it helps the thousands of individuals that visit it each week to explore Congress on the Net has been its own reward.

©1995 Rich Tennant, Federal Computer Week

Who Puts Congress on the Net, and What Do They Put There?

We've developed a proposal which we will bring up in January, that when a conference report or a committee report is offered, when the President sends up a message, they have to be put electronically available at that instant so that every American everywhere in the country has the same access as the lobbyists, has the same opportunity as the insiders, and that information is available automatically for free to the entire country when it's made available to the members of Congress.

Newt Gingrich on National Public Radio,
November 10, 1994

GPO

In May 1993, the 103rd Congress passed the GPO Electronic Information Access Enhancement Act, commonly known as the GPO Access Bill. Senator Wendall Ford of Kentucky and Representative Charlie Rose of North Carolina, chairman and vice-chairman of the Congress's Joint Committee on Printing, which oversees the Government Printing Office (GPO), were the sponsors of the Senate and House versions of the bill. The bill required that the Government Printing Office put the full text of the *Congressional Record* and the *Federal Register* online within one year of the bill's enactment into law.

The Government Printing Office is an agency of the legislative branch that provides printing services to the federal government. The GPO contracts out approximately 80% of this printing to commercial printers and produces the rest in-house. With authorization from the Joint Committee on Printing, executive branch agencies can operate their own printing operations for "specified printing needs," otherwise the job goes to GPO.

For Congress, GPO prints a mountain of material every day: the *Congressional Record*, bills and public laws, committee reports, legislative calendars, and many other public documents. So it was logical for Congress to turn to GPO for the electronic dissemination of the same materials. Since September 1992, the GPO had operated its Federal Bulletin Board System, which enabled "Federal agencies to provide the public immediate, self-service access to Government information in electronic form at reasonable rates." Some of the files on the Federal Bulletin Board were available for free, but citizens had to pay for most of the material. The pricing schedule had a minimum file price of two dollars for a file of less that 50 kilobytes and scaled to fifteen dollars for the first megabyte of data, and an additional ten dollars a megabyte thereafter. File prices were based on a file's uncompressed size, even when the file was stored compressed.

When distributing government information to the public, the Government Printing Office is charged with recovering its costs. This does not necessarily mean that the public cannot locate this information without paying. GPO publications are distributed free of charge to almost 1,400 federal depository libraries across the country. There is at least one depository library in every congressional district. But the Access bill provided no funding for the GPO's new electronic dissemination program. Instead the bill allowed GPO to "recover the incremental cost of dissemination of the information involved."

On June 8, 1994, GPO announced its pricing rates for the initial products to be distributed under the Access Online Service: the *Federal Register*, the *Congressional Record*, and the text of enrolled bills (bills that have already passed Congress and are awaiting action by the president). Subscriptions to either the *Federal Register* or the *Congressional Record* were priced at $60 a month, $200 for six months, and $375 a year. Access to enrolled bills was priced at $60 a year.

Advocates for electronic access to government information, and Internet users in general, usually want things to be free. Many argue convincingly that government information, after all, has been accumulated, compiled, and published at taxpayer expense. Why should the public be charged a second time for the information their tax dollars have already paid for? At the same time, the Internet developed as a culture of free access; free information, free software, free e-mail. Commercial interests are beginning to explore how to sell information, products, and services on the Net, and ultimately they will probably find a way. But in 1994 the culture of free access on the Internet was alive and well, and advocates for electronic access to government figured they were only asking for access to the data their tax dollars had funded. They wanted access to their own data. What could be more American in the 1990s than demanding free access to government information on the Internet?

The GPO pricing scheme was more within the reach of the library and business community, and severely restrictive to the infrequent casual user. How many individuals might take a look at the *Congressional Record* for free? Plenty! How many would pony up $375 a year for the privilege? Not many! In a letter to Michael DiMario, public printer at GPO, the day after the pricing schedule was announced, James Love, director of the Taxpayer Assets Project, wrote:

> *Anyone at all familiar with the debates over these bills knows that the legislation was intended to broaden public access to government information, and to give ordinary citizens opportunities to more fully participate in public policy debates.... However, by requiring the public to buy a subscription service that is really designed for libraries and intensive data users, GPO is creating an insurmountable barrier for episodic users of these databases, and thus frustrating years of efforts to give ordinary citizens convenient and ready access to these materials.*

After meeting with representatives of public interest groups who opposed GPO's pricing schedule, DiMario agreed to look at alternatives such as the hourly rates or "free after six" plans suggested by the Taxpayer Assets Project.

If alternative pricing plans were considered, none was implemented. Instead, free distribution via federal depository libraries was offered as an alternative means for public distribution. Public interest groups who had long campaigned for free public access lauded the program; however, it faced serious limitations in its early implementations. Users at the Columbia Online Information Network (COIN), "the first community-based network in the nation to offer the free service," faced long waits for access and found the system burdensome.

GPO's critics were not limited to the many who were frustrated with their implementation of the GPO Access program. Vice President Gore's National Performance Review had recommended disbanding GPO, as had a General Accounting Office report, as an inefficient solution for meeting the government's printing needs. And GPO's critics in Congress grew in number and power following the election of a new Republican majority in the House of Representatives in November 1994, many of whom were interested in disbanding the GPO and had other ideas in mind for distributing Congressional information.

House Information Systems

Early in 1994, at the direction of Congressman Rose, House Information Systems (HIS) developed a WAIS server to provide public access to the *Congressional Record*, the text of pending legislation, and the U.S. Code. HIS used the WAIS server to demonstrate to GPO how the Internet could be used for public dissemination of congressional documents. When GPO showed no interest in accepting the House's offer of assistance, Rose sent a senior HIS manager to a Depository Library Conference with instructions to let the attendees know that if GPO didn't put this information on the Internet, then the House of Representatives would.

Members of the Republican minority of the House Administration Committee, including ranking member Bill Thomas of California and Pat Roberts of Kansas, protested Rose's efforts to allow HIS to provide information directly to the public. They argued that such an effort would undercut GPO's future ability to develop as the source for electronic dissemination of congressional documents and opposed the use of HIS for nonmember services.

Despite these pressures against independently offering such services, pressure was also very quickly building to offer an alternative to the

GPO's overpriced and highly criticized fledgling efforts with its Access program. Barely a month after the GPO's fee-based Access system was inaugurated, Congressman Rose ordered HIS to release its WAIS server on the Net and began offering free public access to the *Congressional Record*, the U.S. Code, and the text of House legislation. Although not recognized as "official documents," the content of the *Record* and legislation matched that available from GPO. In fact, the information had itself originated from GPO. The House server offered a cost-free alternative to GPO Access. Senate officials insisted that HIS not put any Senate bills on the Net, continuing their reliance on the GPO's much criticized efforts to fulfill that task.

Within days of the 1994 election, Speaker-elect Newt Gingrich gave Representative Vernon Ehlers of Michigan the task of reorganizing the technology infrastructure of the House. Ehlers holds a doctoral degree in physics and served ten years in the Michigan state legislature where he had led an effort to put the state government on the Internet. Ehlers was uniquely qualified for the job. Among his tasks as leader of the GOP transition team for technology were the modernization of House computer systems, the reorganization of HIS, and the development of a system to provide the public with free online access to the *Congressional Record*, the text of legislation, and all other official documents of the House.

Representative Vernon Ehlers – Republican – Michigan, 3rd District

Newt Gingrich chose well when he selected Representative Vernon Ehlers of Michigan to implement his plans for revamping the computer infrastructure within the House and to make congressional information readily available on the Internet. Ehlers's background made him particularly well suited for the job. A Ph.D. in nuclear physics, Ehlers's experience with computers dates back to 1956 when he programmed in assembly language on an IBM 650. A computer user throughout his career as a professor of physics and a state legislator, Ehlers oversaw the integration of new computer systems in the Michigan state legislature where he served for eleven years.

Elected to Congress in a special midterm election in 1992, Ehlers inherited the computers used by his predecessor, and was stunned to discover a dumb terminal on his desk. Believing the House should be on the Internet, he was among the earliest members to establish a public e-mail address, and he also pressed for greater access.

Charged with launching a new congressional information resource on the Internet by the first day of the 104th Congress, Ehlers initiated a project by HIS to establish a site on the Web to fulfill the task. Transferred to the Library of Congress, it became the legislative information system known as THOMAS. With the goal of seeing THOMAS develop into Congress's online "channel to the public," Ehlers acknowledges that there is a lot of work to be done. He says it's being done "the way it should be done, and that takes time." New rules, systems, and procedures will be necessary in order to make more committee information and other congressional information available via THOMAS.

The current most pressing issue is "developing the capability to handle the [E-mail] load that we're now getting." Although fewer than half of the members of the House currently have public E-mail addresses, the amount they've been receiving is growing rapidly and House systems are "just not geared to handle it." Ehlers plans to develop a standard hardware and software infrastructure within the House that meets basic requirements, allows for a maximum of individual freedom for congressional offices, and does not restrict future development.

As Congress considers legislation related to the Internet, Ehlers agrees that members who themselves have Internet experience and experienced staffs are better equipped to understand these issues. The numbers of Net-savvy members continues to increase, particularly among new members, young and old. The sixty-one-year-old Ehlers points out that understanding technology and the Internet is not a matter of age. Perceiving efforts to regulate information content on the Internet as "unmanageable," Ehlers believes in applying "established civil laws to computer users and not to the Net itself."

Ehlers has written that "The policy implications of the Internet would not be so interesting if the potential to transform our world were not so great." Nevertheless, he believes there will still be a place for Congress in that transformed world. "Our nation, as a republic, depends upon the discerning and analytical judgment of information by individual representatives. While information technology promises to enhance the democratic marketplace of ideas, it is appropriate that decisions finally rest with the authority of those elected representatives."

The incoming Republicans did not trust the personnel in place at HIS on which the new Republican leaders would have to rely to succeed in reaching their goals. For years Charlie Rose had overseen HIS as his own pet project. But now the loss of the majority had taken the chairmanship of the House Administration Committee from him, and a losing fight for the position of Democratic Leader against Richard Gephardt had led to his ouster from the committee altogether. Denied the position of ranking member of the renamed House Oversight Committee, Rose was no longer in any position to manage HIS.

In response to Ehlers's request for a system to make congressional documents available on the Internet, HIS staff first suggested further developing the House's existing gopher server, but then proposed that a Web server would better demonstrate cutting edge technology and make a bigger splash. Starting from scratch, with no experience or knowledge of how to develop a Web server or home pages to live on it, HIS began a crash effort to develop a prototype within three weeks. After seeing a demonstration of the prototype, Ehlers instructed the HIS team to continue their efforts to develop a full-blown Web server.

After weeks of working around the clock to study the issues surrounding the creation of a Web server, and developing a resource that integrated existing information resources with a searchable version of the *Congressional Record* and the text of legislation, the House Web effort was ordered to come to a stop by Representative Bill Thomas, the chairman-elect of the House Oversight Committee.

Representative Thomas would now oversee HIS, and serve as vice-chair of the Joint Committee on Printing, which has oversight responsibility for the Government Printing Office. No longer relegated to the role of chief irritant of Charlie Rose, Thomas was now in a position to leave a mark of his own. In a December 20, 1994, letter he wrote with Rep. Jim Nussle of the Republican Transition Team to Public Printer Michael DiMario of GPO and Terry Nugent, the director of House Information Systems, they announced "we envision the Library of Congress as the gateway to make a vast array of information available to the country" and asked both GPO and HIS to transfer documents and resources to the Library of Congress. The Library's new system was officially named THOMAS, in honor of Thomas Jefferson, (whose philosophy and writings have made him the favorite founding father on the Net). The name was also stretched to fill a suitable if somewhat strained acronym, The House Open Multimedia Access System. But others suspected that it was no coincidence that THOMAS shared its name with the new chairman of the House Oversight Committee.

Speaker Newt Gingrich, Representative Bill Thomas, and Librarian of Congress
James Billington inaugurate THOMAS, January 4, 1995

photo credit: Craig Hobson, Library of Congress

The Library of Congress/THOMAS

> *If every Citizen had the access to information that
> the Washington lobbyists have, we would have
> changed the balance of power in America towards
> the citizens and out of the beltway, and this pro-
> gram really is a major step in that direction.*
>
> Newt Gingrich, at the opening of THOMAS

The day after he was sworn in as the first Republican Speaker of the
House in forty years, Newt Gingrich gathered his troops and the
media for a press conference at the Library of Congress for the
unveiling of THOMAS. The timing of the event was critical to his

demonstration that things would be very different in the 104th Congress under its new Republican leadership. Cutting the ribbon on THOMAS allowed Gingrich to stake a claim in cyberspace in a manner that none of his predecessors had. Even though THOMAS didn't initially offer any material not already available on the Internet, the project became a symbol of the many changes that could be expected from Congress's first "Third Wave" speaker.

Among those in attendance were members of the HIS team who had spent the last two months working to develop this resource. They had only grudgingly complied with the order that they turn over their work to the Library and assist in developing THOMAS. With Rep. Ehlers's blessing, they secretly continued their work on the House Web server. Although Rep. Thomas has ordered HIS staff to cease all work on their Web, he was only chairman-elect until January 4th, when he would take command of the renamed House Oversight (previously Administration) Committee. Until that date, they took their orders from Ehlers as head of the transition team for technology, and Ehlers told them to keep working on the Web.

Some feelings of animosity lingered long afterward between the Library and the House. It was not by accident that for several months after their release on the Web, the THOMAS page only contained a link to the House gopher, ignoring the existence of any House presence on the Web (a slight that has since been corrected). And among the HIS staff that developed the House Web, many of whom left the House in the following months, there were long-held hard feelings over the manner in which their work had been taken from them.

Despite the manner in which its development had been pulled from the House and turned over to the Library of Congress, there were some good reasons for the Library to be THOMAS's home. As library to the legislative branch, and to the entire country, the Library of Congress provides a more appropriate symbolic home for the service. If it had originated in the House, it would have been difficult for many to escape the perception that the service was a partisan tool of the new Republican majority. But coming from the Library, it is easier to accept the source of the information as nonpartisan in nature. By rebuffing Speaker Gingrich's desire to post his address to the nation in April 1995 on THOMAS, the Library later demonstrated the willingness and ability to protect the integrity of the service.

The Library also provides a logical home for THOMAS because of the nature of its mission. Public libraries, by definition, make information available to the public. In the information age, distribution on the Net is an obvious avenue by which to fulfill this mission.

While the GPO and HIS are both knowledgeable about the content and the means of distribution, they have fundamentally different missions from the LOC. Although GPO had been working within the guidelines outlined by the GPO Access bill that instructed them to make congressional information available on the Net, the implementation and pricing of the GPO Access program had left many doubtful of GPO's role as the source for this information.

HIS exists to support the computer infrastructure and needs of the House of Representatives. Although Rep. Charlie Rose's enthusiasm for developing public access to congressional information led him to allow HIS a great deal of latitude and to expand its role to providing electronic information to the public, he did so in an effort to force the GPO to accelerate its own efforts. Even though HIS was equipped and capable of distributing information directly to the public, HIS remained an internal House support organization that answered first to the chairman of the House Administration Committee, the party in charge, and the House of Representatives.

The Library already had a number of projects under way for the distribution of Library materials via the Internet, and its LOCIS database catalogs the text of all bills introduced in Congress since 1973. The Library was also the first legislative branch agency with a home page on the Web. Unlike the fee-based resources that GPO put online, the Library did not charge for electronic access to its information.

The media coverage of the early days of the 104th Congress, the transition to Republican majorities in both chambers, and the launch of the 100-day effort to enact the Republican "Contract with America" did not overlook THOMAS, and neither did Net browsers. Stories in the media across the country proclaimed the birth of THOMAS, with the *New York Times* choosing the obvious headline "Mr. Smith Goes to Cyberspace." In his preface to Alvin and Heidi Toffler's book, *Creating a New Civilization: The Politics of the Third Wave*, Newt Gingrich offered THOMAS as evidence of Congress's entry into the Third Wave:

> *On January 5, 1995, the Third Wave came to American democracy in the form of "Thomas," the Library of Congress's online system that allows every citizen to access copies of legislation, committee reports and other congressional documents. During its first four days of operation, 28,000 individuals and 2,500 institutions used Thomas to download 175,132 documents. In fact, more citizens accessed Thomas over a twenty-four-hour period than normally use the Library of Congress in a week.*

While there is no question that its well-reported roll-out helped THOMAS to draw a large number of visitors, a number that continued to grow steadily over the course of the year, such a comparison with the number of individuals who actually visit the Library is very misleading. Keep in mind that only a very small portion of the Library's content are available via the Net. The Library's National Digital Library Program plans on having five million documents digitized for availability via CD-ROM and online access by the year 2000. With the Library's collections currently totaling more than 108 million items and growing at between two and four percent each year, it will be a long time before a virtual visitor to the Library has the same materials available to them than their real-world counterparts do.[1]

---

[1] WIRED, The Future of Libraries, December 1995.

The Speaker's claim that committee reports were available on THOMAS was inaccurate, and their unavailability and the unavailability of other promised items quickly became a point of criticism following THOMAS's brief honeymoon period in the press. The *Boston Globe* wrote of difficulty mastering THOMAS's search engine in an article titled "Room for doubting Thomas" on January 27th, just three weeks after its launch. By August, many of the same groups that had praised Gingrich's efforts to establish THOMAS were now criticizing the Speaker for not making the system live up to its promise. The committee reports the Speaker had claimed were available in January were in fact still not online more than a year later. Committee prints, amendments, and hearing testimonies were among the other promised items still not available online. Government reform groups and more than 650 citizens sent a letter to Gingrich asking him "for a renewed commitment to provide Americans with online access to essential congressional documents." The next month, three of the same reform groups again wrote the Speaker to express their "outrage" over the failure to make a key tax bill available prior to the House Ways and Means Committee mark-up of the bill. A staffer from Committee Chairman Bill Archer's staff referred individuals to a commercial provider (BNA) that was selling the bill for $27. The letter asked:

> *The Archer staffer said the bill runs more than 700 pages. Unless the bill was written by BNA, the House of Representatives must have a copy in digital form. Your promise that congressional information "will be available to any citizen in the country at the same moment it is available to the highest paid Washington lobbyist" is pretty meaningless if the Chairman's Mark for a 700 page tax bill involving billions of dollars isn't available from THOMAS or the Committee before the mark-up. What's the deal?*

If citizens can't get copies of a bill before commit-
tee action, and lobbyists can, lobbyists will con-
tinue to have more access to the legislative process
than ordinary citizens.

There are a number of reasons that THOMAS has yet to live up to
the high expectations generated by the Speaker. There are many who
claim credit for their part in the development of THOMAS, but few
who actually manage its care and feeding. Although the Library only
had a few weeks of notice that it was to develop and host such a
high-profile service for the Congress, the task was given to existing
staff and it competes for time with their existing workload. Some
library staff have actually used their own vacation days in order to
free themselves from their regular work and use the time to work on
THOMAS.

There are widely varying technical capabilities and support for electronic dissemination among committees in both the House and the
Senate that prevent a great deal of congressional information from
yet being made available on the Internet either from THOMAS or the
GPO. Committees are equipped with a variety of hardware, and some
are better able than others to provide GPO with documents that can
be made readily available on the Internet. A large number of congressional documents are submitted to GPO as camera-ready copy, with
GPO only doing the typesetting for the document's cover. Committee
chairman have a great deal of latitude over whether their proceedings
will ever be published electronically at all. Many are hesitant to allow
unedited hearing transcripts to be published, or don't want an electronic version to precede the printed copy.

What You Will Find

The evolution of congressional documents that are available on the
Internet has resulted in a good deal of duplication and overlap in
available content and services. Where is the civic-minded Net surfer

to go in the online quest to track the legislative branch? And will having more than one source for the same information help or hinder that quest? Although the existence of multiple resources for congressional information resulted from politics rather than by design, the result is well suited to the Internet. Mirror sites and multiple archives are familiar solutions for easing the load on heavily traveled sites on the Net. If only to share the load of increasing Internet traffic, providing congressional documents from more than one site is a good idea.

Each of the congressional servers that provide access to the *Congressional Record* and other current legislative information—GPO Access, the House of Representatives, and THOMAS—has some advantages and disadvantages when compared against the others. The Senate's Net offerings do not currently include any legislative information and are limited to information from individual offices, committee and member directories, and educational content.

The Government Printing Office

The Government Printing Office was the original source on the Net for congressional documents. Many of the documents that HIS and THOMAS make available on the Internet (the *Congressional Record*, text of legislation, U.S. Code, and other documents) originate at GPO. The keystrokes take place at GPO, and the files are subsequently provided to the House and THOMAS. Although discussions have taken place about how procedures can be changed to require that congressional documents be prepared electronically by congressional staff, and then provided to both THOMAS and GPO concurrently, this has not yet taken place. As a result, the practical matter is that GPO has the documents first, and is likely to be able to make them available more quickly than the House or THOMAS can.

Additionally, the GPO home page makes most congressional documents available in two formats: plain text and PDF files. Plain text is convenient for quick searches and perusal of many documents such as the text of a bill. But the PDF versions of these documents offer a truly unique view of the same bill not available from either THOMAS or HIS. By maintaining the appearance of the actual printed document, a PDF file can incorporate many of the unique typefaces and styles, such as the strikethru text found in many marked-up bills, that plain text and HTML just cannot approximate.

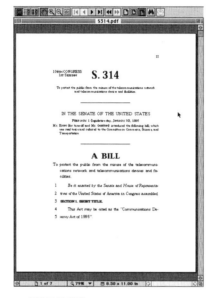
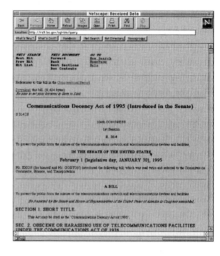

PDF BILL   HTML BILL

The same bill viewed in PDF format (left) available from the GPO Access Web site, and in HTML as found on THOMAS.

While the GPO home page provides access to a great deal of congressional information, the manner in which it is presented is better suited for individuals who know exactly what they are looking for than it is for more casual browsers. Most of the databases of congressional information are accessed via the same uninviting search interface. The search instructions and sample searches are lengthy and complicated, enough to discourage any casual explorer who just popped in to see what Congress was up to lately.

In other instances, the GPO efforts to put information on the Web seem to demonstrate a lack of understanding of the medium, or lack of effort to utilize its features. The online version of the congressional Pictorial Directory offers one example. The Pictorial Directory is a small booklet that would fit comfortably in the palm of you hand. It contains photos of every member of Congress, along with a name, hometown, party, and term in office. No details such as office locations or committee assignments are found in this directory, just names and photos. This small book is a constant companion to many on the Hill including Capitol Hill police officers, elevator operators, and anyone else who could use a quick visual reference to members of Congress. Rather than creating an electronic version of the booklet that takes true advantage of the hypertext and graphical features of the Web, the version that GPO put in place literally consists of full-page scans of the actual printed pages from the booklet. Select Senator Kennedy from the contents, and you'll find yourself looking at his picture as well as those of his fellow members of Congress who happened to be on pages 62 and 63 of the booklet. It's kind of like turning on your TV, and seeing a picture of a radio playing.

But despite such mis-steps, GPO puts a wealth of congressional information on the Internet in a timely and effective manner. GPO is first and foremost a printing operation. Comparing GPO to the Library of Congress is like "comparing a factory to a research institution" in the words of one GPO employee. And so it should perhaps be no surprise that GPO's presentation of electronic document leaves the hand holding behind. For the knowledgeable researcher who is familiar with congressional documents and knows what they are looking for, the GPO is an excellent place to start. But newcomers should beware.

The House of Representatives

The House of Representatives initially began to make congressional documents available on the Net to demonstrate the ability to do so and to help spur a slow-starting GPO to action; it did not imagine for itself a long-term role in delivering information to the public. While the House puts information about individual members, committees, and support offices on the Net, it now finds itself in an awkward position as a result of putting congressional documents on the Net. THOMAS is the resource sanctioned by the House leadership to serve congressional information to the public on the Net, and GPO is required by law to do the same. And yet, the House still makes a large number of congressional documents available via its own WAIS, gopher and Web servers, and does a pretty good job of it.

The greatest strength of the House effort is the comprehensive manner in which it helps visitors to understand the legislative process as a whole. The available documents are put in context as individual steps on the path of legislation. From bill texts, summaries, and a daily status available on the House WAIS server, followed by the same for amendments, committee jurisdictions, hearings, and votes, the House server leads you through the steps for finding items at different points in the process. A number of the described steps are not yet available, such as amendment text and committee hearing transcripts and votes, which remain labeled as "under construction," and their absence leaves some pretty big holes along the way. But even though not all of the pieces are yet in place, a large number of them are.

The search interface for the House WAIS server is no friendlier and no worse than that found at GPO. Once past the explanations of the process, browsers are still faced with a single empty search field in front of them that can be either a help or a hurdle for locating what they need. As with visits to the GPO site, House searchers who know in advance what they are looking for will do best.

The future of the House efforts remains very unclear. Both THOMAS and GPO are tasked with providing public access to this material. But the House is better suited for providing some of documents, particularly those items such as the current floor proceedings and recent actions for the preceding three legislative days for the House and Senate and their committees. This content will continue to be maintained within the House for the use of Representatives and their staffs, possibly making it difficult to remove the content from public access—and it should not be. For students of Congress and of the legislative process, the House has developed a comprehensive tool that combines education with content that will continue to grow in usefulness as the promised unfinished pieces are put into place.

THOMAS

Despite the limited staff resources provided for its support, the Library of Congress's THOMAS server is easily the most user-friendly of these servers. By making good use of the design and implementation of pages that allow both direct searching and browsing of bills, the THOMAS server invites visitors to explore the legislative process in a manner familiar to Net surfers. Legislation can be searched by bill number and keyword. Functions for limiting searches by the bill's sponsor or by the type of legislation are easy options for narrowing the focus of a search and increasing the likelihood of finding what you seek.

In addition to searching for particular bills, THOMAS offers a great many options that allow visitors to browse lists of bills by a number of different criteria. Lists of "Hot Bills" invite the perusal of bills by topic, popular title, short title, bill number, bill type, bills enacted into law, and bills under consideration by Congress this week. The retrieved bills are presented in HTML format, which makes them easy to scan on your monitor, and links to a plain text version and references in the *Congressional Record* are provided as well.

Although it is the easiest to use of the legislative servers, THOMAS was brought about with great fanfare and high expectations that are a long way from being fulfilled. The system still falls well short of what the Speaker promised it would be at its unveiling. THOMAS is likely to continue to develop as the premiere site for public access to congressional documents, and it has made an excellent beginning toward serving that purpose. If given the attention and resources required to complete what has been started, it will develop into a resource worthy of its namesake.

The Senate

The Senate's home page is the youngest of the Hill's resources on the Web, and does not really belong in a discussion of congressional servers that provide access to substantive legislative documents, because it makes no effort to do so. That's not necessarily a bad thing, considering the crowded field of alternatives that exist for this material. The Senate developed a presence on the Web not as an institutional initiative, but at the urging of many individuals Senators who sought a place to put their own home pages. Criticized as being too "touristy," the Senate page was created with an educational role in mind. Even among the dry content that is available such as "A Brief History of the Senate," "A Glossary of Senate Terms" and "A Historical Bibliography of the United States Senate," great care was taken to post only items that were already available in hard copy, such as brochures, to avoid the need for new approvals that might further hinder its development.

Avoiding the substantive content about the workings of Congress provided elsewhere, the Senate Web site provides visitors an opportunity to view some of the statuary and paintings that adorn the halls and hearing rooms and to take a virtual tour of the Capitol building. Together with straightforward committee rosters, and generic home pages for those Senators who do not yet have one of their own, this is about the most that can currently be expected from the ever cautious Senate. The Senate home page was inaugurated with the comment that it will be an evolving resource, designed to meet the needs of the public, and it probably will be. But for now, if you want to know what happened in the Senate today, you'll still do better visiting the House server.

Newt's Net?

The unveiling of THOMAS and the House of Representatives home pages were the first truly significant efforts made by Congress to do more than just pay lip service to the Net and provide access via already outdated tools. The new Speaker of the House Newt Gingrich deservedly received a great deal of credit for making the implementation of these services a top priority for the new Republican-led House. Combined with the frequent emphasis that he put on technology and its role in changing the balance of power in Washington in favor of any citizen with a laptop and a modem, the Speaker has gained a reputation as the man who will lead Congress into the Information Age. Editors espousing his leadership could not resist the inevitable headline announcing the product of the new age, "Newt's Net." It practically wrote itself. As one reporter described her fear at being left behind in the new order that Gingrich was leading us into, "everyone else had disappeared into the virtual democracy, following the virtual Speaker—that pudgy, white-haired Pied Piper of Cyberspace,"[2] or as Time magazine called him in the article naming Newt "Man of the Year" for 1995, the Merry Cybernaut.

But is the reputation deserved? He certainly didn't lead by example. Although he had been among the original seven members of the House of Representatives to establish an Internet e-mail address in June 1993, Newt has taken no further steps onto the Internet since. By August 1995, the Net was no longer just something members of Congress were talking about. The rush was on and members of Congress were announcing e-mail addresses and URLs for their home pages weekly. A special issue of *Internet World* magazine in August

---

[2] Maureen Dowd, "Virtual Democracy," *The New York Times Magazine,*
    February 5, 1995, p. 26.

1995 was devoted to the topic of politics on the Internet, and contained yet another "Newt's Net" headline. It wasn't an article, but "An interview with Don Jones, Newt Gingrich's system integrator and the creator of the THOMAS server." A picture of Jones and Gingrich on the speaker's balcony overlooking the mall and the Washington Monument provided a glowing illustration to accompany the interview about THOMAS. Tired of hearing about Newt's Net, I fired this e-mail off to the interviewer and the editors of *Internet World*.

> Dear Editor,
>
> I enjoyed your special issue on politics on the Net very much. But I'd like to offer a comment about the article titled Newt's Net.
>
> Speaker Gingrich deserves credit for supporting and promoting the Library of Congress' THOMAS service. However, I think it's worth noting that the Speaker is not among the 50 Representatives that as of today maintain gopher directories, or the 32 that maintain home pages on the World Wide Web. As the third highest elected official in the nation, Speaker Gingrich does not post information to the Net as Speaker of the House, nor even as a Representative of Georgia's Sixth district.
>
> I'm sure that eventually he will, but for now the fact is that Newt's Net doesn't exist. The Emperor has no clothes, and the Speaker has no home page.
>
> Regards,
> Chris Casey

I was pleased to see my e-mail appear two months later in *Internet World* under the heading "The Naked Truth." I received a number of e-mail messages from surprised people who asked me why the Cyber-Speaker isn't on the net. The best I could do was suggest they ask him themselves and pass along his e-mail address, knowing their odds of any reply were minuscule. *Wired* magazine put Gingrich on the cover of the August 1995 issue, with an interview hailing him for "getting it." The premiere issue of the political magazine *George* likewise had an interview praising Gingrich as one of about three people in Congress who understands the potentially profound political consequences of the Net. The legend of Newt's Net lives on, while the reality lags far behind.

The Making of a Capitol CobWeb

Although every new home page on Capitol Hill has a story behind its creation, and inevitably politics are involved, most have overcome the battles and succeeded at making a useful contribution to the Net. But others struggle to get started, and then just can't get out of the gate.

The new Republican leaders changed the names of most of the standing committees and some offices in the House of Representatives to reflect the priorities of the new leadership and to act as a symbol of a new and different Congress. After a very brief stint as the Office of Information Resources, HIS ultimately became House Information Resources (HIR). But a name change alone did not change the fact that the Republicans suspected the computer support staff of HIS of holding Democratic sympathies for their deposed masters.

During the first months after the House's official home page became available on the Web on January 4, 1995 (the same day as THOMAS), the listing in its *What's New!* file offered some clue to the Congress's new-found battlefield in cyberspace. Many of the links from the home page led to existing directories on the House gopher server, and in February an entry in *What's New!* indicated the addition of a link to the Democratic Leadership Gopher Service in a section labeled "House Leadership Published Information." Although the Republican leadership maintained no gopher directory, the Republican Conference (HRC) did, only their link from the home page was found in the section on "House Organizations Gopher Services" and not through the leadership section that led to the Democrats. The March *What's New!* file showed the situation to have changed, the link to the Republican Conference gopher had been moved to the leadership section, joining the Democrats.

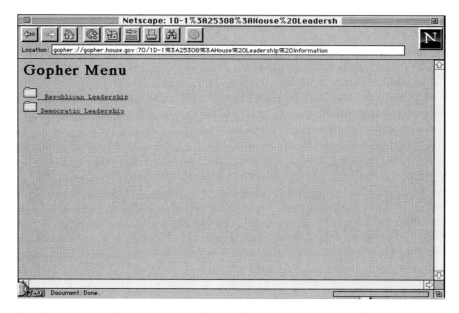

The leadership directory on the House Gopher server. Although Gopher menus aren't necessarily arranged alphabetically, the extra space in the Republican links seems intended to ensure its listing above the Democratic link.

But, by March, staying in the same gopher directory with the House Democrats was not good enough, because the Democratic Leadership and the Democratic Caucus had both unveiled the first home pages put on the House Web server by any member or group. It would be a week before some Republican staffers, browsing the Web late at night, discovered that their Democratic colleagues had beaten them to the Web. In the discovery, they believed they had found validation in their suspicions of HIS, as the memo below from House Republican Conference staff to the Majority Leader's office reflects.

21 March 1995, 12:10 am

Gentlemen:

While working on the Republican Web page this evening, we happened to look at the "What's New" section of the House Web server. We discovered that there certainly is something new there.

What we discovered is a brand new House Democratic Leadership Web site, and a companion House Democratic Caucus Web site. Professionally executed, the pages are complete with red, white and blue donkeys, full color photos of Dick Gephardt and a group of seniors, as well as Rosa Lauro and a group of schoolchildren. It has information on the "GOP Tax Cuts for the Wealthy," tells how "Republicans Wage War on Kids," and even informs the browsing internet surfer that Mfume means "conquering son of kings" It includes a page updated daily by David Bonoir. Curious, since we're quite certain that when we asked about daily updates we were advised that HIS couldn't handle that. Isn't that why Mark Brickman is trying to find a way to allow us to edit HTML (web documents) from the Conference offices?

Curious too, that when we first asked about putting up a home page, it was suggested to us that though we might be able to accomplish that somewhere down the road, it was way off in the future and right now we should stick with the House Gopher.

And like a trip beyond the looking glass, it gets curiouser, and curiouser. The dates on the individual components suggest that the web site has been in production for at least two weeks.

Perhaps somewhere in there, the browsing internet surfer might learn that HIS means "slayer of elephants" in Swahili.

Check it out at http://www.house.gov/democrats/

It may well be that the Democrats hired an outside, professional company to execute their pages, but whatever is going on, the page resides on a "house.gov" computer. Clearly, there is a way to accomplish our goal that HIS chose not to share with us.

Your infuriated collegues,
D.J. & Bob

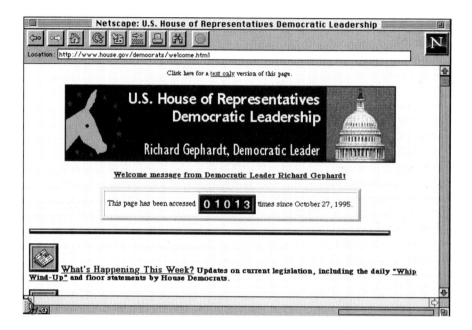

HIS staff insisted that they had shown no favoritism in the development of the Democratic Leadership pages. The Democratic staff, they said, had simply been the first group to request to be put on the Web and had in fact done a great deal of the development themselves.

Still mistrusting of HIS, the Republicans looked for an alternative when they had some content they wanted to share with the Net, an address to America from the Cyber-Speaker himself. Newt Gingrich was to make a prime time televised address to the nation, an unprecedented act for a speaker, to report on Congress's progress on the Contract With America. He wanted to get his words out into cyberspace as well as the airwaves, especially onto the World Wide Web. House Republican staff contacted the Library of Congress and instructed them to prepare to make the text of the Speaker's speech and the accompanying Republican Plan for America's Future available on THOMAS. After all, the THOMAS server had been inaugurated by the Speaker personally, and was touted as evidence of the increased accessibility he was bringing to the U.S. Congress.

The only problem was that the Library staff felt that THOMAS has a mission to provide congressional information in an unbiased, non-partisan fashion. While the text of legislation and the debates that can be found in the *Congressional Record* certainly contain partisan views and arguments, they are the official publications and documents of the institution. If the Library were to post the Speaker's speech and the Republican plan on THOMAS, the credibility of this still fledgling service could be called into question. Library officials contacted the Democratic leadership in the House to offer them the opportunity to post a rebuttal, thinking that providing equal time to the opposition might make carrying out the Speaker's request more palatable. But the Democrats already had a very nice home page of their own, thank you very much, and didn't need any help from the Library to put their rebuttal on the Net. They argued that THOMAS was not an appropriate site for posting the Speaker's speech. The Library's argument against posting the material on THOMAS prevailed, and the Republican leadership was left without a place on the Web for the Speaker.

Unwilling to ask for or accept any assistance from HIS, Republican staff undertook to build their own home page. On the date of the Speaker's address to the nation, April 7, 1995, the *What's New!* file on the House of Representative's home page announced the new House Republican Conference home page. Along with a title graphic and a small picture of the Capitol dome, the Republican Conference home page contained two links, one to a plain text version of the Speaker's speech (a version old enough that it retained the Speaker's reference to the speech's availability on THOMAS), and a very large hypertext version of the Republican Plan for America's Future (loaded with large, slow-to-load charts).

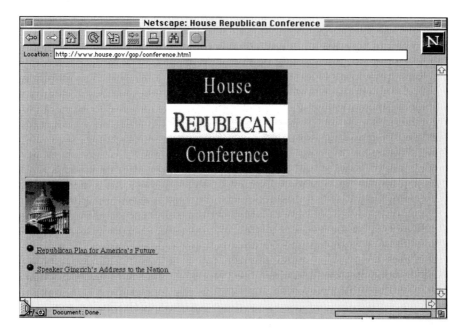

The posted text version of the Speaker's speech contained a number of references to the promise of high technology, complete with visual aids, and an analogy was made between the vacuum tube technology still found in some FAA computers and the advanced microchip of today. The Speaker said,

This is a Federal Aviation Administration vacuum tube. Good solid 1895 technology. This is the up-dated mid-1950s version. When you fly in America, vacuum tubes in the air traffic control system keep you safe. Our purchasing rules are so complicated and so wasteful that our government has not been able in seven years to figure out how to replace vacuum tubes with this. This is a microchip that has the computing power of three million vacuum tubes. So today's government operates this way [tube]; af-ter we remake it, the government of the future will operate this way [microchip].

The posted version of the speech also includes the Speaker's claim that "We are making this speech and our briefing on the budget available through the Library of Congress at THOMAS on the Internet," offering some indication of how late the switch from the plan to post it on THOMAS to instead using the House Republican Conference page came.

But this story doesn't end here, or maybe it does, because the posting of the Speaker's speech and the Republican Plan for America's Future might have been the beginning of an active presence on the Internet for the Republican leadership in the House. The HRC home page might have provided daily updates, links to the policies, position papers, and statements of the members of the Republican majority. But it did not. A week later the page still contained only the same two links, a month later there was nothing new, seven months later the page remained unchanged. The HRC home page was a CobWeb. An untended home page, starved for new content, and unlikely to find itself a regular stop on any Net surfer's hotlist. Given the opportunity to create an up-to-date and useful information resource, the House Republican leadership built a vacuum tube.

Roll Call, a newspaper covering Congress and Capitol Hill, reported that the two conference aides responsible for creating the site had left for other jobs, and had been told to pack up their hardware and "stow it somewhere out of the way." Interest in developing a full-service site with information for the public, and secure areas for Republican members and interest groups, faded with their departure, and the page remained unchanged for more than seven months.

On November 10, 1995, the House Republican Conference home page made a second appearance in the *What's New!* file on the House home page. The listing read "House Republican Conference Home Page has been UPDATED." Now, the file is called *What's New!*, not *What's Updated!* By that logic anything that changed on any of the home pages on the House server would rate a whole new roll out; every new posting made, new image added, or turn of the hit-counter would rate a listing in *What's New!*. But apparently someone realized that the only way to breathe life into a completely dead home page was to resurrect it with a re announcement. The updated House Republican Conference page was a big improvement over the original, complete with new graphics, backgrounds, blinking headers, and a fourfold increase from two to eight links. The Speaker's speech and the Republican plan for the future were replaced by links such as "Republicans Keeping their Promises," "White House Out to Scare Veterans," and "The President Has Been AWOL, Absent Without Leadership." Unfortunately, or maybe fortunately, none of the links worked. None of the listed items below the blinking headers lead to anything. Click all you want, nothing happened. A hypertext dead end. A few days passed before the links were fixed and actually began pointing to the promised items.

The site also overlooked one of the most useful features that characterizes the World Wide Web, links to any other sites beyond the House Republican Conference. This is a cul-de-sac on the info superhighway. And in another inexplicable move, the new Republican Conference home page used a different file name from the earlier version, which remained in place and reachable on the House server. For any other home pages on the Web that contained links to the long moribund HRC page, those links very likely remained unchanged and continued to point to the old page, unaware that a new version existed. Webmaster wanted.

What to Look for on Member Home Pages

Without question the World Wide Web has been the hot property for any person or organization seeking to establish a presence on the Internet. Although a bit slow to spot the trend, members of Congress eventually recognized the Web as the place to establish an office in cyberspace. In November 1994, there was a single member of Congress on the Web, Senator Kennedy of Massachusetts. A year later, in November 1995, more than 120 members of Congress had home pages on the Web.

The House and the Senate have taken different approaches toward helping members get a home page on the Web. The House's computer support office, House Information Resources (HIR), has a Web shop with staff who are available to assist offices in the development of a home page for the Web (this doesn't mean that there aren't any House offices that have developed their own home pages, or staff capable of writing their own HTML, only that a resource exists to help an office get on the Web if the necessary skills don't exist within the office itself). The Senate Computer Center (SCC) offers no such support, and in fact thirty-four Senators had established their own home pages before the Senate itself did, so there was much more Web experience within those offices than could be found in the computer center. Only one member of the House, Representative Peter DeFazio of Oregon, had established a home page for his office prior to the institution. Considering the larger staffs and resources available to Senate offices, a Senator's home page is more likely to have been completely conceived, developed, and created within the Senator's own office, whereas a Representative's is more likely to have been the collaborative work of House support staff working with the office to create a home page for them.

After three years in Senator Kennedy's office, helping to make him one of the first members of Congress to utilize the Internet, and then working to help put his campaign online and seeing him reelected, I was ready for an opportunity to help advance Congress' use of the Internet even further. I spent a large amount of my time assisting other offices undertake their own Internet efforts, and enjoyed that aspect of my work more than the day-to-day work of a systems administrator.

Shortly after the November 1994 elections Senator Tom Daschle of South Dakota became the new Democratic Leader. A strong advocate for further developing Internet use among his Democratic colleagues, Daschle led by example and became the second member of the Senate to establish a home page. As Democratic leader, Daschle made the development of new uses of technology a high priority and directed resources to support Senate Democrats' efforts to employ them. He created the Democratic Technology and Communications Committee (DTCC) as part of the Democratic leadership structure in the Senate. Chaired by Senator Jay Rockefeller of West Virginia, the committee's task was to support the efforts of Senate Democrats in communicating their message using both traditional and new media.

I participated in the meetings that helped define the DTCC's goals and needs, and wrote the description for the position of Internet evangelist for all Senate Democrats. The job was to be exactly what I had already been spending an increasing amount of my time doing from Kennedy's office, assisting other offices in their efforts to follow the example Kennedy had set on the Internet. Unable to pass up the opportunity to take the position that my efforts had helped to create, I left Senator Kennedy's office to work with Jeff Hecker, forming what has come to be known as the "Net Squad," helping Senate Democrats get online. The short-term gain of claiming bragging rights to getting online first and being the majority in cyberspace eventually diminished as more Senators went online, but the long-term payoff in experience will remain an advantage to Senate Democrats for a long time to come. The success of this effort has been evident in the larger presence Senate Democrats have on the Net, as well as in widely reported stories in the press about the dominance of Democrats on the Net.

Generic and Genuine Home Pages

Not every home page for Members of Congress found on the House and Senate's Web sites is the result of any effort on the part of the Members they describe. The House and Senate sites contain directory and generic home pages that offer basic information about individual Members of Congress that are distinct from Member's own home pages. But just as the mineral pyrite (fool's gold) led many forty-niners to believe they'd struck it rich, net surfers frequently mistake these generic home pages for the real thing. Knowing what to look for can help the discriminating net surfer distinguish the genuine from the generic.

Although the House Web site hosts home pages for a steadily growing number of individual Representatives (just over 100 at this writing), it also contains a "Member Directory" that leads to a generic home page for every single Representative, including those who maintain a separate home page of their own. These directory pages contain basic information about Representatives including office address, phone, e-mail address, member service history, committee assignments, and links to lookup legislation sponsored and co-sponsored by the Member described. House directory pages do not contain any graphics or links to the Member's own home page if one exists. These directory pages should not be mistaken as the product of each individual Representative, they are not.

Similar looking at first glance, New York's Senate delegation illustrates
the difference between generic and genuine Senate home pages. Senator
D'Amato's SCC-created page is a basic directory listing with a
biography. In contrast, Senator Moynihan's office created page includes
that and a great deal more information including links to press releases,
sponsored legislation, and other related Web sites.

When the Senate developed its home page, there was some concern
that the 66 Senators who had not already developed their own home
pages would not appreciate a Senate home page that noted their own
absence from the Web. The solution was for the SCC to create a
generic home page for every Senator, allowing a Rules committee
staffer to brag, "Now, *everybody* has a Web page." Well, yes, every
Senator has a home page on the Senate's Web server, but many are
simply these generic pages. Generic Senate pages can be spotted by
the graphic banner that appears at the top of the page and is common
to all of the Senate's pages. These generic pages contain office
addresses, phone numbers, and (when available) e-mail addresses.
They also include the Senator's photograph, committee assignments,
and biography from the GPO's *Congressional Directory*. Senators
have the option of replacing their generic home page with one of their
own creation, and more than half have done so at this writing. As
more Senators develop their own home pages, and the ratio of genuine
to generic changes in favor of genuine, a sharp eye will be needed to
spot the dwindling number of generic ones.

The Clue Is in the URL

Every home page on the Web has a unique address called a uniform resource locator, or URL. Usually a string of characters that begins with http://, a URL will lead your Web browser directly to the directory and file for the home page that it designates. URLs often (but not always) offer insight into about the location and source of the content found on a home page. A glance at the URL for the home page for a member of Congress will tell you a lot about what you are looking at.

The URLs for home pages maintained by Members of the House of Representatives generally follow the same formula: *http://www.house.gov/lastname/welcome.html* (in cases where more than one Representative shares the same last name, the directory is: *http://www.house.gov/firstnamelastname/welcome.html)*

For example, the home page maintained by Representative John Spratt of South Carolina's 5th Congressional District is found at: *http://www.house.gov/spratt/welcome.html.*

A generic directory home page exists on the House Web server for every Representative. The URLs for these generic pages follow the formula: *http://www.house.gov/mbr_dir/STATEDISTRICT.html*

So the directory page for Rep. Spratt would be found at: *http://www.house.gov/mbr_dir/SC05.html*

URLs can also determine the difference between genuine and generic home pages in the Senate. Generally, the URLs for home pages developed by Senators themselves follow the formula:

http://www.senate.gov/~lastname

Generic home pages created by the Senate Computer Center for those Senators who have not yet put themselves on the Web are revealed by a URL that delivers you to another directory in which all the generic pages are kept and appears as:

http://www.senate.gov/senator/lastname.html

A handful of home pages for members of Congress are found at URLs that don't follow these formulas. This is the case for those members who maintain home pages on Internet sites other than the House and Senate servers. Senator Kennedy's home page, for example, remains at MIT where it has been since long before the Senate had a Web site. Similarly, the home page for a member of the House, Representative Peter DeFazio of Oregon, continues to be hosted by a Web server at the University of Oregon (a complete listing of member URLs is found in the Appendix).

Home pages for members of Congress generally have three things in common. First, they provide links to information provided by the member such as statements, press releases, and constituent service information. Second, they provide links to information resources in the member's state or district such as state government or university home pages. Third, they provide links to other government resources such as the White House and the Library of Congress. These three general categories of information can be combined in a number of ways, allowing members to further customize their home page. For example, many members provide links that perform searches on the *Congressional Record* and legislation available via THOMAS that will return all bills sponsored by or floor statements made by that member.

Members with home pages, which by necessity all begin by covering these three general areas, often struggle to find a way to set their Webs sites apart from all of the rest. Here are some Web watcher's hints for looking closely at a member of Congress's home page.

One frequent mistake in Web design that is not unique to the Hill is the inclusion of unnecessarily large graphics. Although graphics provide one of the most appealing features of the Web, most good Webmasters try to keep their graphics to a manageable number and size, in consideration of Net browsers who ride in the slow lane at 14,400 baud or slower speeds, or who don't have the benefit of graphics at all (e.g., LYNX users).

Virtually every member's home page has their official portrait as the first and most essential element. Usually a smiling picture of the member with an American flag or the Capitol dome in the background, a member's official portrait will be reproduced in scores of directories, newspaper articles, newsletters, and other places. Signed copies will hang on the walls of constituents, contributors, restaurants, and barber shops. For that reason members of Congress often agonize over their portrait, and when they've settled on one they like, it gets used everywhere. Member home pages often include these images, and sometimes they make the mistake of making it too big. One example is the home page unveiled by Representative Ben Cardin of Maryland in August 1995. Visitors to this page faced a moment of uncertainty on their arrival, seemingly looking at an empty background. But once their browser had been given a moment to churn on the GIF (image) file, their monitor would slowly be filled like a movie screen being lowered with an extreme close-up of the congressman's smiling face. Not a word of text could be found anywhere without scrolling down past his chin and tie. It was as if your monitor had turned into a mirror through which Rep. Cardin was looking back at you. Scary. A few months later the page was updated, the picture reduced to a much humbler size.

Senator Leahy of Vermont, one of the earliest members of Congress on the Web, chose a much different type of photo. The first version of his home page showed him visiting a classroom of small children, sitting at a small table talking with them. Later this photo was replaced with a photo of a casually dressed Leahy hoisting his young granddaughter. These informal pictures present a much warmer and welcoming view of the Senator than any desk-and-flag photo could. Although it is hard to break the habit of the official photo, members could go a long way toward improving their home pages by following Senator Leahy's example.

As more home pages on the Hill take advantage of advanced graphics features such as backgrounds, tables, and button bars, it's worth noting those that have shown their understanding of the varied capabilities of different Web browsers and provided a text-only version of their page as an alternative. Some designs, such as a busy background image, can actually make it more difficult to read and locate information on the page, and is more of a distraction than an enhancement.

Many pages are now getting fancier with their topmost graphic. Custom graphics that incorporate the portrait together with other elements such as the member's name, state/district name, and perhaps a scenic photo or a state/district map are becoming the nameplates on many member home pages, rather than a portrait alone. Such custom graphics are often very attractive and effective at conveying more than a photo alone can, subject to the same design considerations when it comes to size.

Probably the most important thing to look for on any member's home page is the availability of timely information. A close look can help you determine if the page is an actively maintained resource with up-to-date content, or an attractive facade that hides empty rooms behind it and contains only static content and links to other sites. The most positive sign you can find is the existence of any type of "What's New" file. Commonly found on home pages across the rest of the Web, the existence of a "What's New" file on a member page is a clear demonstration of an office's intention to add new content to the page frequently and a brave willingness to prove it. You won't find many on the Hill.

If there is no "What's New" file, the next item you should look for when carbon-dating member home pages are dated press releases. Members spend a tremendous amount of time trying to keep their name in the paper and their face on TV. They employ skilled press staffs who churn out press releases, statements, and media advisories every single day. The promise of finding a new audience for many of these press releases and statements, an audience that can gain direct access unfiltered by any media intermediaries, is often the prime factor in leading a member of Congress to establish an Internet presence. But for many offices it has not yet become routine to see that every press release, or even a selected few, are regularly posted to the Net. Often a congressional office's Internet effort begin with the best of intentions and a handful of items are posted. But routines for the upkeep of the site are not established and postings are sporadic or fall off completely. If you can't locate a press release that's less than a week old, and you see no evidence that items are regularly uploaded, it's a good clue that you're visiting a dormant site. Press release directories on the Senate's gopher are established with a default 45-day expiration on posted files. The stated intention, to preserve disk space on the server, has been completely unnecessary in light of the minimal disk space currently being used by Senate offices, and the low cost of adding more if necessary. The unstated reason is the concern of some offices that they will be leaving too much material on the Net, making it easy for their opponents to examine a long historical record of their statements and actions. Whatever the reason, if you find yourself looking at an empty press release directory on the Senate's server, it's a safe bet that nothing has been posted by that office for at least six weeks. It's an even safer bet that no member of Congress has gone that long without having something to say.

A few members actually create an Internet presence and make no effort at all to post any current press releases or statements. Content to get their picture, some generic information, and a few links to other sites out on the Web, they don't even try to provide up-to-date information on their activities in Congress. House Majority Leader Dick Armey provides an example. Deserving credit for finding his way to the Web early on with a single-issue "Flat Tax Home Page," Armey eventually established a page for his office, making him the highest ranking House member on the Web. You'll find a biography and facts about Texas's 26th District on Armey's home page, as well as pictures in "Armey's Actions Shots" and a collection of "Armey's Fun Links." But don't look for his statements to the press, his speeches, or current updates on his legislative activities. They aren't there.

Armey is also among the few members of Congress who have disregarded the interactive nature of the Net and chosen to post information without also establishing a public e-mail address at which to invite feedback. Representative Barney Frank's home page made its debut on the Net in January 1996. Frank is frank about why he does not accept e-mail, stating:

> *I do not maintain an e-mail address. The significant increase in mail volume that would result would place too great a strain on my resources and my staff's ability to keep up with their already heavy work load. However, I will, as always, gladly respond to any question, comment or inquiry received by letter or phone call. Thank you.*

I am sympathetic to the additional work load that handling e-mail places on congressional staff, and applaud Frank for addressing the question of why he has no e-mail address rather than ignoring it as some other members have. But I disagree with members who want to reach the Net without providing netizens the opportunity to reply in kind. Someone on Frank's staff has time enough to manage the development and upkeep of his home page and the material found there, they also ought to find the time to read constituent e-mail.

Members of Congress should not treat the Internet as a broadcast-only medium, pumping it full of their speeches and statements, if they are not prepared to allow for feedback. A public e-mail address should be the first Internet service made available by any congressional office. Any other effort to make information available on the Net should be released concurrently or subsequently, but not prior to e-mail.

Congressional Committees

Whereas members of Congress have begun moving quickly to establish their personal offices on the Internet, the committees on which they serve and where a great deal of the workings of Congress takes place have come online more slowly. Committees receive and produce a wealth of information essential to the legislative process. At hearings on legislation, subcommittees and full committees accept testimony from experts and other interested individuals. Mark-ups of bills and committee reports determine what form legislation will take before consideration by the full membership of either chamber of Congress. Access to this material would be of much greater value to individuals seeking to monitor congressional actions than the home pages of any individual members of Congress could be, and most of it could be made available relatively easily.

Divided into majority and minority staffs and offices, congressional committees and subcommittees are essentially the domains of their chairmen who are responsible for their staffing and operation. Committee staffs often operate as extensions of the personal staff of their chairmen. And if a committee is on the Net, it is probably there because the chairman and his staff made it so.

Most of the committee material that is currently available on the Internet is on the House and Senate gopher servers. Only a few committees have developed a presence on the Web. Via gopher and the Web, House committees are making a great deal more information available on the Internet than their Senate counterparts.

At this writing, twelve out of twenty standing and select committees in the House of Representatives maintain directories on the House gopher server, and six of those also have home pages on the World Wide Web. Within House committee gopher directories you will find a wide variety of information. Some with little depth may include only a roster of the committee's membership, or press releases from the chairman. But others are much more thorough and include up-to-date committee and subcommittee schedules, testimony submitted to the committee by witnesses, and viewpoints from the members of the minority. The disparity is illustrated by the House Committee on Resources whose directory contains fourteen subdirectories with information about the activities of each of its subcommittees, hearing schedules, and minority views. In contrast, the House Oversight Committee directory is empty except for a notice that it is still under construction.

The home pages for House committees generally provide a graphical storefront on the Web that leads to their gopher directories. Of the six House committees that currently have home pages, four of them (Economic and Educational Opportunities, Government Reform, Judiciary, and Science) prominently display a photo of the committee's chairman. Among those four, only the Science committee chairman has a home page for his personal office, a strong indication of how members often promote their efforts more in terms of their roles as committee chairmen than as individual Representatives. The House Science Committee's page is the most interactive House committee page, utilizing Web-based forms to accept internship applications and invite guest comments. The delays in developing these advanced features may have been what led the Science Committee Democrats to develop the first Committee Minority home page on the House, beating the full committee to the Web.

Eleven out of twenty standing and select committees in the Senate have directories on the Senate's gopher server, but four of them are currently completely empty, while six more have five or fewer posted items, often items that are several months old. Senate committee directories are almost completely devoid of the useful hearing schedules and witness testimony commonly found on the House side. This disparity is a reflection of the slow manner in which Senate Republicans have approached the Internet in their own offices. Of the four committee's I found with empty gopher directories (Agriculture, Commerce, Labor, and Small Business), three are chaired by Senators who have not yet established an E-mail address or any other Internet presence for their office (Senator Pressler, chairman of the Commerce, Science & Transportation Committee, does have an E-mail address and a gopher directory, but is not yet on the Web). When Senator Kennedy was chairman of the Senate Labor and Human Resources Committee in the 103rd Congress, I posted committee press releases and other materials into the committee's gopher directory. But those postings stopped under the new majority in the 104th Congress, and the directory has remained empty ever since.

A look at House and Senate gopher directories offers another insight into the different approaches to the Net taken by the two chambers. House members and committees are permitted to develop whatever subdirectory structure best suits their needs. A quick trip through the House gopher reveals a wide variety of subdirectories. Senators and Senate committees who want to make information available on the Senate gopher lack this freedom to develop their own organization. Originally Senate offices were provided with two subdirectories (general and press releases). Months later, after many offices requested greater flexibility and much discussion and debate (nothing happens in the Senate without it), the number of available directories was expanded to seven (general, press releases, briefs, hearing notices, reports, testimony, transcripts). After this long exercise in coming up with a selection of directory names suitable to every office, Senate offices continue under a constraint not imposed on the House side. Although this limitation may result in a simpler and more uniform presentation of directories on Senate servers, such restrictions and delays caused by micromanaging such details have also stunted the development and use of the Internet by the Senate.

In both the House and the Senate, the policy committees have been at the forefront of Internet use. Unlike all of the other kinds of committees in Congress (standing, select, special, and joint), policy committees are partisan in nature, composed of members of the same party. Policy committees provide a foundation for the leadership structures of the majority and minority parties in both the House and Senate. The House Democratic Leadership and Democratic Caucus established two of the earliest home pages on the House Web server, and the Senate Democratic Policy committee was the first Senate committee on the Web. The House Republican Conference, Senate Republican Policy, and Senate Republican Conference all likewise developed an Internet presence very early. In seeking to utilize the Net to promote the programs and positions of their parties, these partisan committees have been quicker to utilize the Net as a communications medium than the "regular" committees have.

One Senate committee that stands out for actually having witness testimony available on the gopher, and for being the first standing committee in the Senate on the Web is the Energy and Natural Resources Committee. The committee's systems administrator, Chris Kimball, has created what is probably the best home page for any congressional committee in terms of utilizing the Web's abilities. Complete with hearing schedules, witness testimony from past hearings, and status of legislation under the committee's jurisdiction, the home page also includes links to the full-text versions of each bill via the Library of Congress's THOMAS server.

Two of Congress's four joint committees have home pages on the Web. The Joint Committee on Printing has a home page maintained by the Government Printing Office, the agency over which the committee has oversight, but it is little more than a static photo roster of the committee's members and contains no other updated content. The Joint Economic Committee is disjointed on the Web. This committee has two separate home pages, one on the House and the other on the Senate's web server, and no link between them.

All congressional committees will slowly find their way onto the Internet, a couple of paces behind their chairmen and other members who are only now learning the medium. Individual members of Congress rightfully exercise broad latitude over the material that they choose to post to the Net. But committees ought to be required to meet some minimum standard of items that they must make available online. New rules and procedures would be required in the House and Senate to require that all committees make their fundamental information and documents such as schedules, witness testimony, and reports available. Once this information is available from every committee, the public's ability to follow Congress on the Net will improve dramatically.

A basic item that all committees could quickly and easily make available on the Internet is the prepared testimony submitted by witnesses who appear before congressional committees. Congressional hearings are one of the most fundamental means by which members of Congress receive input on the wide array of legislation and other issues subject to their consideration. The Senate's role of confirming presidential nominations and ratifying treaties brings additional importance to the hearing process. And congressional investigations, whose work is often carried out by temporary committees, also often hear testimony from witnesses in public hearings as they did during the Iran-Contra and Whitewater investigations.

Expert witnesses, concerned citizens, and many others interested in any particular piece of legislation are regularly invited to share their expertise in hearings held by committees considering legislation. These witnesses are routinely asked to prepare and submit a written statement prior to the hearing for inclusion in the hearing record. Often a witness's spoken testimony is simply a direct reading from prepared remarks, followed by questions from the committee members. Depending on whether it is a subcommittee or a full committee hearing, and on the expected interest in the hearing, witnesses are regularly asked to submit multiple copies of their testimony, usually between fifty and a hundred copies. This testimony is quickly grabbed up by committee members and their staffs and the press, with what is left available to the attending public (often a gang of bicycle couriers who have been paid by law firms and lobbyists to wait in line at the hearing and be sure to get a copy of the testimony).

At least one commercial services currently works to gather copies of submitted testimony which they then digitize with a high-speed scanner and make available on the Net to those who can afford the steep subscription costs. The Govline Congressional Committee Transcript Service offers delivery of testimony via a Usenet feed, delivering the testimony "into about 60 [news]groups corresponding to current US Congressional Committees." The service doesn't come cheap, with prices that range anywhere from $6,000 to $12,000 a year depending or the type of organization and number of users that will use the material. Such high prices demonstrate the value that is placed on timely online access to this material, particularly considering that these are only the prepared statements submitted by witnesses and members, and not true verbatim transcripts of the hearings as they occurred.

These same statements could and should be made available on the Net directly from the committees themselves. It would be a simple matter for submitted testimony to be made available on the Net by the committees themselves, and at no cost either to Congress or the end user.

It's safe to assume that the majority of the witnesses who submit testimony have prepared it on a personal computer, and that making the additional request of them to submit a copy of their testimony on computer diskette would not be unreasonable. Many committees already request a copy on disk so that they can more easily store and reproduce witness testimony, and a few make that submitted testimony available on the Internet. If all witnesses who testified before Congress were requested to submit a copy of their testimony on diskette (assistance could be provided for the few who could not), and all congressional committee put those prepared statements on the Internet immediately following the hearing at which it was offered, a wealth of useful information about the issues of the day would be available to millions.

As I've pointed out, a number of House and Senate committees do make testimony and other information available on the Net. But until new rules require it, or new practices prevail, the availability of current material from committees will remain haphazard.

A couple of home pages on the Hill offer a peek at some of the inner workings and support offices in the legislative branch. One of the best and most complete home pages in the Senate is maintained by the Office of the Legal Counsel, an office created by the Ethics in Government Act of 1978. The page, built by Barbara Thoreson, describes the role of the legal counsel, with hypertext links to the relevant sections from the U.S. Code. "The Ethics Act provides for four major activities of the office:

1. defending the Senate, its committees, Members, officers, and employees in civil litigation relating to their official responsibilities or when they have been subpoenaed to testify or to produce Senate records;
2. representing committees of the Senate in proceedings to aid their investigations;
3. appearing for the Senate when it intervenes or appears as amicus curiae in lawsuits to protect the powers or responsibilities of the Congress; and
4. advising committees and officers of the Senate."

The page includes a list of cases in which the counsel was involved, and demonstrating an understanding of how the Web can best be utilized, provides hypertext links to the decisions in these cases when available. The Legal Counsel home page is currently available only via ftp, as the Senate struggles with the nonissue of allowing this page onto the Web server.

Another home page most Congress-watchers may have missed belongs to the Office of the Chief Administrative Officer (CAO). The office was created in 1992, in the wake of the House banking scandal and other institutional problems, to administer the internal operations and support of the House. Containing information that is primarily directed to House staff interested in utilizing the services provided by the CAO, this home page offers a quick glimpse into the internal organization and operations of the House of Representatives.

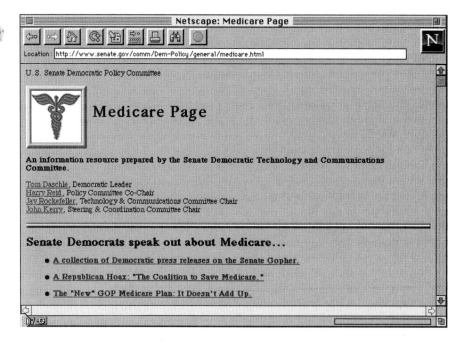

Another emerging genre of home pages on the Hill is the single-issue effort. Representative Dick Armey's "Flat Tax" home page, and Representative Vic Fazios "Save McClellen Air Force Base" effort on the Web were among the earliest examples of this type. Newer pages are being developed that are designed to provide a common message and shared content for more than one member to utilize. The Senate Democratic Policy Committee's (DPC) "Medicare" home page is one example. The DPC used this page in the Medicare fight to bring together DPC issue briefs and legislative bulletins, statements by

Senate Democrats and the President regarding the fight over Medicare, and other Internet resources related to Medicare and of interest to seniors. The home page was unveiled during an online meeting at which three Senate Democrats (Bingaman, Kennedy, and Reid) took questions online about Medicare from the members of SeniorNet, an organization of computer-using senior citizens. Many of the personal home pages maintained by Senate Democrats added links to the DPC Medicare page, helping to make it the most frequently visited Internet resource the committee developed.

The Republican delegation from the State of Washington developed their "Balanced Budget Web" as a resource to promote the Balanced Budget Act of 1995 and to provide links to other resources supporting their bill. The counter on the page advertises almost 3,000 visits in the first two months since it became available on the Web in mid-November 1995.

Single-issue pages that help to promote the positions of the majority or the minority, a state's congressional delegation, or a special interest caucus are likely to become a more frequently utilized means for creating resources that can be shared by more than one member on the Net.

SIX

---⭐---

Tales from the Trenches

April Fools or Real Life?

In March 1994, an acquaintance forwarded to me an e-mail message he had received from a mailing list to which he subscribed. The message referred to a column by John C. Dvorak that appeared in the April 1994 issue of *PC Computing* magazine, and the column described a legislative effort under way in the United States Senate.

Senate Bill 040194 was said to be a bill "designed to prohibit anyone from using a public computer network (Information Highway) while the computer user is intoxicated," and also make it illegal to "discuss

153

sexual matters." The bill, sponsored by Senator Patrick Leahy and co-sponsored by Kennedy, was crafted by members of Congress who know so little about computer networks that they think the "Info Highway" is an actual road. The column reported Senator Pat Moynihan asking "if you needed a driving permit to 'drive' a modem on the Information Highway! He has no clue what a modem is, and neither does the rest of Congress."

One ominous result of the bill was the FBI's plans to conduct wiretaps "on any computer if there is any evidence that the owner uses or abuses alcohol and has access to a modem." A new law enforcement group called the Online Enforcement Agency was said to be placing want ads soliciting wiretap experts.

With strong support from Baptist Ministers and no member of Congress either willing or able to understand technology or "come out and support drunkenness and computer sex," the bill was on the fast track to passage. Readers were told they could register their complaints with Ms. Lirpa Sloof in the Senate Legislative Analysts Office, whose "name spelled backwards says it all."

I would have probably found the column to be more amusing had I not been frustrated at how it had chosen to pick Senator Kennedy as a target. But the last thing I'd expected was that anybody could actually believe it to be true. I did have the advantage of certainty. I *knew* this story was not true. And there were plenty of clues in the story itself to help reader reach that conclusion. The title, "Lair of Slop," is an anagram for April Fools. At the end of the column, "Lirpa Sloof...Her name spelled backward says it all.," April Fools. And the bill number itself, 040194, a date, April Fools Day. But even these clues did not prevent a large number of people from believing it. It didn't take long after *PC Computing* hit mailboxes and newsstands before the first calls and e-mails began arriving in Kennedy's office, followed shortly by faxes and letters. The offices of the other senators mentioned in the article also started hearing from outraged constituents.

I was surprised that people could believe the story, but my surprise grew even more when people I knew personally and who knew of my efforts to put Senator Kennedy online told me of their concern over this bill. Even Jonathan Gourd, sysop of North Shore Mac, the BBS on which Kennedy's online efforts had begun, posted a message to his system encouraging readers to contact Congress and protest this bill. The whole tale was taken as fact by an even wider audience after initial messages of alarm, posted by people who'd read and believed the article, convinced many others of the Senate's evil intentions without them having had the opportunity to read the story and perhaps catch the clues for themselves.

It was apparent that this story had the potential to become an "urban legend" of the Net. Just like other oft retold and wildly inaccurate stories such as the one about the proposed FCC modem tax or the dying boy who wanted Get Well cards, the Senate's Information Highway Drunk Driving Bill was proving to be a tale with legs that could rapidly traverse the Net.

In an attempt to prevent Dvorak's column from spawning another net legend, I posted an explanatory message (with the article included) to the ACE groups mailing list and encouraged readers to repost it where appropriate to help prevent the rumor's spread. This message did get around and was reprinted in the widely read *RISKS-FORUM* Digest among other places. On March 30 a brief article about the hoax appeared in the *Washington Post*. These efforts seemed to work, calls from concerned constituents decreased.

In late October I received an e-mail message from a gentlemen who described himself as a Ph.D. in physical chemistry and an Internet user. He wrote that he had read the article and was concerned about this bill. Explaining passionately why he felt the bill was wrong, he offered his own expertise to Senator Kennedy as a scientific consult-ant to help prevent such misguided legislation. I e-mailed him an explanation and by that afternoon he'd sent a note expressing his own embarrassment at having missed the clues and believed the story. He was the last person I heard from on the subject.

In the year following Dvorak's April Fools stab at the Senate, the Senate passed the Digital Telephony or wiretap bill. It's purpose is to protect the government's ability to eavesdrop on the Information Superhighway. In June 1995 the Senate passed the Communications Decency Act, a bill sponsored by Senator Exon of Nebraska, an effort to "clean up" the dark alley's of the Internet and make them safe for children.

I have a much better understanding now of the people who didn't see the humor in John Dvorak's April Fools joke. Ironically, Senator Leahy has been the Senate's most outspoken advocate for protecting the Net from misguided and damaging government intrusion, and not the sponsor of such as Dvorak's column made him. Kennedy and Moynihan, both made out as ignorant of the Net in the article, were actually both among the 16 Senators to oppose the Exon bill when it came to a vote in the Senate.

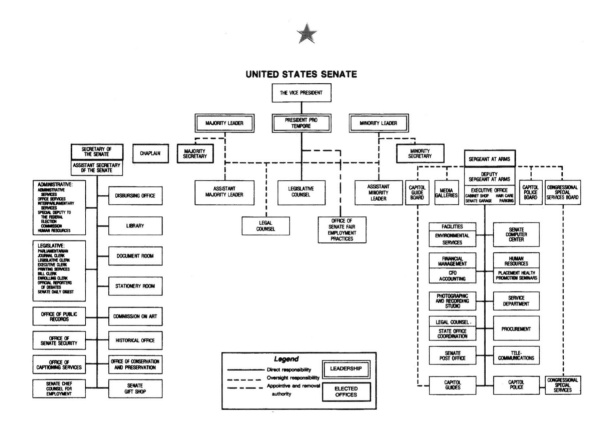

UNITED STATES SENATE

Rules

The Senate Rules Committee is responsible for the operation of the Senate. An organizational chart of the Senate may show that the Sergeant at Arms manages the day-to-day administrative minutiae of keeping the Senate running, overseeing the offices of Facilities, Financial Management, Human Resources, the Service Department, Telecommunications, the Recording and Photographic Studio and the Senate Computer Center. But nothing happens to change the operations of the Senate without the explicit instruction of the Rules Committee.

Before Senator Kennedy's office first began posting information to bulletin board systems and then to the Internet, our office made an inquiry to the Rules Committee to see if there were any guidelines or restrictions on such an activity. "Nobody's ever done that before," was the response. There were no rules. Our office would be exploring uncharted waters in cyberspace, and our experiences would likely set precedents for other offices that would eventually follow in our path. The burden was on us to make the most out of this new medium, without doing anything to give the Rules Committee cause to prohibit us.

One Senate Computer Center staffer has described the Senate's efforts to apply old rules to new technologies as akin to "trying to make airplanes stop at railroad crossings just because the busses do." But rules governing other Senate facilities and operations did exist, and some of them would impact our use of the Internet. In particular, there is a rule restricting a Senator's use of certain Senate facilities during the sixty days prior to any primary or general election for which the Senator is a candidate for office. One of them, known as the Mass Mailing rule, prohibited Senators facing an election from using the franking privilege to send out any mass mailings (500 or more pieces) during the restricted sixty-day period prior to the election. Another rule prohibits the use of certain Senate facilities such as the recording studio during the same period. The obvious reason for these rules is to prevent the appearance that Senate resources could be misused for campaign purposes.

One hurdle that many on the Hill have trouble overcoming in understanding electronic mail is that word "mail." The handling of postal mail plays such a vital role in the operation of any congressional office, and is of such great importance to every member, that the word itself takes on a greater meaning. The words "mail" and "correspondent" can be found in almost every job description for congressional staff positions and in a number of the job titles as well. The franking privilege, which allows members of Congress to send mail out with no more postage than their signature on the envelope, itself demonstrates the great amount of importance placed on the mail as a means for reporting to and responding to constituents.

So how does the frank apply to electronic mail? Or does it apply at all? Unlike a typical mass mailing of newsletters to every constituent in the district or state, e-mail was only being used to respond to incoming messages, or in a few cases to send messages out using listservers that reached only those individuals who had specifically requested to be on the mailing list. Any effort by a member of Congress to send an uninvited mass e-mailing into the computers of their constituents would certainly invite their wrath rather than their support.

The posting of files to the Internet or a computer bulletin board system (BBS) has nothing in common with sending information out in the mail. Nobody would find their way to Senator Kennedy's conferences on a Massachusetts's BBS, his ftp archive or home page at MIT, or his directory on the Senate gopher who had not themselves sought that location out and brought themselves to it. Unlike a mass mailing appearing in a mailbox unexpected and uninvited, postings to the Net are much more closely related to tacking something up in a public place where anyone interested could read it. They're called computer "bulletin boards" for a reason.

Several months prior to the 1994 elections, the Rules Committee determined that the Senate's Internet server would be subject to the same election rules that applied to other Senate facilities, and that sixty days prior to an election all files placed on the Senate server by a Senator running for office would be erased.

But these distinctions were difficult for some to understand. In late July 1994, sixty days prior to the Massachusetts Democratic Party's primary election, the Senate Computer Center was preparing to implement the directions of the Rules Committee and completely erase all files in Senator Kennedy's directory on the Senate's ftp/gopher server. I contacted the computer center and requested to see what explanatory message they would be leaving behind so that visitors to the Senator's directory would know why it was suddenly empty. I was told that the Rules Committee had argued against any such message, claiming that no such explanation would be necessary.

What?! During its first six months the Senate gopher had logged more than 80,000 visitors. Kennedy's directory had been the first one on the server and material had been available in it from the beginning. And now everything in it was to suddenly be deleted, leaving an empty directory, and without explanation?!

One Rules Committee staffer argued that "You don't send a mass mailing out to tell people you aren't going to be sending any more mass mailings." They just didn't get it. I argued in reply, "No, you don't close up shop during business hours without hanging a 'gone fishing' sign on the door." Eventually, a single-line explanation was posted. It read, "Senate policy restricts a Senator's use of the Senate Internet servers during the 60 days before an election."

In an apparent effort to prevent those Senators who were not facing reelection from being tempted to act as conduits to the Net for any of their restricted colleagues, *every* Senator was subject to the sixty-day restriction from the Internet during the final sixty days prior to the November election.

Our office faced another decision. The Rules Committee could tell us what we could do on the Senate's server, but neither the bulletin boards in Massachusetts to which we posted nor the Internet host at MIT are subject to Senate rules. Kennedy's office could have continued posting materials to these sites. To avoid confusion and any appearance that the Senator was sidestepping Senate rules, it was decided that we would stop posting any new material to our other online outlets during the restricted period, but that we would not delete all of the existing materials as had been done on the Senate server. On Senator Kennedy's home page at MIT, still the only one for a member of Congress, and now the first for a member seeking reelection, a message was posted at the top of the page indicating that the page would be "frozen" in compliance with Senate rules. As an additional touch that I liked, the word "rules" was a hypertext link to the precise language from the Standing Rules of the Senate that mandated the restriction.

We had complied with the Senate's rules, but the reaction from users of the Senator's online information was entirely opposed to this election freeze. Messages from constituents who had become used to getting information about his activities in the Senate directly from Kennedy's office indicated their frustration with having that source cut off for more than three months.

The sixty-day rule did not restrict access to Internet resources for Senate committees. Since committees are staffed and run by the committee's chairman, they are essentially an extended staff for their chairmen. This could be a potential loophole for Senators who find their own access to the Internet restricted, but remain able to post press releases and other materials in the committee's directories. In 1994, in following the decision to halt all postings to the Internet during the restricted period, the Senate Labor and Human Resource Committee, then chaired by Senator Kennedy, stopped posting material to the committee's directory on the Senate gopher.

The mass-mailing rule does not apply to any mailing that "consists entirely of news releases to the communications media," allowing Senators to continue sending franked mail to the traditional media letting them know all about their accomplishments in Congress, right on up to election day.

Most Senators are posting the very same press releases and statements to the Internet that they provide to the media. The consequence of the way the rule is applied to the Internet is to force a media filter over information coming out of a Senate office by cutting off direct online access from the public during the very period a constituent is most likely to wish to learn more about their Senator's activities in Congress. In many cases, the old rules are just as likely to prove impractical when applied to using the Net in Congress.

The House of Representatives did not raise any issues regarding rules governing the use of the Internet prior to an election. It was not until a few weeks before election day that the House Administration Committee approved a plan allowing members to establish a local gopher directory on the House gopher. Prior to that, members who wished to establish a gopher directory were encouraged to make some arrangement with a university or other organization in their district. The fact that these directories did not live on House computers may have helped make it easier for the House to choose not to attempt to restrict their use. With every single member of the House facing reelection, and several running for Senate seats, the House Administration Committee chose a hands-off approach toward Members' use of the Internet.

It remains unknown how the sixty-day rule will be implemented in the 1996 election year, as more members of the Senate establish home pages on the World Wide Web that are hosted by the Senate's Web server. In 1994 the Senate had only a gopher server, and the rule as implemented led to the deletion of every file posted by every Senator (committee directories remained unrestricted). If the same "delete everything" approach is taken in 1996, the home pages created by Senate personal offices will cease to exist when the HTML files that create them are deleted. A better approach would be to "freeze" the home pages as Senator Kennedy voluntarily did with his in 1994, leaving them in place and intact and restricting only the posting of new material. Better still would be to reexamine the restriction and consider lifting it completely. There's no need for this plane to stop at the train tracks.

The Access Fight Grinds On

Almost two years after Senator Kennedy's office first began posting information to the Net, Internet services available to staff within the Senate remained woefully inadequate. Electronic mail was still the only service available to all staff, access to ftp and telnet services were still restricted to three staff members per personal office and six per committee. The ftp/gopher server that the SCC had established at the end of 1993 remained the only means for posting to the Net from within the Senate.

Despite the fact that the Senate had not yet followed the example of virtually every other significant government agency or institution from the White House to the House, from the Pentagon to the Bureau of Mines, a number of Senate systems administrators began teaching themselves the fundamentals of Hypertext Markup Language (HTML) and posting home pages on the Senate ftp server. Although a Web server is certainly better suited for hosting a home page, an ftp server can deliver up a file to the Web, albeit clumsily.

Our bosses were certainly not blind to the huge amount of positive coverage that the Internet, and the Web in particular, continued to get in the media. The Library of Congress' THOMAS home page had been unveiled to great fanfare in the first week of the new Republican-lead Congress, and stories about access to Congress on the Internet were plentiful. Members of Congress who still had only the vaguest understanding of the Internet began instructing their staffs to put them there.

After years of having our requests for more Internet access within the Senate fall on the deaf ears of the Senate Rules Committee, the budding interest in the Internet that began to find expression from Senators themselves provided Senate systems administrators an opportunity to bring their bosses' power to bear in the battle.

Freshman Republican Senator Bill Frist of Tennessee was no stranger to technology. As a heart/lung transplant surgeon, he had used it daily saving lives, and he intended to use it to serve his constituents. At a dinner hosted for Senators by the Library of Congress, Frist saw a demonstration of the World Wide Web (including a look at CapWeb) and decided to put his own office on the Web. He followed up with the Library the next day, looking for more information about how to get on the Web, and was surprised to discover the limited access to the Internet provided within the Senate. Senator Frist drafted a letter, which fourteen of his fellow Senators also signed, to Senator Ted Stevens, chairman of the Senate Rules Committee which oversees the use of computers and communications within the Senate. The letter made five specific requests for improving Internet services within the Senate and asked that they be implemented "quickly and efficiently."

The Senators requested that the Senate do the following:

- Provide Senate staff access to the World Wide Web,

- establish a Senate Web server (several offices had already established home pages and placed them on the Senate's ftp server),

- permit offices to directly administer their directories on Senate Internet servers,

- provide staff with access to Usenet news groups, and

- increase the number of staff in an office permitted access to the Internet.

The official response was that the Rules Committee requested that the Sergeant at Arms prepare a "cost/benefit" analysis regarding the development of additional Internet services within the Senate. The unofficial response was to treat the letter as the work of fifteen renegade systems administrators who'd gotten reckless with their bosses' auto-pens. When the Senate Systems Administrator's Association (SSAA) was asked by the computer center to contribute to the analysis by preparing a report explaining "why" Senators wished to be on the Internet, some lively e-mail exchanges resulted. Why?! What's next? Will Telecom be asking us 'why' we need phones? Or the Architect of the Capitol ponder 'why' our offices need doors? Jeff Hecker, systems administrator to the Democratic Policy Committee, was well known within the Senate for his knowledge of UNIX (very rare in the Senate), his logical arguments in favor of improved Internet access, and his biting retorts to arguments against it. In one message to the SCC in response to the request for input, Jeff developed a cost/benefit analysis of his own.

Tom—you've got to be kidding

I'm really tempted to say something that I'll likely regret, so instead, I'll pass along a very quick benefit/cost analysis:

Costs:
Internet feed from ANS or equivalent
alternative supplier: Already
installed. Additional cost $0.00
IP firewall hardware, software, staff,
floor space, electricity: Already
installed. Additional cost 0.00
Inter-office IP backbone, fiber,
routers, network monitoring
software, electricity: Already
installed. Additional cost 0.00
Local workstation TCP/IP software:
Already installed. Additional cost 0.00
Workstation browser software available
from the National Center for Supercomputing
Applications. Cost 0.00
                                                 _____
Total cost $0.00

Benefits:
Ability for concerned staff to click on a picture
of Socks the cat, and listen to its
"meow." Value $0.01
Ability for interested staff to benefit from
the wisdom of alt.rush.limbaugh. Value 0.01
                                                 _____
Total Benefits $0.02
Cost / Benefit ratio: 0.00 / 0.02 . . . . 0.00
Benefit / Cost ratio: 0.02 / 0.00 . . . . (infinite)

If SCC really thinks it's necessary, a more detailed analysis can be provided. What is the time frame for the SCC's internal analysis?

I hadn't realized that after two and a half years of presenting "Stand by for the Internet" seminars, the SCC has yet to perform any evaluation of its cost/benefit for senate offices.

When we make future requests of the Senate Computer Center, such as the purchase of a new software update, or the repair of a malfunctioning piece of equipment, should we also include a similar benefit/cost analysis? I'll alert our staff of the new procedures right away.

jeff

Frustrated but undeterred, the members of the SSAA prepared a detailed memorandum titled "Considering the Expansion of Senate Office Internet Access" and delivered it to the Senate Computer Center and the Rules Committee on March 15, 1995. The report detailed the potential benefits a Senate office could realize with meaningful access to the Internet and dispelled the most common excuses offered in explanation of the Senate's snail pace toward the Net; "there will be viruses everywhere," "hackers will break into the Senate," "we can't afford more bandwidth and must be careful when making any withdrawals from our available bandwidth bank account," were among the most frequent. The report concluded "The SSAA, and more specifically, those Senators who co-signed Senator Frist's letter, believe that his requests are modest, inexpensive, trivial to implement, have been hinted at during SCC presentations for two years, and should be implemented without delay."

The Frist letter had been handled as the forged effort of staff rather than a genuine request of Senators, and the word was that it would see no action. To again push their request for improved Internet services, at least a half dozen of the letter's signers sent personal follow-up notes, some hand delivered, to Senator Stevens to leave no doubt as to the authenticity of their desire to get on the net.

But despite these efforts, the chairman's reply, which came a month after the Frist letter had been sent, promised only the prospect of a "pilot project to analyze the cost and benefit of providing additional services." Nobody held their breath.

Senator Bill Frist – Republican, Tennessee

Although he describes himself as just a computer user and "not a guru at all," among members of the Senate the users are the gurus. In his previous career as a heart/lung transplant surgeon, Freshman Senator Bill Frist had used computers since his residency in medical school for word processing, statistical analysis, and communicating with his fellow scientists in the rapidly growing field of transplantation across the country and around the world.

During his campaign for the Senate, he discovered how little information about Congress and its members was available online. And when he arrived in the Senate to take his place in the 104th Congress he was surprised at how far behind the Senate was in using technology. "[T]his environment's very similar to that of medicine and the research world in that there's new information coming in every day which adds to the whole...and there's no way to access it in the legislative arena, where in the scientific arena there is."

Frist helped bring the Internet to the attention of his fellow Senators, and pressed for the development of greater access of Senate staff and enhanced services to allow Senators to make information available to the public on the World Wide Web. Pleased with the progress that has been made, he still recognizes that the Senate has "a lot of catching up to do." The first Republican in Congress to establish a home page on the Web, Frist has set an example that many members now seek to emulate. As chairman of the Senate subcommittee on disability policy, Frist is particularly interested in the benefits that computers and other assistive technologies can provide to those with disabilities who might otherwise prevent their gaining access to information that is critical to them.

As a means of staying attuned to his constituents' positions on various issues, Senator Frist uses e-mail to send questions and obtain responses from field representatives in his state, who are in more direct contact with constituents. Frist says this feedback gives him a "much more accurate read" on his constituents' thoughts than the often generated phone calls and mail campaigns to his office. "To me if there's one area that has been of particular interest or help as a public servant, it has been being online with my entire seven field offices around the state."

Lacking any immediate prospect of gaining access to the Web from the Senate itself, many offices began to gain access to the Internet the same way that millions of individuals have, by purchasing a dial-in or SLIP/PPP account with an Internet service provider. Unused analog phone lines and modems are in very short supply in most Senate offices, but they were easier to come by than Internet access using the Senate Fiber Network from behind the Senate's firewall. For most organizations that connect themselves to the Internet, a firewall is an essential piece of security hardware designed to keep unwelcome visitors from the Net off of their networks. But in the Senate, more time was spent making sure that the firewall was configured to keep most staff in, to keep them off the Net.

System administrators were finding themselves looking at a situation similar to the one they faced when the Senate's ftp/gopher server had been made available for use by personal and committee offices in the Senate. While this had given offices the ability to get material onto the Internet, staff did not have enough access to view their own postings. Now the World Wide Web was in the news, and members of Congress and their staffs could not help but read about it—the Web efforts of Kennedy, the White House, THOMAS, the House, all had been written about and noticed. Members of Congress who still had little understanding of what the Internet was, were instructing their staffs to put them there, and "there" meant the Web. And the Web was someplace Senate staff could not get to.

Information about how to find an Internet service provider and how to install and configure the necessary software needed to get on the Web was shared among many offices, and more than a few managed to get their own access to the Net. The experience that Jeff and I had gained in creating CapWeb had helped us to develop some basic skills with HTML, the language used for building Web sites. We spread those skills among other interested systems administrators by arranging tutorials and providing whatever assistance we could to other interested offices.

One thing that had occurred to Jeff late in 1994 was that the lack of a Senate HTTP server (Hypertext Transfer Protocol, a Web server) didn't necessarily have to prevent a Senate office from creating a presence on the Web. And Jeff's solution did not require an office to seek outside assistance from a university as Senator Kennedy and Representative DeFazio had with MIT and the University of Oregon. Jeff realized that we could make the most of the facilities available to us, by putting our home pages on the existing Senate ftp server. Web browsers such as Mosaic and Netscape allow access to ftp servers, and though it wasn't the best way to serve up a home page, it was the only way we had available. We started helping offices to write their own HTML, build their own home pages, and then put those files onto the Senate's ftp server.

The Democratic Policy Committee placed the first HTML files on the Senate's ftp server in December 1994 and was followed shortly by the new Democratic Leader, Tom Daschle, in January. As word spread of this means to make the most of the ftp server, and HTML skills began to develop among a handful of sys admins, a few of the Senate offices most interested in the Net quickly developed home pages. Senators Leahy, Rockefeller, Bingaman, Robb, Frist, Breaux, and Kerrey all established home pages in March. While gopher accesses had previously far outpaced ftp requests on the Senate's server, the presence of HTML files being served up to the Web via ftp soon led it to outpace gopher as the most used path to the Senate's Internet server.

The Great Senate Web Hack

An interesting thing happened amidst all of these roundabout efforts to put Senators on the Web and repeated requests for increased Internet access for staff. Somebody in the Senate discovered that access wasn't being restricted at all. Essentially they had simply tried the doorknob on the firewall, and instead of finding it locked as expected, they found it wide open and began surfing the Web. Word spread quickly and quietly among offices, and many began hooking their staffs up and enjoying the very access to the Web they'd been told they could not have. I had a dozen staffers in Kennedy's office connected, each of whom benefited from the resources they found after a five-minute lesson in using a browser.

For about two months an increasing number of Senate staff enjoyed access to the Web. Previous warnings about lack of bandwidth, a frequent excuse for restricted access, proved false. Office LANs did not come grinding to a halt as we'd been warned. For weeks nobody in Telecommunications, the department responsible for the Senate's firewall and Internet connection, even noticed the increased outbound Net usage. But eventually they did, and the door was slammed shut. For a couple of weeks, a few staff had found their way to the Web, and then they were locked in again.

The best explanation for the firewall's failure that we could find was that the firewall crashed and a technician made a house call to revive it. Presumably, the technician returned the firewall to its default security settings, settings that allow outbound traffic, rather than the more restrictive Senate settings that allowed almost nothing.

Once the jig was up, word of the clandestine Web access spread quickly. Those offices and staffs that had begun to make use of the Internet as a resource, quickly came to miss it when it was gone. And the fact that none of the oft warned of problems such as lack of bandwidth, viruses, or hackers resulted was used to great advantage by those of use who advocated access to the Net. Three days after an overly dramatic headline in *Roll Call* read "All Senate Offices Soon to Get "Web" Access After Hackers Break Into Computer Center," the Rules Committee announced its approval of Web access for staff (subject to the same restrictions as ftp/telnet, three personal staff and six committee staff), and the development of a Senate Web server and home page. Months would pass before either actually became available, but their authorization was itself a great step forward for the Senate on the Net.

Later, it quietly came out that some Senate staff had taken a peek at the adult side of the Web during the spree, a fact that must have come from an exhaustive analysis of log files after the open firewall had been discovered. While discouraging to learn that what Senate offices do on the Internet would be monitored, it's little wonder that some became curious considering the hoopla that was arising in the Senate over pornography on the Internet.

Once access did become available to three individuals per office, a Hecker solution that lived within the letter of the law, if not the spirit, helped many offices deliver access to their entire staffs. The Senate's firewall restricted outbound access to the Internet by checking the requesting machine's IP address, allowing only three "blessed" machines per office to get out to the Net, and preventing every other computer from gaining Net access. Senate offices, whose staffs generally number twenty to thirty individuals, found that allowing only three staff members to have Internet access was restrictive. The standard reply was that the office should set up a common computer in an open area within the office and make it one of the three blessed machines, allowing any staffer who needed to get to the Net to line up at the public machine and wait for a turn.

Taking this idea one better, Jeff began helping offices take old 386s that were marked for extinction and configure them with a public domain version of UNIX called LINUX. The LINUX boxes were set up to be one of the three blessed machines, with an IP address that was permitted to pass the Senate's firewall to the Internet. Once in place, all staff within the office could now link to the LINUX box from the computer on their own desk, and that old 386 would forward their requests out past the Senate's firewall and onto the Internet, allowing entire staffs to gain Net access. With Jeff's assistance, a large number of offices slipped past efforts to restrict them, gaining Internet access for as many staff that they deemed needed it. Knowledge of

LINUX has very slowly begun to grow among Senate systems administrators, and many more offices are on Jeff's list for help.

Another benefit of the LINUX box will continue even after all access restrictions are lifted in the Senate. With entire offices gaining access to the Net via the single IP address of the LINUX box, that machine alone will leave footprints in the Senate's log files. Any future monitoring or review of the sites a Senate office's staff have visited on the Net will lead only to the LINUX gateway rather than to any individual's desktop. This additional security will preserve for the office the task of developing appropriate use policies for Internet usage among their staffs, and protect individual staff from any concern that their work on the Net is being monitored from outside their office.

©1995 Etta Hume, Fort Worth Star-Telegram

Pornographers and Terrorists

For many Netizens, the U. S. Senate earned itself the distinction of being the most widely reviled and disparaged of all government institutions of 1995. The reason was a piece of legislation introduced on February 1st, sponsored by Senator Jim Exon of Nebraska, that was known as the Communications Decency Act. A year earlier, John Dvorak's April Fools column was joking that Congress was trying to regulate sexually related content on computer networks. Now Senator Exon wanted to pass a law to do just that.

In his press release announcing the bill, Exon said, "I want to keep the information superhighway from resembling a red light district."

But Internet users generally agreed with Harvard law professor Laurence Tribe's description of the bill as "a frontal assault on the First Amendment."[1] The general impression was that Exon and his supporters were rushing to regulate a medium that they did not understand. A *Washington Post* editorial, entitled "Censoring Cyberspace," described the bill as having been "written without hearings on the new technologies and without a full appreciation of how differently they work."

Following the Clinton administration's Clipper Chip proposal to help maintain the government's ability to read the contents of encrypted communications, and the passage of the Digital Telephony bill that would enhance the FBI's ability to perform wiretaps, the Communications Decency Act was received by the Net as yet another government assault against the Net. It was the first issue over which an Internet-based, widespread, organized, grassroots opposition movement emerged.

By early March only two letters had arrived in Senator Kennedy's office regarding the Communications Decency Act, one from a Massachusetts constituent that opposed the bill, and one from Texas in support. But hundreds of e-mail messages had arrived from across the country and around the world. Virtually all of them were opposed to the Communications Decency Act. Many who were not constituents of Kennedy's wrote to him regarding their opposition to the Exon bill simply because they were aware of Kennedy's Internet efforts and expected his knowledge of the Net would make him likely to oppose the bill. Others wanted to express their views electronically but found their own Senators did not yet have an e-mail address, so sent their messages to Kennedy with requests that he forward them to their Senators (something that was easily done as most offices that didn't have a public address were reachable on the Senate's internal network). As described earlier in this book, the e-mail received on this issue provided the first instance where Kennedy's office sent a

---

[1] Quoted in "On a Screen Near You: Cyberporn," *Time* magazine, July 3, 1995. p. 42.

specific reply in response to e-mail (a message stating his opposition to the Exon bill) rather than just the standard auto-acknowledgment followed by a snail mail reply.

One of the dilemmas of the online opposition campaign was that the bill's supporters, most notably Senator Exon and Senator Coats of Indiana, were not accessible via the Internet. While this situation was no surprise to many who felt it demonstrated their unfamiliarity with the medium, it also left them untouched by e-mail campaigns, updates, or other online opposition efforts.

Senator Patrick Leahy of Vermont became the most outspoken opponent of the Exon bill and was among the most knowledgeable members of Congress on Net-related matters. He offered legislation with an alternative approach to Exon's, mandating that the government study whether new legislation was necessary (the Justice Department said existing laws were sufficient and that the Exon bill would actually hamper efforts to halt obscenity and child pornography on the Net), and explore what parental control solutions might be created to take the task of censoring the Net away from the government and put it in the home. He linked his own home page to an online petition drive sponsored by the Center for Democracy and Technology that gathered more than 115,000 signatures in opposition to the Exon bill in less than five months.

A staff member from Exon's office contacted me, seeking to borrow the color printer from Senator Kennedy's office. I let them know it could be tricky to configure properly and asked what application they would be printing from. "Netscape," was the reply. I had left Kennedy's office by this time, so I referred them to my successor who declined their request for assistance. But apparently they did find some help, and on the day that the Senate was to vote on the Communications Decency Act, Senator Exon came to the floor armed with a blue binder stuffed with sordid screen shots and images from the Net to shock his fellow Senators. The Senate's Chaplain, Dr. Lloyd John Ogilvie, offered the following prayer, seeking divine guidance to fill the gap left where informed consideration was missing.

Almighty God, Lord of all life, we praise You for the advancements in computerized communications that we enjoy in our time. Sadly, however, there are those who are littering this information superhighway with obscene, indecent, and destructive pornography. Virtual but virtueless reality is projected in the most twisted, sick, misuse of sexuality. Violent people with sexual pathology are able to stalk and harass the innocent. Cyber solicitation of teenagers reveals the dark side of online victimization.

Lord, we are profoundly concerned about the impact of this on our children. We have learned from careful study how children can become addicted to pornography at an early age. Their understanding and appreciation of Your gift of sexuality can be denigrated and eventually debilitated. Pornography disallowed in print and the mail is now readily available to young children who learn how to use the computer.

Oh God, help us care for our children. Give us wisdom to create regulations that will protect the innocent. In times past, You have used the Senate to deal with problems of air and water pollution, and the misuse of our natural resources. Lord, give us courage to balance our reverence for freedom of speech with responsibility for what is said and depicted.

Now, guide the Senators as they consider ways of controlling the pollution of computer communications and how to preserve one of our greatest resources: the minds of our children and the future moral strength of our Nation. Amen.

The vote in the Senate was 84-16 in favor of the Exon amendment. Senators with little or no understanding of the Net themselves had little on which to base their decision. Their staffs who advised them on the vote, who likewise had no meaningful access to the Internet, could only offer the most simplified summary of the legislation as a vote to protect children from computer pornography. Not big on supporting pornography, the votes in favor of censorship poured in. Not surprisingly, among the sixteen Senators who opposed the amendment were the Senators who had taken the greatest strides in using the Internet in their own Senate offices: Leahy, Kennedy, Bingaman, Robb, Lieberman, Levin, Wellstone, Biden, Simon, and Feingold, one of the Senate's most vocal supporters of protecting the Net from government intrusion.

Senator Patrick Leahy – Democrat, Vermont

Senator Patrick Leahy is considered by many to be one of the most Internet savvy members of Congress, and it is a well-deserved reputation. Well known for his efforts to protect the Internet from government restrictions, Leahy has also sought to utilize the Internet in his own office to communicate with the public. He has led the fight against legislative efforts to restrict content on the Internet, and as chairman of the Judiciary Committee's subcommittee on Technology and the Law in the 103rd Congress he held hearings examining the Clinton Administration's Clipper Chip proposal, an effort to enhance the government's ability to view encrypted data that is strongly opposed by many Internet users.

Within the Senate, Leahy has been a vocal advocate for increasing access to the Internet for staff and has kept his own office on the leading edge of online constituent communications. Not the first time he has sought to find new ways to encourage his constituents to let him know what they are thinking, Leahy was the first member of the Senate to establish an 800 number for the citizens of his state. He blames what he calls "the quill pen nostalgia attitude" of some Senators for the institution's cautious approach to the Internet. "This is a whole new way of doing things for a lot of these people and they don't want to learn the new way." But Leahy says he will continue to utilize any new means to communicate with his constituents "so that people can let me know what they think."

In addition to having been one of the first members of the Senate to establish a public e-mail address and to post information about his activities to the Senate's Internet server, his home page on the World Wide Web is among the best. Leahy believes the Internet offers members of Congress the opportunity to bring attention to challenging and substantive issues, and to invite the public's feedback. His own home page includes information about his efforts to ban land mines, and he says the feedback he's received has aided him in gaining support among his colleagues. According to Leahy, those members of Congress that don't attempt to understand this medium and try to put online the same kind of purely self-promotional material found in many congressional newsletters will find that on the Internet "it won't go over very well."

Attention quickly turned to the House, where Senator Leahy's alternative approach had passed by the overwhelming margin of 420-4. Of the Senate bill Speaker Newt Gingrich said, "It is clearly a violation of free speech and it's a violation of the rights of adults to communicate with each other. I don't agree with it and I don't think it is a serious way to discuss a serious issue." Many, including Senator

Exon, believed the Speaker's opposition would kill the Communications Decency Act.[2] But the amendment remained when the Senate's version was adopted over the House's in the conference committee vote on the issue. Gingrich made no effort to strike the language from the House bill, damaging his high-tech credentials among those who were looking for him to halt the bill. As *The Hill* reported, "people from the online community say that, for all his stumping on behalf of technology, Gingrich let them down in their hour of need."[3]

Joining the fray in June, Senators Grassley and Dole introduced their own bill titled the Protection of Children from Computer Pornography Act of 1995, which sought to prevent "indecent material" from reaching anyone under 18 years of age. Like Exon's bill, legal experts said the Grassley/Dole bill "appears to violate constitutional rights to freedom of speech and the press."[4] On July 24, the Senate Judiciary Committee held a hearing on "Cyberporn and Children: The Scope of the Problem, The State of the Technology and the Need for Congressional Action." Recognizing the concern that the online community had for the issue, Senator Kohl's staff attempted to arrange for a real-time transcript of the hearing to made available on the Internet via Internet Relay Chat. When that was not permitted by the committee's chairman, Senator Orrin Hatch, Democratic staff instead posted the prepared statements submitted by witnesses to several Usenet news groups including *alt.politics.datahighway* and *alt.politics.usa.congress.* The effort was well received and provided a glimpse of what should be a routine example of Congress providing information to the Net rather than a rare occurrence.

On the morning of April 19, 1995, a rented truck was parked in front of the Alfred Murrah Federal Office Building in Oklahoma City,

---

[2] Kara Swisher and Elizabeth Corcoran, "Gingrich Condemns On-Line Decency Act," *The Washington Post*, June 22, 1995, p. D8.

[3] Craig Karmin, "Newt is caught up in an (Inter)net," *The Hill*, December 20, 1995, p. 7.

[4] Ellen Messmer, "Sen. Dole backs new Internet antiporn bill," *Network World,* June 12, 1995, p. 12.

Oklahoma, and the homemade fertilizer bomb it contained detonated. One hundred and sixty-nine people were killed in the blast, and 600 more were injured, many of them children who had just arrived at the day care center that was completely destroyed in the explosion. Americans who have long felt secure from terrorist acts that seem only to happen in foreign countries, now experienced the shock, horror, and outrage of the Oklahoma tragedy. In the wake of the World Trade Center bombing of 26 months earlier, the frightening realization set in that even our country's heartland was not safe from a random act of violence of such a massive scale. Initial assumptions that the bombing was the work of foreign terrorists proved to be premature, as evidence pointed to the explosion as having been the work of homegrown extremists rather than the more widely presumed foreign terrorists. When Americans learned this was allegedly the work of another American, outrage turned to fear.

President Clinton spoke out immediately, promising that justice would be "swift, certain and severe," and the Congress vowed to take quick action on anti-terrorism legislation that would give the FBI greater ability to prevent it.

Amidst the huge amount of positive media coverage that the Internet had been receiving for many months, something of a backlash had begun. Although there was no indication that the suspect held in connection with the Oklahoma bombing used computer networks, new attention was focused on the use of the Internet and computer BBSs by extremist militia and hate groups, and the easily accessible information carried on the Net, such as instructions on how to build bombs.

The Senate Judiciary Committee, of which Senator Kennedy is a member, scheduled a hearing on terrorism at which FBI director Louis Freeh was to testify. I had only the week before begun a new job as an Internet evangelist for Senate Democrats on the newly created Democratic Technology & Communications Committee, but was still keeping a foot in both jobs as I had not yet been replaced in Kennedy's office. Less than an hour before Senator Kennedy was to attend the hearing, his legislative director gave me a call. He told me that he had heard about bomb-making information being available on the Internet and asked me if I could locate something that the Senator could display at the hearing. I cautioned him that they should tread very lightly in this area. Senator Exon had already demonstrated how a well-intentioned but misguided effort to restrict objectionable content on the Internet could paint him as a politician with no understanding of or experience with the Internet, as someone who would recklessly introduce legislation that would have little real impact in the area it claims, and would instead have a chilling effect on free speech on the Internet and actually threaten its future. For Senator Kennedy to point out that bomb-making information is available on the Internet would be one thing, but to suggest that Congress take some action to restrict it would be quite another.

Having offered that warning, I passed up the opportunity to just lie and avoid the issue. I could have told him I did not think I could find any such material on the Internet. Instead I figured the best thing to do was acknowledge the truth, and accepted his request as a challenge to my search skills. I needed to come up with something in a hurry before the hearing began. Connected to my personal Internet account, because we still had only negligible access to the Net from within the Senate, I first went to one of the more popular search pages on the World Wide Web. My first search proved to be a bit too direct. A search on the word "bomb" returned a list of dozens of links to different variations of a graphic that people on the Web might incorporate into their home page in the place of a plain horizontal line divider.

I also turned up a link to instructions on how to build a nuclear bomb, complete with ASCII illustrations of a hydrogen bomb in cross section. But figuring that there aren't too many people around who actually have the means and the resources to build a nuclear device, this find was rejected as impractical.

Determined to succeed, I took a new tack and did a search on the word "anarchy" and ended up with a list of promising-looking links to Internet sites on the subject. The Anarchy home page that I visited was located in the Netherlands and contained a great number of links to various political writings and theory. It also had a link near the top, inviting those only interested in destruction to click on the word "bomb" for more info. That link led me to two promising looking files, *The Anarchist's Cookbook* and *The Terrorist's Handbook*. Not having time to compare the two for content, I choose *The Terrorist's Handbook*, only because of the title. This was, after all, for a hearing on terrorism.

I downloaded the file and gave it a look. It contained a wealth of information for any home-grown terrorist with access to the usual items under the kitchen sink or on a garage workbench to build some pretty lethal toys such as pipe bombs, book bombs, phone bombs, and other things that explode.

The Terrorist's Handbook filled 73 pages when printed. I was aware that such material existed and had long been available in printed form, produced and sold by underground publishers and available in some libraries and bookstores. I had in my desk an example of such a publication that had been mailed into our office by a constituent long before and that I had kept as a morbid curiosity. It was a thin red booklet with the straightforward title, *How to Kill, Vol. 3*, and contained pages of instructions of various ways to commit murder. The Internet had not brought about the existence of such materials, it had merely provided a new means for their widespread distribution.

The same week of the Judiciary Committee's hearing, the *Boston Globe* reported that police in Randolph, Massachusetts, were investigating several youths who were allegedly selling "a manual containing information downloaded from the Internet that details how to build a bomb" to other students at school.

Senator Kennedy began his remarks at the hearing by expressing thanks to the firefighters and rescue workers who had shown "extraordinary dedication and bravery and courage and tireless devotion." He went on to thank the witnesses who were testifying at the hearing, Louis Freeh, director of the FBI, and Jamie Gorelick, deputy attorney general, for "advancing these sensible and responsible initiatives by the President." The Senator went on to say "with speech as with other rights and liberties of our citizenship there are important responsibilities. And those that fuel the darker side of human nature and the pools of hate really are going to be held accountable for their actions."

Turning to the subject of the Internet, Senator Kennedy held up *The Terrorist's Handbook*, and said it was something his staff took only ten minutes to find on the Internet. Before briefly describing some of the information in the document, he said, "And we're all making moves towards — stop pornography on the Internet, and we ought to stop terrorism too."

Even to those who knew that Senator Kennedy was on the record as being opposed to Senator Exon's Communications Decency Act on the grounds that its restrictions would violate free speech protections, his statement at the hearing sounded as if he had turned away from that position and now advocated similar restrictions on bomb-making information. The next day's *Washington Post* carried a story headlined "Advocates of Internet Fear Drive to Restrict Extremists' Access" and reported that to many online activists Senator Kennedy's remarks were "like a shot across the Internet's bow." Kennedy's press secretary had been able to add later that the Senator wanted only to raise the point that such material existed for debate, and had proposed no actions that would damage the First Amendment by restricting free speech.

Within minutes after the Senator's remarks had been broadcast on C-SPAN, the first e-mail message commenting on them had arrived. During that afternoon and evening about a dozen more messages arrived. A couple strongly protested any suggestion that Congress enact legislation restricting the Internet. Others were friendlier and politely cautioned against letting post-Oklahoma passions lead to bad legislation. As we worked on drafting the Senator's reply to these messages, one message stood out. With a subject line that read simply "Gratitude," came a note from a 15-year-old young man in Oklahoma who thanked Senator Kennedy for raising the issue and said he was appalled by how easily someone as young as himself could "gain information on destructive and violent material on the information super highway in this day and age." He said that he would be writing his own Senators on the subject, but pointed out that they did not have e-mail addresses "as of yet." As I worried about and worked to avoid the "Exonization" of Kennedy on the Internet, I remained struck with this note of concern from a young Net user who was himself concerned with what was out there.

The Senator's reply, which we also posted to several appropriate Usenet news groups and to our own Net sites to be sure it was widely available, included the following:

> *We have only just begun to consider these complex issues in Congress, and clearly we must do so with the full regard for freedom of speech and other basic liberties protected by the Constitution.*
>
> *As I have stated many times in the congressional debate on pornography on the Internet, we must exercise the utmost caution if we are to legislate in this area. The constitutional right of free speech clearly applies to electronic communications, just as it applies to written or spoken communications.*

A number of my friends on the Hill and in the online community identified me as the likely suspect when they saw or read Senator Kennedy's remarks that a staff member of his had located this information on the Net, and some scolded me for having done so. I personally felt that if members of Congress are ever to truly come to understand the Net, the best thing to do is to introduce them to it, warts and all, and work through whatever issues might be raised along the way.

As for the antiterrorism bill, the Judiciary Committee held another hearing, this time specifically on the issue of "The Availability of Bomb-Making Information on the Internet." At that hearing Senator Feinstein claimed the spotlight by speaking out most strongly in favor of legislating restrictions against the availability of such information on the Internet. She later proposed an amendment to the antiterrorism bill to criminalize the distribution of material such as that found in *The Terrorist's Handbook.*

Introducing her amendment on the Senate floor, Senator Feinstein said:

> *In today's day and age, when violent crimes, bombings, and terrorist attacks are becoming too frequent—2,900 bombings a year, 541 in California alone in the year 1993—and when technology allows for the distribution of bomb-making material over computers to millions of people across the country in a matter of seconds, I believe that some restrictions on speech are appropriate.*
>
> *Specifically, I believe that restricting the availability of bomb-making information for criminal purposes, if there is intent or knowledge that the information will be used for a criminal purpose, is both appropriate and required in today's day and age.*[5]

---

[5] Congressional Record, June 5, 1995, p. S7684.

The final language of the amendment contained no reference to the Internet but generically prohibited the distribution of bomb-making material by any means "if the person intends or knows" that it will be used for a criminal purpose. Senator Biden had the following congratulatory words for Senator Feinstein's efforts.

Mr. BIDEN. Mr. President, let me say that the Senator from California never ceases to amaze me. I say that with genuine respect. When she zeroed in on this problem when Senator Kennedy came to the hearing and presented a 60-, 70-, 80-page document—I forget how long it was—of information that the staff had pulled off the Internet for him on how to do these things, one of the things that I admire most about her is her incredible common sense.

I remember her sitting there looking at us and saying, "You mean you can do this? I mean, why are we allowing this?" All of us who were supposedly hopefully good lawyers all looked and said, "First amendment problem, Senator." And we all did say that. We all knew because of our reverence for the first amendment. Those of us who are conservative, liberal, and moderate alike all said, "First amendment problem." We all kind of went on to other things.

As she always does, she went back to her office, and I am sure she turned to that able staff member next to her and said, "Wait a minute, there has to be a way to do this. There has to be an answer to this." As usual, her instinct is almost always right. And when I have dealt with her, it has been unerring. Not being a lawyer, she went out and got some fine lawyers and said, "How can I write this thing because I, Dianne Feinstein, don't want to amend the first amendment either, but I do want to deal with this foolishness."

She did it. I compliment her. And remind me, if I ever forget, never to underestimate her. She always gets it done. We are all better for it. I again congratulate her.[6]

But not everyone was as satisfied as Senator Biden that the First Amendment concerns raised by the Feinstein amendment had been satisfactorily dealt with. In his online newsletter *Cyberwire Dispatch*, Brock Meeks wrote of the Feinstein amendment,

What Sen. Dianne Feinstein's amendment does is open a chilling precedent for regulating content on the Internet. It is the break in the dike; the trickle that could become a river of regulatory hammers meant to turn the rough and tumble, open and free-flowing online discourse into something with all the appeal and intellectual acumen of Tofu. The cyberspace equal of the domino effect.[7]

The issues raised by Congress in 1995 concerning the regulation of content on the Internet have yet to be resolved. Congress will continue to consider legislation that can have a tremendous impact on the Internet, not only in the regulation of content, but in other areas such as controls over encryption technology. In every case Congress will attempt to meet the task by considering the concerns expressed by all sides, bringing their own experience and expertise to the question, and attempting to find an appropriate compromise. Despite Senator Exon's Blue Book and my terrorist handbook, a Congress that itself

[6] Congressional Record, June 5, 1995, p. S7686.

7 Brock Meeks, *Cyberwire Dispatch*, June 7, 1995.

utilizes the Internet in a day-to-day manner, gathering input from the public, posting information on issues, and using the medium as a routine means of communications, will be best equipped to understand and appreciate the concerns of the Internet community when faced with these issues.

SEVEN

★

Campaigns and Opposition

New technologies often demonstrate their utility in the political arena. Americans have become accustomed to getting information about campaigns and elections by the latest means that technology has to offer. In his book *InfoCulture*, Steven Lubar wrote about one of the earliest examples, the use of Morse's telegraph line under construction between Baltimore and Washington, DC, on the Senate side of the Capitol building.

191

> *One of the first uses of Morse's Telegraph line was
> to relay news of the presidential ticket selected at
> the Whig convention in Baltimore from Annapolis
> Junction (the furthest point the line then reached)
> to Washington. The crowd at the Washington station
> was skeptical, until the train brought the news an
> hour later.*

In 1920, the first news story broadcast on the first commercial radio station was of Warren Harding's election to the presidency. The desire to quickly know an election's results was pushed to new extremes when a UNIVAC computer was challenged to predict the outcome of the 1952 presidential election. The computer picked Eisenhower, and it was right, but of course the odds of a correct guess were even.

Television's impact on campaigning has been such that today its importance to any serious candidate cannot be underestimated. Lubar wrote, "The televised presidential debates between Democrat John F. Kennedy and Republican Richard M. Nixon were a turning point in the history of American politics. Surveys concluded that Kennedy benefited most from the four televised debates. His gains were greatest after the first debate in which he showed himself at least a match for Nixon, who had been considered more skillful in the use of television. Ironically, many radio listeners thought Nixon won the debates."

The technical ability to put a presidential or congressional campaign on the Internet existed for years before the Internet population and consciousness of the Net had reached a high enough level to make it practical. Unsuccessful efforts were undertaken in 1984 and 1988 to get candidates for President to post information to the Internet. In 1992, putting the presidential contest between George Bush, Bill Clinton, and Ross Perot on the Internet had been an experiment at MIT. In 1994, a small but significant number of candidates took their first steps into cyberspace in a number of different ways. In 1996, the candidate who makes no effort to utilize the Internet may be the exception rather than the rule, and the development of a campaign Internet presence will be as obvious an undertaking as printing and distributing yard signs and bumper stickers. The roads to the White House and to the Hill have merged with the Information Superhighway.

The impact that the Internet will have on campaigns remains unclear. All candidates on the Net have the potential to reach millions of people, to invite voters to learn more about them and their agendas, and could even encourage more active participation in the process prior to election day. But Net campaigns will also run the risk of being only so much political bunting hung in cyberspace, home pages with attractive facades that hide a dearth of useful content within, and outreach that fails to connect to potential supporters or respond to opponents.

1992

It's no exaggeration to say that the presidential campaign of 1992 set in motion a series of events that spurred the White House, the Congress, and virtually the whole federal government to get on the Internet much sooner than they otherwise might have.

Each of the major commercial services made room on their systems for campaign information. Compuserve supplied each campaign with accounts to allow e-mail between the campaigns and voters, and on election day, Prodigy's tracking service for local and national elections logged almost a million calls, the highest one-day count in the system's history.[1]

---

[1]Grame Browning, "Hot-Wiring Washington," *The National Journal*, 6/26/93, p. 1625.

Late in the summer of 1992 a graduate student at MIT, Eric Loeb, turned his attention to the coming presidential election. Long a believer that "society itself had some sort of intelligence," Eric longed to take his efforts out of the realm of theory, and out of the lab, and combine them with a passion for politics to bring them to the Net. He began making contacts with Clinton-Gore supporters online and at MIT, and started writing some shell scripts that would allow for the distribution of campaign documents and discussions in different subject areas.

Eric proposed an experiment, to make an Internet-based document distribution and discussion list available to each of the presidential campaigns. While the Clinton campaign agreed immediately, a few weeks passed before the Bush campaign signed on, allowing the experiment to proceed and the domain *campaign92.org* to join the Net. During the lag, another doctoral candidate at the AI Lab, John Mallery, reimplemented Eric's UNIX-based shell scripts using LISP.

This description was attached to all of the automatic forms generated by the campaign experiment's servers:

> *The Presidential Campaign Information Service is a non-partisan service operated at M.I.T. to make campaign information available, facilitate electronic discussion of the issues, and to study the use of electronic mail as a component of a presidential campaign. The service can neither control who reads what you write in public, nor how they may use your written words. For our part, we store most messages, and we will make them available after the election for scientific study. Names and any other identifiers will not be released; they will be omitted or replaced with random symbols.*

Using a computer-generated form submitted via electronic mail, individuals could subscribe to specific lists to receive documents, speeches, and state-by-state volunteer information for the Bush, Clinton, Perot,

Marrou, and Hagelin campaigns. They could also choose to participate in economic policy, foreign policy, social policy, and political
philosophy discussion groups for each campaign.

Although it didn't get up and running until less than a month before
election day, word of the service spread quickly on the Net. MIT's
servers held 10 megabytes of political positions and other campaign
information that the candidates' campaigns had sent out, and delivered these materials as well as the discussions in response to about
2,000 queries each day.

The service was most heavily utilized by the Clinton campaign, which
actively participated in its discussion groups and responded to all
e-mail inquiries. Input and comments from the discussion groups
helped contribute to the campaign's position papers on some issues.
And the well-known rapid response team from the Clinton campaign
saw that their opponents' charges and challenges were quickly rebut-
ted and corrected, using the Net to distribute their responses and
prove their motto "speed kills."

The Bush campaign provided materials for distribution, but did not
utilize the service far beyond that passive dissemination. The Perot
campaign was similarly disinterested, but the Marrou and Hagelin
campaigns, perhaps recognizing the egalitarian nature of the Net for
candidates, were both active.

Although it would be a stretch to assume that MIT's Campaign
Information Service affected the outcome of the 1992 presidential
campaign, it certainly proved the viability and effectiveness of the
Internet as a communications resource for candidates. Even more
importantly, the service helped lead an online campaign to become
the first wired White House, putting the Net in the realm of politics
as never before and laying the groundwork for all who would follow.
Two years later Eric would put his experience in a national campaign
to use at the state level.

1994

By the late summer of 1994 I began to have a better understanding of one of the inevitable facts of life for any congressional staffer, elections. One unique aspect of working for a member of Congress is the reliance that continued employment has on the boss's perform-ance at the polls on election day. Come November 7th, the voters of Massachusetts would make a judgment on whether or not to send Edward Kennedy back to the Senate for another six-year term, or send him home, and me along with him. I had tremendous confidence that Senator Kennedy would win. Kennedy was the fourth ranking member of the Senate. He had a 6-0 campaign record and had served thirty-two years in the Senate, longer than I had been alive. The thought that he might not win reelection seemed unthinkable to me.

But then things began to seem less sure. Many were already foretell-ing a Republican landslide, and the Senator seemed a ready target. The same longevity in office that I found reassuring was viewed by many people as a tremendous negative, particularly in light of public support for congressional term limits. Kennedy's opponent, Mitt Romney, was a young successful businessman whose campaign was gaining national attention in stories that said this campaign might be the end for the senior Senator from Massachusetts. When my own friends and family asked me what would happen to me if Kennedy lost, I brushed their concerns aside with a confident reply that he would win by much more than people expected him to. But I did become concerned. The polls showed the race a dead heat in September.

There are strict rules that govern what activities congressional staf-fers can take on behalf of their employer's reelection campaigns. Until that fall, I'd had very little contact with the campaign except to brief them on what the Senator's office was doing on the Internet, just as I frequently did for anyone who asked.

The campaign had arranged for some basic Internet service through a service provider in Massachusetts with the intention of having a campaign e-mail address and posting some files to Usenet and a gopher directory, but had not yet done much with it and had no plans for anything very elaborate. In the hubbub of a growing campaign headquarters, little thought was being given to what could or should be done on the Net. As many congressional staffers understandably do, I worked on my own time as a volunteer in my boss's reelection effort, taking on the unique challenge of seeing that the campaign utilized the Internet in the same successful manner that Kennedy's Senate office had. From the basement of my home in Virginia, I worked to reach voters in Massachusetts through cyberspace. I began sending replies to the small amount of e-mail that had accumulated and attempted to gather campaign materials to put online, something that proved difficult to do without a strong ally in place among the clamor of campaign headquarters in Boston.

Less than a month before election day, I learned that the Democratic Senatorial Campaign Committee (DSCC) had established itself on the World Wide Web and was building home pages for each of the 17 Democratic candidates running for Senate. In most cases they were doing so with little assistance from the campaigns beyond gathering some background material and issue papers to post. But the DSCC was aware of Kennedy's efforts to put his office on the Web and invited us to take an active part in developing a home page for the campaign.

At about the same time I came across a message from a prospective volunteer whose help I knew we could use. It was an offer from Eric Loeb to help get the campaign online. Almost immediately after receiving my reply accepting his offer, Eric was at campaign headquarters in Boston where he began to gather the content we needed to get on the Net and much, much more.

Eric quickly developed two mailing lists, one for volunteers and the other for press. The volunteer mailing list received updates regarding every aspect of our volunteer efforts, from updates about events and rallies to information about our election day get-out-the-vote effort. The press mailing list received campaign press releases, statements, and position papers. Eric also made the same materials available via ftp and gopher using the campaign's local service provider, and posted updates into the Usenet news group *ne.politics*, the same news group to which Kennedy's Senate office posted material and in which the Massachusetts Senate race was being hotly debated. I took the same material and made it available in the Massachusetts election forum on America Online (AOL) and on several bulletin board systems.

With a great deal of assistance from Tim Nelson of the DSCC and Ken Deutsch and the staff of Issue Dynamics Inc., the company through which the DSCC was reaching the Web, and finally armed with some campaign material, I built a respectable home page for the campaign. In addition to the expected internal links containing content from the campaign, the page also had links to other election-related resources on the Net including the Massachusetts Online Election Server, which had information about every initiative and candidate that citizens of the Commonwealth would find on their ballots, and the Project Vote Smart home page.

Kennedy's virtual campaign did a number of things right and wrong, but generally made an effort that other campaigns would do well to emulate. First off, we worked to make campaign information available by as many means as possible. Material from the Kennedy campaign could be obtained on several bulletin boards, the largest commercial service provider (AOL), via electronic mail, Usenet, ftp, gopher, and the World Wide Web. Although some of these resources, particularly the home page, received more attention than others, it was important that to a basic degree the campaign could be found at as many levels as possible in the online world.

By using a local service provider, the campaign made an important statement to Net users in the state. The World in Brookline, Massachusetts, is the oldest public access Internet service provider in the country, and by using their services and those of another Massachusetts Net provider, TIAC, the Kennedy campaign put its own Net use in the state where it belonged. The campaign's e-mail address, *TedK94@world.std.com,* was immediately recognizable to Internet savvy citizens of the state. But Romney's e-mail address (his only online presence) was found in a neighborhood on the Net that suffers the consequences of "domain-nameism" and is looked down on by many who consider themselves genuine Net surfers. Mitt Romney's e-mail address was *Romney94@aol.com.*

By participating in the Usenet news group in which the Senate race was being debated, Kennedy's campaign not only succeeded in providing the readers (and voters) of the news group with the Senator's positions on the issues and other campaign updates, but likewise sent an underlying message that Kennedy was the candidate more in tune with the medium in which they were all participants. By posting material into *ne.politics* at all, Kennedy made a connection with online voters that his challenger missed out on by his absence.

But participating in Usenet in an essentially "broadcast-only" mode was a mistake we made. As the campaign's Netheads, Eric and I posted material to the net, but neither of us were campaign spokespersons who were authorized or capable of responding to many of the questions and responses that our Usenet postings drew. Just as I had when the Senator's office first began reaching Usenet, we did our best to respond to the easy stuff, but some questions directed at the campaign in Usenet went without response. Those on the campaign who could have done so were plenty busy with the more proven and effective means of communicating in the campaign's final days. There was nobody with the time or the inclination to devote any time to responding to online challenges. By participating in Usenet, we ought to have been better prepared to engage in a two-way dialogue than we were.

Our other mistake was getting such a late start. With more forethought we could have developed a much more extensive and useful online campaign presence. Our mailing lists would have had time to grow in size and mature in usefulness, but our late start never let them gain more than a couple dozen subscribers each.

A number of other candidates and campaigns discovered the Net in 1994. In Minnesota an online debate was conducted among all of the candidates running for the U. S. Senate. Conducted via e-mail and mailing lists, the debate ran over a five-day period starting on Halloween. It posed three questions to each of the candidates and allowed them to rebut the responses of their opponents. To secure the participation of all candidates, the event's organizers at Minnesota E-Democracy allowed candidates to have staff answer questions, which led to an online regurgitation of the candidates' stump speeches and television commercials rather than the hoped-for online dialogue. But third-party candidates who had been excluded from the televised debates reveled in the equality that the Net finally provided to their campaigns and were enthusiastic participants in the online debates. The event gained national attention in the press and the participation of Vice President Gore, whose online endorsement of Democrat Ann Wynia was not enough to prevent her defeat.

A significant number of congressional campaigns went online in 1994. Many were long-shot candidates from third parties, or challengers to secure incumbents, who were able to bring some attention to their campaign by virtue of the fact that they waged it on the Net. As explorers in the unknown realm of cyberspace campaigning, the Clinton-Gore campaign in 1992 and other early adopters in 1994 had discovered and opened up the medium for the land rush of candidates that would follow them in 1996.

1996

Although many members of Congress discovered the Net first as a means for communicating with constituents, others discovered it first as a means of seeking votes. For incumbent members of Congress seeking reelection or higher office, the promise of reaching voters on the Internet has in many cases been more compelling than the need to reach constituents for the offices they hold. Senator Dianne Feinstein had an elaborate, professionally developed home page on the Web to support her successful reelection effort in 1994, months before her Senate office established an e-mail address or posted anything to the Net. Among Senate Republicans seeking to win their party's nomination to challenge President Clinton in 1996, Bob Dole, Phil Gramm, Richard Lugar, and Arlen Specter all had developed Web sites for their presidential campaigns more than a year before election day, and yet among them only Specter had by that time established any Internet presence for his Senate office to serve the constituents of his state. His directory on the Senate gopher contained three files; a biography, a listing of his offices in Pennsylvania, and a single press release dating from June 1995.

On September 26, 1995, the "Dole for President" home page was unveiled to a great deal of media attention and hype. Some early press reports quickly rated it the best of the home pages maintained by candidates vying for the Republican nomination for President. The site for Candidate Dole is stocked full of press releases, sound and video files, games and screen savers, a detailed explanation of the campaign's utilization of the latest in technology, and the ability to pledge a donation to the campaign complete with an example of what your contribution would allow the campaign to buy, for example, $100 = 100 yard signs.

And yet Dole the Senator is completely absent on the Net. As Majority Leader of the Senate, and one of that body's longest serving and best known members, there can be little question that Senator Dole is aware of the Internet services available to him as a Senator. The campaign has a listserver to allow individuals to subscribe to campaign updates delivered right to their electronic in-box. Why is no e-mail address available for his constituents in Kansas to send their concerns electronically? The campaign has a wealth of information about this presidential hopeful available at the click of a button. Why does no gopher directory or home page exist through which interested

Americans can learn more about the Senator's positions on the issues and his agenda for steering the U. S. Senate?

When a politician is more interested in the Net as candidate than as an officeholder, he may be revealing a telling insight into his attitude toward the medium. A Senator, carrying out the task of governing, daily considers legislation that impacts the entire nation and world as the representative of the citizens of his states, and may find no practical reason to put his office online. But if, when turning into a candidate for reelection or for another office, he suddenly touts the virtues of cyberspace while seeking to reap support, contributions, and votes on the Net, one might question what truly motivates him. The 1996 elections will offer an interesting opportunity to see how many incumbents find that the quest for reelection brings them to the Net more readily than their time in office did.

Things change so rapidly with technology and on the Internet that normal measures of age don't apply. The Internet ages in dog-years. Apple's Macintosh computer was introduced little more than a decade ago, and today one sits in the Smithsonian's National Museum of American History along with the original "Old Glory" and Charlie McCarthy. Mosaic, the first graphical browser for exploring the World Wide Web, was introduced in 1993, but to many millions of Net surfers who've never known a non-point-and-click net, that's a fact for the history books. The White House got on the Internet in the first days of the Clinton administration, and on the Web in 1994, and Americans have quickly become used to direct electronic access to 1600 Pennsylvania Avenue (even as nutty fence climbers and the threat of more serious harm led to the closing of the "real" Pennsylvania Avenue in front of the White House).

But has an electronic White House become so ingrained an idea that it could not be reversed? Do the candidates who utilize the Internet imply that they will carry their use of the Net into office with them? For the White House, I suspect it does. The 1996 election will bring about some of the first virtual transitions to congressional offices on the Internet. Even as it becomes routine for congressional offices to have some online presence, it has not happened overnight and without question some offices will lag behind.

One example of such a transition backsliding came in 1994 when Sam Coppersmith, the Democratic Representative of Arizona's high-tech first district, gave up his House seat in a failed bid for the Senate. Coppersmith was well known for his pioneering efforts to make his congressional office available on the Internet, being among the first members of Congress to establish a public e-mail address and gopher directory. His successor, Republican Matt Salmon, had not taken any steps to maintain online access to his office. With no e-mail address and no online postings from his office more than a year after taking office, the doors on the fist district of Arizona's congressional office in cyberspace have apparently been closed.

The Race for the White House

As political campaigns begin to utilize the Internet as a means for reaching voters, none will draw more attention than the efforts put forth by candidates running for President. A full year before election day, the use of the Net by every candidate running for President in 1996 already dwarfed the 1992 MIT experiment that had helped bring presidential candidates online just weeks prior to election day. Nine months before the first Republican primary, and eighteen months before election day, Senator Phil Gramm of Texas and former Governor Lamar Alexander of Tennessee each claimed bragging rights to being the first presidential candidate on the Web. Their campaigns were soon followed onto the Net by Senator Richard Lugar of Indiana, Pat Buchanan, and Senator Arlen Specter. Later they were joined by Senator Bob Dole and many other candidates, both familiar and unknown, all seeking votes on the Net.

Among the crowded field of Republican challengers and a few third-party candidates, President Bill Clinton has the distinct advantage of being unchallenged within his party, unless you count the write-in campaign being waged on the Net by Bruce Daniels. A professor of history at the University of Winnipeg, Daniels holds dual U.S.–Canadian citizenship and is running his Net campaign for the White House from Canada. Daniels' home page makes it clear that this candidate has no expectation of actually defeating Clinton in the New Hampshire primary, but hopes that any votes he receives there and as a write-in candidate in subsequent states will help send a message to the President. In his "Declaration of Candidacy," Daniels' states:

> *I do not expect to beat President Clinton in the New Hampshire Primary—although I would be pleased if I did. I would like to affect his campaign, however, and I would like to be able to influence his second term in office if he is reelected. By voting for me, New Hampshire citizens will send a message to President Clinton that liberalism is politically viable and that people will support the Democratic Party's principles if they are presented honestly and implemented consistently.*

We may never know if President Clinton receives the message that Bruce Daniels is trying to send to him, but the Net has increased Daniel's odds of reaching the President and anyone else considerably.

Facing no significant challenge from within his party, the President has enjoyed the luxury of staying on the sidelines. While the Republicans candidates raced to put themselves on the Web, a "Clinton-Gore '96" home page is not expected until the President formally announces his re-election campaign sometime in early 1996. The President has the advantage of being presidential, using the White House to reach the public as President rather than as a candidate. The State of the Union Address (the first one broadcast live on the Net) delivered by Clinton in January 1996 was well received by the public, while Senator Dole's reply was widely criticized, slowing his campaign's momentum going into primary season. The White House also gave its home page a new look early 1996, providing new information and ease-of-use to its already highly-rated web site.

Even before their official campaign presence is felt on the Net, the Clinton-Gore team can be expected to hold a strong advantage when they take their reelection campaign to cyberspace. The experience gained from their online efforts in the 1992 campaign, and three years worth of experience developing the White House's Net presence, just cannot be matched by any of Clinton's challengers. The Clinton team will also have had the advantage of watching the home pages of the Republican challengers develop over several months, monitoring their development and content, before unveiling their own home page on the Net. As cyber-savvy incumbents faced by net-newbie challengers, expectations will run high that the Clinton-Gore campaign will make good use of the Net in their quest for reelection. Describing the possibilities of organizing Net support for a campaign, former White House Net head Jock Gill said, "If you look at cyberspace as a sort of 51st state, and you organize it as effectively as you'd organize, say, Tennessee—ward by ward, precinct by precinct by precinct—then guess what happens."[2] What happens is you just might activate enough supporters to make the difference in a close election.

Running a national campaign on the Internet has a unique advantages over campaigns for statewide or other lower offices. The global nature of the Internet allows any candidate for President the ability to make their campaign available to every wired citizen in the country, a rapidly growing population of individuals whose demographic profile (higher than average incomes, highly educated) suggests an increased likelihood that they are also voters. The low costs associated with establishing a presence on the Internet pales in comparison of producing and airing television spots and employing other traditional campaign strategies, increasing the Net's appeal as a level playing field on which all candidates compete equally. The Net provides candidates a place to provide meaningful information about their candidacies and their positions on the issues for the curious Net browser/voter that could never be matched in a 30-second television

---

[2] Grame Browning, "Presidential Debates on the Net?", *National Journal*, February 3, 1996, p.281.

commercial. A candidate's Net content is also more likely to remain positive in its focus, explaining the reasons why the candidate is deserving of support, than are television commercials which rapidly resort to mud-slinging and name-calling.

In the end it is uncertain if an Internet presence will make any difference on which candidate ultimately prevails, but no candidate will be willing to bet that it won't. It would be foolish for any candidate to pass up such a cost-effective means for distributing information and demonstrating themselves to be in touch with the electorate. The Net will certainly bring previously unavailable exposure to lesser-known candidates. Dozens of politically oriented web sites that link to the home pages of every presidential candidate will include links to third-party and fringe candidates who could never have previously gained such exposure. The equalizing nature of the Net has already led many lesser-known candidates to embrace the technology more quickly than their mainstream counterparts. Dr. John Hagelin, the Natural Law Party's candidate for President, and Libertarian Harry Browne, have gained more exposure than their parties' candidates have ever known before, and more attention to their platforms as well.

Third-party candidates may find their enthusiasm for the Internet matched by those who find themselves low in the polls or altogether unknown. The risk-averse front-runners will avoid the unknown at all costs, careful to avoid any unforeseen missteps that might halt their momentum, while those at the back of the pack will have nothing to lose and everything to gain by more aggressively exploring the Net as a campaign forum.

An effort by Jim Warren to organize an Internet-based debate among the Republican candidates for the White House was canceled after only three of ten invited candidates expressed a willingness to participate. Jim had implored the readers of his *GovAccess* newsletter to contact each of the Republican campaigns and encourage them to participate, arguing that an online Republican primary debate would lay the groundwork for "substantive online presidential debates" prior to the general election. Warren proposed a week-long online debate in which each candidate would daily question the others, respond to questions and offer rebuttals within length and time limits agreed upon by all. The three willing participants; Richard Lugar, Charles Collins, and Maurice Taylor, could each have brought themselves much needed attention by participating. Lugar's campaign was struggling at the bottom of the polls, and Collins and Taylor were both virtually unknown candidates. None of the other well-known Republican candidates—Dole, Gramm, Alexandar, Buchanan, or Forbes—were willing to participate. Apparently 1996 will be the year of the campaign home page; they provide a safe and controlled outlet for a candidate to promote themselves. But at this point in the race for the White House, the prospect of utilizing the Net for a more meaningful exchange of ideas among candidates is still enough to scare off all but the desperate.

A seat in Congress, particularly the Senate, is often a stepping stone for a run at the White House. At least eleven Senators in the 104th Congress are either currently or have previously been candidates for President. Although many Senators from both parties have made a run for the White House, none have succeeded since John F. Kennedy won the election in 1960. Most presidential campaigns are short-lived, the candidates calling it quits for lack of support or money. Some fall before a single primary vote has been cast. Only two campaigns are destined to last until election day, and many of the rest will return to serve in Congress and await another day. In 1996 we will see if upon their return failed candidates for the White House will bring to their congressional offices the enthusiasm for the Internet that they demonstrated in their respective campaigns. Or, discouraged at the failure of their online efforts to help take them all the way to the White House, might they sour on the Net and determine not to utilize it in Congress?

House and Senate Campaigns

The speed with which all of the candidates seeking their party's nomination to challenge President Clinton in 1996 have put themselves on the Internet is strong evidence that the Net is now widely recognized as a powerful communications medium that a candidate for our nation's highest office cannot ignore. The 1996 race for the presidency will be the first in which both candidates develop a substantial Internet presence designed to reach an ever-growing, nationwide online audience in the millions.

But while the global reach of the Internet is among the most appealing feature of the medium, its use by candidates for public office will not be limited only to presidential hopefuls or even to statewide races for public office. While it is obvious why such campaigns would benefit from the Net's far reach, candidates in local level races are putting their campaigns on the Net in growing numbers as well. Candidates running for state legislatures, mayor, and other local offices showed up on the Web frequently in the off-year elections of 1995. In Prince William County, Virginia, I was able to pay a virtual visit to at least two local candidates running for the County Board of Supervisors. Running in different districts, one was an incumbent seeking reelection and the other was a challenger. Both recognized that the Net was a medium worth exploring in their search for votes in a very localized geographic area. And both learned that just being on the Net won't necessarily make the difference. Both lost.

If their online campaigns are meant to be substantive efforts to reach out to voters, candidates for Congress and their staffs will have to think very carefully about how their Internet-based efforts will be seen by their own potential voters. Senate candidates will have an easier task targeting a statewide audience than will their House counterparts. Representatives are responsible to the roughly 600,000 residents in their own congressional district. Among those 600,000, the potential target audience that can be reached on the Net shrinks rapidly. Among those of voting age, a smaller percentage will be registered voters (although encouraging and assisting individuals to register is certainly possible and likely to be widespread on the net), and fewer still will have access to the Internet with varying degrees of access. A candidate reaching the masses of the Net is fine, but if the masses reached can't cast a ballot for you, then it's not going to do a lot of good.

Individuals browsing the World Wide Web find a site by one of two ways; they either know the URL of the site and go to it directly, or they get there via a link from another site on the Web. In both cases it is a deliberate act, unlike a campaign's television commercial, mass mailing, or bumper sticker, which can place themselves in front of individuals who didn't seek them out. Such power remains with the individual on the Net, and only those that seek to see a candidate's home page on their computer screen will.

Helping and encouraging individuals to make that visit is essential to an effective Net campaign, and every effort should be made by a campaign to spread the word about their Internet presence. Press releases from the campaign should include a URL (WWW address) and an e-mail address to encourage reporters to utilize the site. Coverage of the Net campaign in print and broadcast media can help spread the message of a campaign's utilization of technology to an audience much larger than those that will ever actually utilize it, increasing general awareness of the effort among voters and concern for its impact among the opposition. Online supporters should be recruited to spread awareness of the site in appropriate places on the Net to help other Net browsers discover the campaign, and to demonstrate the site to others in public places and to their less wired friends and neighbors.

Every candidate's site on the Internet should seek to inform voters who the candidate is, what office they seek, and what their political philosophy and positions on the issues are. The content should seek to energize supporters to support the campaign actively with more than just their vote, and to arm them with material with which to campaign on the candidate's behalf. The site should seek to convince the undecided why they should become supporters, and be an up-to-date informational resource for media covering the campaign.

Tom & Jerry Preview Campaign '96 on the Net

On December 15, 1995, a special election was held to fill the unfinished term of retiring Democratic Congressman Norm Mineta of California's 15th Congressional District. Republican Tom Campbell and Democrat Jerry Estruth faced each other in the race to succeed Mineta as Representative of this high-tech district that encompasses California's Silicon Valley. The race earned national media attention and close attention from Congress watchers because of Democrat Estruth's efforts to make the campaign a referendum on Republican House Speaker Newt Gingrich, a strategy expected to be put to wide use in 1996 by Democrats seeking to take advantage of the Speaker's rapidly declining popularity.

California's special election might have been the first congressional race in which both candidates maintained campaign home pages on the World Wide Web. These pages also offered a preview of what you can expect to find from other congressional candidates on the Web in 1996, as well as illustrating some do's and don'ts.

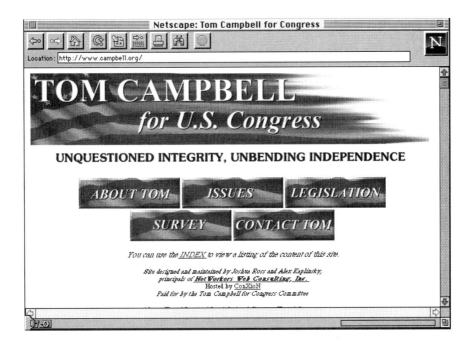

Formerly a member of Congress, Tom Campbell gave up his seat to pursue a race for the Senate in 1994, but settled instead for a seat in the State Assembly after his Senate bid failed. Seeking to return to the House of Representatives, Campbell's campaign opened an office in cyberspace, hiring a professional consulting firm to develop the home page shown here. Among the first things you noticed visiting the site is the address, *www.campbell.org,* which tells you that they've made the effort to register their domain name to give their page an easy-to-remember address. This may be worth doing, but isn't essential, and isn't a guarantee that the site is an official effort of the campaign (the bogus "Dole for President" home page has the seemingly official domain name of *dole96.org*). Going with just *campbell.org* rather than *campbell95.org* was a good call because it keeps the name available for next year's election and other purposes that may come up.

Looking at the "Campbell for Congress" home page, prospective Net voters found themselves faced with a dearth of useful information about the candidate. We know the candidate's name, and that he's a candidate for Congress of "unquestioned integrity" and "unbending independence" (what candidate for Congress wouldn't claim those traits), but nowhere is it apparent which party the candidate represents, or even what state he's in or the congressional district he seeks to represent! A deeper look into the pages offered enough clues to learn that Campbell was running for a Bay Area seat in California, but I could find no specific mention identifying the congressional district nor any reference to the fact that Campbell is a Republican. The lack of party identification may well have been intentional, especially for a candidate who already has high name recognition and whose challenger was trying to tie him closely to his party's leader. But by failing to quickly identify the district in which Campbell was a candidate, this home page probably left most Net voters who visited it wondering if they could even vote for Campbell. I sent an E-mail message to the address provided by the page under the "Contact Tom" link asking what party Campbell was a member of and what congressional district he was running in, but did not receive a reply.

But most surprising of all, there was no indication on the page that this was a special election that was to take place in December 1995, rather than during the regular election cycle in November 1996. Other candidates for Congress across the country had by this time already begun to establish their campaign pages as well, and nothing was apparent on the Campbell page to indicate that he needed election day support eleven months earlier than the others.

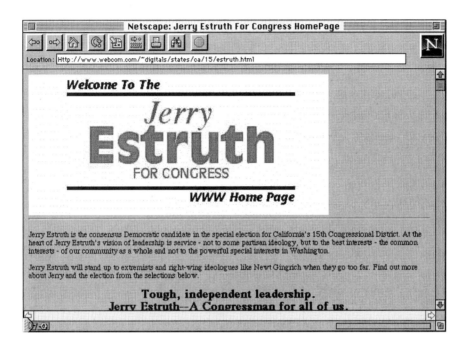

Although the Campbell home page contained flashier graphics, the Estruth home page easily won the contest to provide visitors from the Net with more useful information. The Estruth page was created by a 14-year-old junior high school student and other volunteers who were members of a grassroots group called Digital Democrats, which also hosted the home page on their server. Although not as slick looking as Campbell's page visually, it was nothing to be ashamed of either. In terms of providing essential information right up front, the Estruth page succeeded where Campbell's had failed. The first sentence on Estruth's page answered the questions that Campbell's did not: what district is he running in, what party does he represent, and what election is he running in? "Jerry Estruth is the consensus Democratic candidate in the special election for California's 15th Congressional District."

Exploring Campbell's and Estruth's pages more deeply turns up the kind of information you'd expect—issue statements, press releases, and information on how to contact the candidate. Campbell's page had a longer and more substantive collection of his positions on selected issues than did Estruth's. Campbell also made good use of electronic access to legislation put on the Internet by the State of California, allowing him to highlight his recent efforts as a state Senator. Fill-in forms on his page invited individuals to offer their opinions on particular issues, and to volunteer their assistance to the campaign. Estruth's page contained briefer position statements and, not having held elective office for many years, left him with less of a legislative record to run on. Estruth's page was the only one to go negative, providing links labeled "Who's REALLY Pro-Choice?" and "Top 20 Reasons Not To Vote For Tom Campbell." I found no mention of Estruth on Campbell's page. And remaining the better of the two for providing practical information, Estruth utilized Net lingo and included an Election FAQ (Frequently Asked Questions) with information about the date of the special election, how to register to vote, and a list of zip codes contained within California's 15th district.

Campbell's home page now includes a picture of a newspaper headline proclaiming his victory. It appears that the page may continue on as Representative Campbell's official home page because the "Legislation" link now includes a promise of soon-to-come updates on Campbell's efforts in Congress. But in my consideration the Estruth home page won on the Web. It proved that a volunteer effort can be better than a professionally developed one. While Campbell's page may have been slicker and more attractive, Estruth's demonstrated a better understanding of the Net and did a better job of providing essential information to Net browser's who encountered it. That may be small consolation to Jerry Estruth, but it won't be the first time that style has won over substance in politics.

Another special election, the January 1996 Oregon Senate race to complete the unfinished term of Senator Bob Packwood, has already offered another illustration of the unique impact the Internet can have on congressional elections. Voters Telecom Watch (VTW) "is a volunteer organization, concentrating on legislation as it relates to telecommunications and civil liberties." VTW utilizes the Net to spread the word about legislative issues that will have a negative impact on free speech to those interested in following the latest developments, and Congress has given them plenty of legislation to watch over.

In an effort to determine what a candidate's views are on issues of concern to the online public, and to offer that information to voters, Shabbir Safdar and Steven Cherry of VTW came up with The Technology Pledge. Calling it "a political platform for the technological public," the pledge consists of four statements that candidates are encouraged to support:

> *THE TECHNOLOGY PLEDGE*
>
> *While in office, I pledge to support parental control instead of government censorship on interactive services.*
>
> *While in office, I pledge to support online availability of government information to the public free of charge as an additional standard method of government publication.*
>
> *While in office, I pledge to advocate a consistent national policy on the regulation of the online commerce industry.*
>
> *While in office, I pledge to support market-driven standards for cryptography instead of anti-competitive government regulation.*

The issues raised by the pledge are the ones of most concern to a large majority of individuals on the Net, and that have already come under attack either by Congress or the executive branch in the eyes of many. The pledge offers an educational opportunity for candidates who may be unfamiliar with the issues and is considering them for the first time, and it offers netizens an opportunity to learn where a candidate stands on these issues. Candidates for offices might make many promises in their quest for elective office, and may well break them once in office. But the pledge at least puts them on the record, and President George "No New Taxes" Bush will tell you that politicians break them at their peril.

Both candidates for Oregon's Senate seat, Democrat Ron Wyden and Republican Gordon Smith, have taken VTW's technology pledge. Within the "Oregon U.S. Senate Voters Guide" that VTW distributed via the Net, this "Internet Candidate Matrix" could be found.

INTERNET CANDIDATE MATRIX

Candidate	Stated Support for Internet Issues		Has Voting Record To Back It Up	
Ron Wyden (D)	Y	|	Y	|
Gordon Smith (R)	Y	|	N	|
Karen Shilling (A)	Y	|	N	|

VTW cannot urge you strongly enough to vote for the candidate that is most likely to defend the Internet as an open medium. This matrix should make your choice obvious.

Oregon's special election was unique not only due to the role that the Internet played during the campaign (both candidates maintained home pages built by volunteers), but also because the voting was carried out entirely by mail over a two-week period. The results were impressive. Sixty-five percent of all ballots were returned, an incredible participation rate particularly for a special election. The day after the result's were announced, VTW claimed a share of Ron Wyden's success, stating that "the closeness of the vote in Oregon's special Senate election justified the attention given to the cyberspace vote by the Wyden campaign. Wyden's 1% margin of victory represented fewer than 20,000 votes."

How many more candidates for Congress will likewise give to the cyberspace vote will offer an indication of the strength of the voice that "the technological public" has begun to discover and to use.

One more aspect of online campaigning to watch is whether all of the candidates who put themselves on the Web will pack up their home pages when the election is over or leave them in place. A number of sites from the 1994 and 1995 elections remain available long after all the votes have been cast and counted. While to some this may seem no better than leftover posters remaining on telephone poles after election day, they may prove useful as a reference either for individuals taking another look at the campaign, or for the candidates themselves who may seek to revive them for another run at office and want the site to remain where it was the first time around.

Other post campaign sites have sprung up, offering a historical perspective to congressional campaigns. Jed Lewison, press secretary to Rod Sims's failed race for the Senate in Washington in 1994, has created the "Sims for Senate WWW Archive" and filled it with RealAudio sounds from Sims's campaign ads and news coverage of the Senate race. Of his effort, Lewis writes, "I've established the Sims for Senate WWW Archive for the teeming masses bent on learning more about this wonderful man and his first statewide campaign."

Watch, Opposition, and Unofficial Home Pages

Among the reasons I have offered to members of Congress and their staffs about why they should develop a presence on the Internet, a particularly powerful one I use is this. I tell them, "If you don't put yourself on the Internet, be assured that someone else will do it for you." I don't bother adding, "and they still may even if you do." Members of Congress are frequently the subject of home pages on the Web that seek to expose their missteps or misstatements, their perceived failures or inadequacies in the job, or simply to make a mockery of them.

Probably the best known of this category is a home page called NewtWatch. Making its Net debut in March 1995, NewtWatch has helped spawn a number of similar "watch" pages that seek to follow the activities of a particular member of Congress and utilize the Net to share the magnifying glass of close scrutiny with online citizens.

In the above artist's rendering, House Speaker Newt Gingrich reacts to a perceived slight he suffered aboard Air Force One which shut down the American federal government.

(Cover illustration by Ed Murawinski, *New York Daily News*, October 16, 1995.)

Your Source for Information on Newt Gingrich

NewtWatch has set a high standard to follow and is easily among the most professionally executed of the Watch sites. That may be no surprise, because this site is managed by a professional political consultant, Matthew Dorsey, who maintains NewtWatch as a Political Action Committee (PAC) registered with the Federal Election Commission. The amount of information available is enough to keep anybody interested in a close look at the Speaker busy for days and includes:

- the full text of all seven ethics complaints filed against Gingrich,

- reports of office and staff salary expenditures for the Speaker's office,

- listings of PAC and individual contributors,

- Gingrich's financial disclosure reports, and even

- review's of Gingrich's book *1945*, as well as

- links to other Gingrich related Net sites, both pro and con.

Much more information is likewise available at this site, which invites individuals to contribute to the effort online or through the mail.

NewtWatch has gained widespread attention in Washington and also reactions from the Speaker's office. Using his boss's frequently repeated future talk, Gingrich's press secretary Tony Blankley said of NewtWatch creator Dorsey, "I think this person is Third Wave slime."[3]

Newt Gingrich is not alone in the glare of scrutiny from the Internet. Other Watch pages have sprung up on the Net, focusing their attention on individual members of Congress. Most aren't as slick or thorough as NewtWatch, probably because they are not usually professional efforts and are instead simply the work of individuals who are particularly opposed to the member of Congress on which they've focused.

---

[3] Craig Karmin, "It's fundraising in cyberspace as 'NewtWatch' joins the Internet," *The Hill*, March 15, 1995, p. 14.

House Minority Leader Richard Gephardt is the focus of one such Watch page, as is California Senator Dianne Feinstein, whose efforts and actions in Congress are challenged on a page that titles itself "The Unofficial Senator Dianne Feinstein." At least a half dozen other members of Congress have found themselves the focus of these grassroots efforts, including Senator Jesse Helms, who has a collection of past quotes repeated for him on "The World According to Helms" home page, and Senator Jim Exon, for whom several memorial home pages contain pictures that certainly would be found "indecent" under his bill. The Arizona Democratic party's home page maintains "Hayworth Watch," which focuses on the former sportscaster and current Representative of Arizona's 6th District, and shares items such as Hayworth's inclusion on the "Ten Dimmest Bulbs in Congress" list.

In the coming elections of 1996, it may be no surprise to see such Watch pages evolve into opposition pages that encourage support of anybody challenging the spotlighted member of Congress. In 1994,

Tom Foley of Washington became the first House Speaker not to be reelected in 134 years. An online campaign called "De-Foley-ate Congress" (DF8) which was born in opposition to Foley's pro-gun control votes, used E-mail and Usenet news groups to gather and redistribute information critical of Foley, distribute summaries of his opponents positions, and solicit funds to help defeat the Speaker. The DF8 campaign raised almost $30,000 that was spent on advertising in print and radio, and Foley lost a squeaker by less than 4,000 votes. Foley's campaign made no effort to monitor or respond to the DF8 campaign, ceding the online battle for supporters to the opposition. Learning a lesson from Foley's narrow defeat, future challengers running for Congress are likely to seek out and encourage any grass-roots opposition efforts that focus on the incumbent, while incumbents will do well to pay close attention to what's being said about them on the Net and reply in kind by using it to defend their records.

The appearance in 1995 of several official-looking campaign pages for presidential candidates that were in fact parodies of the real thing is a strong reminder that things may not always be what they appear to be on the Net. A parody of the Dole campaign is found at the domain name *www.dole96.org*. To many Net surfers, the domain name alone might reassure them of the authenticity of the site, just as *whitehouse.gov* or *harvard.edu* would offer an indication of where on the Net they had landed. Who but the Dole campaign would be at *www.dole96.org*?: a couple of online satirists who also set up sites lampooning other candidates for President, that's who (the real Dole campaign site is at *www.dole96.com*). For any Net browsers exploring what they think is a member of Congress's or a candidate's home page on the Net, let the browser beware. You may not be seeing what you think you are. For member pages, you should look to see if it's hosted by *senate.gov* or *house.gov*, the congressional Internet servers on which most (but not all) member pages are hosted. On campaign pages, look for some indication that it's an "official" site authorized and paid for by the campaign.

It seems as if the political instinct to "go negative" proves valid even on the Internet. Besides their own congressional home pages, or official campaign efforts, there are few notable efforts on the Net designed to offer support for any individual member of Congress. House Speaker Newt Gingrich seems to draw the most attention, with at least a half dozen pages that focus on him, some in support. In contrast to the already mentioned NewtWatch, there is the Newt Gingrich WWW Fan Club and a handful of other pro-Gingrich sites to be found on the Net. But few other members of Congress have yet rated such online displays of support, and it seems as if the negative trend will dominate.

Can the Net Make a Difference?

The Net provides an unobtrusive medium for reaching potential voters, unlike television commercials that bombard voters in their homes with ever-increasing frequency as election day approaches, signs and bumper stickers, which are an unavoidable sight for anyone venturing outside in late October, and campaign mailings and flyers stuffed in mailboxes and front doors by fundraisers and volunteers. A proactive effort on the part of the user is required to locate a candidate's home page or to read their postings elsewhere on the Net. A campaign Web site can provide the opportunity for a candidate to present a much more complete picture of themselves and their reasons for seeking office than can ever be offered during a 30-second TV commercial or delivered during the split second a driver passes a sign on the highway. The challenge for the developers of these sites is to build a resource at which visiting voters will linger, a place in which they'll be informed and even entertained, and hopefully stirred to vote or even to greater action through volunteering for a campaign or contributing financially. The risk for candidates that fail to succeed at this is that their Net presence will be immediately stale, an unnoticed billboard on the info highway.

Brock Meeks, chief Washington correspondent for HotWired and Wired Magazine, has described the current batch of home pages for presidential candidates as "junk" and "nothing more than a gimmick." But he also believes that a Net-based constituency could possibly be mobilized into making a difference. He writes "Maybe the '96 election will see the rise of a new, powerful block of swing votes. The Net, with its rabid independent and anarchist leanings could, if mobilized, even swing a close election. Don't forget that Hubert Humphrey lost to Nixon in 1968 by a margin of only 499,074 votes. That's less than a couple of well-trafficked news groups and mailings lists."[4]

Congressional races often hinge on much smaller margins, with races decided on vote margins in the few thousands, hundreds, and sometimes in single digits. In 1994 freshman Republican Andrea Seastrand earned the right to represent California's 22nd district with less than 2,000 votes to spare, while her fellow California Representative, Democrat Jane Harman, was returned to Congress for a second term by a vote margin of 812 votes. But the closest shave of '94 went to "Landslide" Sam Gejdenson of Connecticut, who won an eighth term in Congress with only 21 votes to spare. Twenty-three current members of Congress were elected with less than 50 percent of the vote, ninety-seven with less than 55 percent.[5] With such close margins, votes gained by a campaign's Internet presence could have enough impact to change the outcome of an election.

But the use of the Internet by members of Congress, by candidates for office, and by the government in general does not portend the

---

[4] Brock Meeks, "Muckraker", *HotWired*, September 1995.

[5] Philip D. Duncan & Christine C. Lawrence, "Politics in America 1996: The 104th Congress", *Congressional Quarterly Press*, 1995, p. 1533.

demise of the traditional means by which government and politicians make information available to the public. Candidates will still produce radio and television commercials, offer press releases and interviews to the print media, and press the flesh in face-to-face encounters with voters. Members of Congress will still travel back to their states and districts frequently, meet with constituents and lobbyists in their offices to hear their concerns, and promote their own legislative agendas and accomplishments with traditional media. The authors of the book *White House to Your House: Media and Politics in Virtual America* examined the impact that new technologies have had on their predecessors. "After the hyperventilating about 'revolutionary media' subsides, Gutenberg still will coexist with the Internet. New media are additive; they increase the consumers' options, rather than subtract from them. Selective consumers have usually adjusted these tastes and habits to fit in a new medium, when its price was deemed reasonable, its technology more convenient than daunting, and the product enjoyable and/or useful."[6]

---

[6] Edwin Diamond and Robert A. Silverman, *White House to Your House: Media and Politics in Virtual America*, The MIT Press, Cambridge, MA, 1995, p. 22.

EIGHT

---★---

What's Ahead?

What's ahead for Congress on the Internet? Plenty. While the efforts of the last few years by those members of Congress and congressional agencies that have ventured into cyberspace have been very slow in coming, it seems clear that the Internet is not likely to be just a fad on the Hill and that instead it will continue to be developed as a communications medium. At this writing, many members of Congress still aren't on the Internet. Eventually they will all get there, and no one will long remember or care who was the first with an e-mail address or a home page. Being on the Net will be no more remarkable than having a phone or a fax in the office.

What will matter more in the long run is who is doing it better. When the Net land rush is over, and 535 members of Congress have home pages on the Web, you can expect to see greatly varying degrees of quality, content, and usefulness among them. Members of Congress will discover that after all of their hesitation, getting onto the Internet is the easy part. But it's the development of a thing of substance that is the real challenge.

One glimpse of what's ahead for the Hill on the Net is provided by the Congressional Memory Project established by the Internet Multicasting Service (IMS), well known for having developing radio programming that is delivered both live and on-demand from its studio in the National Press Building in Washington, DC. Seeking to develop something like the online version of C-SPAN, IMS makes live feeds of the proceedings of both the House and Senate available via multicast for those on the Net properly equipped to receive it. House proceedings are stored in a searchable database, permitting individuals to search out and download their favorite sound bites from the House floor. The Senate's sounds are not yet available. In July 1995, IMS demonstrated how this technology could bring the activities of a congressional committee online, when it broadcast the proceedings of a Joint Economic Hearing on the Economy in the 21st Century out to the Net, and invited questions submitted via e-mail. Even more useful than the ability to listen to the event in real time is the fact that all of Congress's proceedings can be saved in such a way, and any congressional researcher or interested citizen can search, retrieve, read, and listen to what's going on in Congress after the fact, on their own time.

For Congress as an institution, an abundance of information that can and should be made available on the Internet still remains unavailable. While the THOMAS system at the Library of Congress has broken new ground in advancing electronic access to the *Congressional Record* and the text of legislation, much, much more remains to go online. Hearing testimonies, bill mark-ups, committee reports, legislative agendas, congressional directories, and many other congressional documents would prove to be invaluable to researchers, students, and citizens alike. A great deal of information that Congress could make available finds its way online subject to the whim of individual members of Congress, particularly committee chairmen. Hearing testimonies, transcripts, and reports may soon find their way to the Net, but doing so should be a requirement for all committees, rather than the piece-mail efforts of a forward-thinking few. Other material, such as Congressional Research Service reports, are already available on the Net to congressional staff but remain unavailable to the public. Until recently, the financial reports of politicians on file with the Federal Election Commission (FEC) were available only via a prohibitively expensive BBS. On Valentine's Day, 1996, the FEC launched a home page on the Web, improving access to much of this material. There is no shortage of congressional information that could be made available on the Net, but long-standing rules and procedures for the dissemination of such information will have to be changed or done away with to make it happen, and change in Congress is often glacially slow.

The idea of utilizing technology for the further development of our American democracy is not at all new, but has had many proponents who've envisioned various degrees of a future in which technology allows citizens to directly participate in and vote on the questions that our elected officials do today. In 1978, in the second volume of The People's Almanac, Laurel Schonfield described her vision for *Instant Democracy in Your Living Room:*

> *One television set in each household in the U.S. would be wired with an extra channel—the government channel. And this TV would be attached to a remote-control voting box. For most of the day, this new station would broadcast debates on different bills and proposed programs. Then, for one hour a night, this station would be turned over to actual voting on the issues of the day....Congresspeople would no longer make any major decisions. Their job would be to carry out the decisions that had been made by the daily voting of the people.*

Laural's vision of a future form of direct democracy based on interactive television very closely resembles scenarios that descriptions of cyber-democracy offer today. Some of her predictions have already come to pass. The channel that she describes that would be installed on a television set in every household, and on which debates and programs would be debated all day, currently exists in the form of C-SPAN and C-SPAN2, which broadcast the proceedings of the House and Senate as well as other public policy-related forums and debates. The only thing missing from Laural's ideal of direct democracy is the direct, remote-control voting by citizens.

Does increased ability for direct citizen participation in the policy-making process mean the end of our representative form of democracy? For members of Congress, often known to demonstrate their skills of self-preservation, such a prospect can be frightening and offers a reason to look at increased access to Congress on the Internet with skepticism. Representative Charlie Rose of North Carolina, a longtime advocate of increasing electronic access to government information, described the reaction of another senior member to the availability of a database of available government grants to the public. "Hell, if that database goes too far, those people won't even have to come to me anymore" was his reaction.[1]

As chairman of the Senate Rules Committee, Senator Ted Stevens was capable of advancing or delaying the development of Internet access within the Senate. Having represented the State of Alaska since 1968, Stevens was known as a protector of Congress's ability to send mass mailings and for the need for government-funded public broadcasting, and was the second member of the Senate to post information to the Senate's Internet server. But despite these hints that he might encourage increased Internet access within the Senate and public access to congressional information, Stevens remained skeptical. At a demonstration of the World Wide Web arranged in the Senate for his benefit, Senator Stevens was said to have remarked that this technology was "leading to Cyber-Democracy, people voting at home and not needing us at all."

---

[1]Kristin Spence, "Getting Wired on Capitol Hill," *WIRED,* May/June 1993, p. 25.

But despite such concerns, the fact is that as interactive digital technologies succeed in bringing the public closer to their government, they will inevitably expect to be able to perform a more active role in governing themselves. In his 1995 book, *The Electronic Republic*, Lawrence Grossman wrote:

> *Interactive telecommunications now make it possible for tens of millions of widely dispersed citizens to receive the information they need to carry out the business of government themselves, gain admission to the political realm, and retrieve at least some of the power over their own lives and goods that many believe their elected officials are squandering.*

In mid-1994, a small blue booklet was mailed to Members of Congress. Titled *The Telecom Coup: The Computer-Driven Political Revolution That Will Rejuvenate American Society In the Years Just Ahead*, the author, McKinley Conway, predicted that "During the mid-1990s the much-promised electronic communications breakthrough will arrive. Technological developments will give the long-suppressed majority a means of expression and organization. The data highway will open a new route to Washington." But despite the dramatic title and words, this booklet predicts a form of cyber-democracy that's not quite as far reaching as Laurel Schonfield's vision of direct democracy via interactive television.

Conway argues that there has been a shift away from majority rule in America, and that special interest groups which are corrupted by power and focused so narrowly on their own particular concern that they don't work in the majority's interest, now drive the decision-making process in Washington. The ballot initiative process that allows voters in some states to put items directly on state ballots is an outgrowth of voters who are represented by legislators who are more beholden to special interests than they are to the majority of voters, but such initiatives faced severely limiting restrictions.

The missing link, according to Conway, is the need for "an official national referendum that would allow voters to place on the record their agenda for the nation." Such a national referendum would do what elections and polls today try and fail to do: "to reveal how the majority of voters feels about any certain question."

The possibilities for the future development of a truly wired legislative branch are many, from continued access to individual members and congressional committees and their workings, to the development of a wide variety of advanced means by which the public can let Congress know how it feels about issues; in ways such as online hearings and national referenda that will make the e-mail messages of today seem quaint by comparison. While their continued development may seem inevitable, nothing is a certainty in this most unique of government institutions. An informed citizenry that utilizes the resources that are currently available, and lobbies in favor of those that are not, will be necessary to make sure that the Hill on the Net develops into a resource to strengthen our democracy, and a place worth visiting in cyberspace.

Epilogue

The story of the Hill on the Net is far from over. At best this book has attempted to describe the early chapters. Even as I write, new developments arise daily, challenging my efforts to find a place to finish. I cannot, because the story isn't over. But as calendars provide an artificial ending to the continual passage of time, I will let the following chronicle of events end this part of the Cyber-Congress story. The events of December illustrate what a busy year it was for the Hill on the Net, and there's no sign that it is slowing down.

December 1, 1995

In its year-end special issue, *Newsweek* magazine proclaimed 1995 as the "Year of the Internet," pointing out that the World Wide Web had grown by more than six times since January 1995.[1] For its look

---

[1] Levey, Steven, "The Year of the Internet", *Newsweek*, December 25, 1995, p. 26.

back at "The Best and Worst of 1995," *Internet World* magazine repeatedly put the U. S. Senate in the Worst category. However, the distinction was earned as a result of legislative efforts to regulate content on the Internet, and not for the Senate's own online efforts.

Also on December 1, 1995, the Government Printing Office announced that it was scrapping all subscription fees for electronic access to congressional information via GPO Access. Paid subscription fees would be refunded, and while federal depository libraries would continue to be "an essential link between GPO Access and the public," they were no longer the only free option. In the press release announcing the policy change, Public Printer Michael DiMario was quoted as saying, "We believe the public should have timely access to vital information about the activities of their government without charge." The success of free access via federal depository library gateways had led to the demise of the subscription service. As the number of gateways providing free access increased, the need for anyone to pay for a subscription continued to diminish in the face of widespread free access from a gateway. By allowing free access directly from GPO in addition to the gateways, a final hurdle to even more widespread free access was removed and the administrative costs for maintaining paid subscriptions were eliminated.

December 7, 1995

"An Agenda for the Information Age: Managing Technology in the Senate" was the subject of the first Rules Committee hearing under the chairmanship of Senator John Warner of Virginia. Warner was an early adopter of the Internet in his own Senate office, joining Senator Robb to make Virginia the first state that had both of its Senators on the Web. And the topic of his first hearing was a positive indication that he intends to put the Senate on the "cutting edge of technology."[2]

Results of a commissioned study on the Senate's state of preparedness for meeting "its strategic objectives for information resource management" include the conclusion that "An inefficient organization and lack of customer focus have slowed the introduction of such important technologies as Internet access," and rates Senate organization and planning as "poor."[3]

Among various witnesses from AT&T, Mobil, and the U.S. Navy who discussed their own efforts at managing technology within their organizations, was Kimberly Jenkins, executive director of Highway 1, a nonprofit organization dedicated to helping Congress understand and use technology. Two paragraphs included in the fifty hard copies of testimony submitted to the committee (and also on diskette) by Ms. Jenkins mysteriously disappeared from the copies distributed at the hearing. The deleted testimony, echoing the conclusion of the commissioned study, began:

> *The technology system in the Senate is badly broken, not just in terms of equipment, but in terms of organization and management. The problem is bad enough that it is no longer sufficient to say, "It's broken and I don't care," or "It's broken. Drop me a memo when it is fixed." The Rules Committee has the authority and responsibility to fix the system and bring the Senate into the 21st century with the rest of America. I encourage you to do it as soon as possible.*

---

[2] Juliet Eilperin and Mary Jacoby, "The Senate's New 'Mayor'" *ROLL CALL*, September 14, 1995, p. 20.

[3] U.S. Senate Information Technology Infrastructure Review, Executive Summary with Findings and Action Plan, Performance Engineering Corporation, November 21, 1995, p. iv.

Senator Warner announced at the hearing that the existing restrictions that limited only three staff at a time in a Senator's office to have access to the Internet were to be lifted. A minor victory for staff access considering the many offices that had already defeated the restriction by sidestepping it with a LINUX box. Nevertheless, staff access to Usenet news groups remains the only unfulfilled request from the letter sent to Rules by Senator Frist and his colleagues in February, 1995.

December 12, 1995

In reaction to developments in the House-Senate conference committee that appears close to approving language to the telecommunications reform bill that would restrict "indecent" content on the Internet, a group of public advocacy groups organized The Internet Day of Protest, and encouraged individuals to phone, fax, and e-mail their opposition to members of Congress. Organizers estimate that up to 50,000 phone calls and faxes were generated to Congress and report that the offices of targeted members have been "overwhelmed" with handling them. Already backed up with a huge influx of e-mail related to the budget stalemate and government shutdown, House and Senate e-mail systems became even more backlogged under the new wave of protest messages (and the outbound wave of auto-acknowledgments).

December 21, 1995

Shortly after celebrating his 93rd birthday, Senator Strom Thurmond became the 69th member of the Senate to establish a public e-mail address (*senator@thurmond.senate.gov*). Fewer than one-third of the members of the Senate do not yet have a public e-mail address. The House needs about fifty more members to reach the halfway point to ubiquitous member e-mail.

December 22, 1995

The House Republican Conference home page made its *third* appearance in the *What's New!* page on the House of Representatives's site, announcing that it has once again been updated. This time it lead visitors to a special holiday page, "A Holiday Gift for the American People," with two links outlining the Republican commitment to a balanced budget and real welfare reform. The graphics are nice, the content is about what you'd expect, the pages are both dead ends. All in all, getting a little better. At least there's some new life here. Maybe by their fourth appearance in *What's New!* it will be worth a bookmark. [Late update: That fourth appearance came less than a month later, when in January 1996 *What's New!* announced another HRC update, this time announcing the availability of the Republican Response to the President's State of the Union address. After three appearances by the HRC homepage in *What's New!* in three months, the House Democrats decide to begin playing by the same rules and at their request are added to *What's New!*, pointing out that their *Whip*

Windup report changes daily. A story in *Roll Call* brought attention to the battle over *What's New!*, and may have brought an end to this particular twisting of a Net convention for political purposes. Stay tuned.]

December 29, 1995

Senator Larry Craig became the fortieth member of the Senate to establish a home page in 1995.

CompuServe blocked access to more than 200 Usenet news groups from its subscribers worldwide after prosecutors in Germany claimed that their content was in violation of German pornography laws. [In February 1996, President Clinton signed the Telecommunications Reform Act, with the included Communications Decency Act, into law. Within weeks a federal judge temporarily enjoined enforcement of the provision, ruling that the word "indecent" is unconstitutionally vague and not defined in the act.]

Stay tuned . . .

In order to keep readers up-to-date with what's happening with the Hill on the Net, I have created a mailing list to which I will send periodic updates and information. If you are interested in adding yourself to this list, send an e-mail to *hillnet@casey.com* with the word "subscribe" in the subject line.

Appendix

Grace York's
Congressional E-Mail Addresses
and Web Sites

3-4-96

104th Congress
1995/96

United States Senate

State	Party	Name	E-Mail Address
AK	R	Stevens, Ted	senator_stevens@stevens.senate.gov
AK	R	Murkowski, Frank	email@murkowski.senate.gov
AL	R	Shelby, Richard	senator@shelby.senate.gov
AR	D	Bumpers, Dale	senator@bumpers.senate.gov
AZ	R	Kyl, Jon	info@kyl.senate.gov
AZ	R	McCain, John	senator_mccain@mccain.senate.gov
CA	D	Boxer, Barbara	senator@boxer.senate.gov
CA	D	Feinstein, Dianne	senator@feinstein.senate.gov
CO	R	Brown, Hank	senator_brown@brown.senate.gov
CO	R	Campbell, Ben N.	data@nighthorse.falcontech.com
CT	D	Dodd, Christopher	sen_dodd@dodd.senate.gov
CT	D	Lieberman, Joseph	senator_lieberman@lieberman.senate.gov
DE	D	Biden, Joe	senator@biden.senate.gov
FL	D	Graham, Bob	bob_graham@graham.senate.gov
FL	R	Mack, Connie	senator_mack@jec.senate.gov
GA	R	Coverdell, Paul	senator_coverdell@coverdell.senate.gov
IA	D	Harkin, Tom	tom_harkin@harkin.senate.gov
IA	R	Grassley, Charles	chuck_grassley@grassley.senate.gov
ID	R	Craig, Larry	larry_craig@craig.senate.gov
ID	R	Kempthorne, Dirk	dirk_kempthorne@kempthorne.senate.gov
IL	D	Simon, Paul	senator@simon.senate.gov
IL	D	Moseley-Braun, Carol	senator@moseley-braun.senate.gov

State	Party	Name	E-Mail Address
IN	R	Lugar, Richard	lugar@iquest.net
KY	D	Ford, Wendell	wendell_ford@ford.senate.gov
KY	R	McConnell, Mitch	senator@mcconnell.senate.gov
LA	D	Breaux, John	senator@breaux.senate.gov
LA	D	Johnston, J.Bennett	senator@johnston.senate.gov
MA	D	Kennedy, Ted	senator@kennedy.senate.gov
MA	D	Kerry, John	john_kerry@kerry.senate.gov
MD	D	Mikulski, Barbara	senator@mikulski.senate.gov
MD	D	Sarbanes, Paul	senator@sarbanes.senate.gov
ME	R	Cohen, William	billcohen@cohen.senate.gov
MI	D	Levin, Carl	senator@levin.senate.gov
MI	R	Abraham, Spencer	michigan@abraham.senate.gov
MN	R	Grams, Rod	mail_grams@grams.senate.gov
MN	D	Wellstone, Paul	senator@wellstone.senate.gov
MO	R	Ashcroft, John	john_ashcroft@ashcroft.senate.gov
MS	R	Cochran, Thad	senator@cochran.senate.gov
MT	D	Baucus, Max	max@baucus.senate.gov
MT	R	Burns, Conrad	conrad_burns@burns.senate.gov
NC	R	Faircloth, Lauch	senator@faircloth.senate.gov
NC	R	Helms, Jesse	jesse_helms@helms.senate.gov
ND	D	Conrad, Kent	senator@conrad.senate.gov
ND	D	Dorgan, Byron	senator@dorgan.senate.gov
NE	D	Kerrey, Bob	bob@kerrey.senate.gov

State	*Party*	*Name*	*E-Mail Address*
NH	R	Gregg, Judd	mailbox@gregg.senate.gov
NH	R	Smith, Bob	opinion@smith.senate.gov
NJ	D	Bradley, Bill	senator@bradley.senate.gov
NM	D	Bingaman, Jeff	Senator_Bingaman@bingaman.senate.gov
NM	R	Domenici, Pete	senator_domenici@domenici.senate.gov
NV	D	Reid, Harry	senator_reid@reid.senate.gov
NY	R	D'Amato, Alfonse	senator_al@damato.senate.gov
NY	D	Moynihan, Daniel P.	senator@dpm.senate.gov
OH	R	Dewine, Michael	senator_dewine@dewine.senate.gov
OH	D	Glenn, John	caroline@cua3.csuohio.edu
OK	R	Nickles, Don	senator@nickles.senate.gov
OR	D	Wyden, Ron	wyden@teleport.com
PA	R	Santorum, Rick	senator@santorum.senate.gov
PA	R	Specter, Arlen	senator_specter@specter.senate.gov
RI	R	Chafee, John	senator_chafee@chafee.senate.gov
SC	R	Thurmond, Strom	senator@thurmond.senate.gov
SC	D	Hollings, Ernest	senator@hollings.senate.gov
SD	D	Daschle, Thomas	tom_daschle@daschle.senate.gov
SD	R	Pressler, Larry	larry_pressler@pressler.senate.gov
TN	R	Thompson, Fred	senator_thompson@thompson.senate.gov
TN	R	Frist, Bill	senator_frist@frist.senate.gov
TX	R	Gramm, Phil	info@gramm96.org
TX	R	Hutchison, Kay	senator@hutchison.senate.gov

Senate Committees

Senate Committee on Small Business
committee@small-bus.senate.gov

Senate Special Committee on Aging
mailbox@aging.senate.gov

Senate Republican Policy Committee
webmaster@rpc.senate.gov

United States House of Representatives

State	District	Party	Name	E-Mail Address
AL	2	R	Everett, Terry	everett@hr.house.gov
AL	5	D	Cramer, Bud	budmail@hr.house.gov
AL	6	R	Bachus, Spencer	sbachus@hr.house.gov
AR	3	R	Hutchinson, Tim	timhutch@hr.house.gov
AR	4	R	Dickey, Jay	jdickey@hr.house.gov
AZ	2	D	Pastor, Ed	edpastor@hr.house.gov
AZ	5	R	Kolbe, Jim	jimkolbe@hr.house.gov
AZ	6	R	Hayworth, J.D.	hayworth@hr.house.gov
CA	1	R	Riggs, Frank	repriggs@hr.house.gov
CA	3	D	Fazio, Vic	dcaucus@hr.house.gov
CA	6	D	Woolsey, Lynn	woolsey@hr.house.gov
CA	7	D	Miller, George	gmiller@hr.house.gov
CA	8	D	Pelosi, Nancy	sfnancy@hr.house.gov
CA	10	R	Baker, Bill	bbaker@hr.house.gov
CA	12	D	Lantos, Tom	talk2tom@hr.house.gov
CA	13	D	Stark, Pete	petemail@hr.house.gov
CA	14	D	Eshoo, Anna	annagram@hr.house.gov
CA	15	R	Campbell, Tom	campbell@hr.house.gov
CA	16	D	Lofgren, Zoe	zoegram@lofgren.house.gov
CA	17	D	Farr, Sam	samfarr@hr.house.gov
CA	19	R	Radanovich, George	george@hr.house.gov
CA	22	R	Seastrand, Andrea	andrea22@hr.house.gov

State	District	Party	Name	E-Mail Address
CA	25	R	McKeon, Howard	tellbuck@hr.house.gov
CA	36	D	Harman, Jane	jharman@hr.house.gov
CA	42	D	Brown, George E.	talk2geb@hr.house.gov
CA	47	R	Cox, Christopher	chriscox@hr.house.gov
CA	48	R	Packard, Ron	rpackard@hr.house.gov
CA	49	R	Bilbray, Brian	bilbray@hr.house.gov
CO	2	D	Skaggs, David	skaggs@hr.house.gov
CO	6	R	Schaefer, Dan	schaefer@hr.house.gov
CT	2	D	Gejdenson, Sam	bozrah@hr.house.gov
CT	4	R	Shays, Christopher	cshays@hr.house.gov
DE	AL	R	Castle, Michael	delaware@hr.house.gov
FL	5	D	Thurman, Karen	kthurman@hr.house.gov
FL	6	R	Stearns, Cliff	cstearns@hr.house.gov
FL	9	R	Bilirakis, Michael	truerep@hr.house.gov
FL	12	R	Canady, Charles	canady@hr.house.gov
FL	15	R	Weldon, Dave	fla15@hr.house.gov
FL	20	D	Deutsch, Peter	pdeutsch@hr.house.gov
FL	23	D	Hastings, Alcee	hastings@hr.house.gov
GA	3	R	Collins, Mac	rep3mac@hr.house.gov
GA	4	R	Linder, John	jlinder@hr.house.gov
GA	6	R	Gingrich, Newton	georgia6@hr.house.gov
GA	8	R	Chambliss, Saxby	saxby@hr.house.gov
GA	10	R	Norwood, Charlies	ga10@hr.house.gov
GU	AL	D	Underwood, Robert	guamtodc@hr.house.gov
IA	2	R	Nussle, James	nussleia@hr.house.gov
ID	1	R	Chenoweth, Helen	askhelen@hr.house.gov
IL	1	D	Rush, Bobby	brush@hr.house.gov

State	District	Party	Name	E-Mail Address
IL	4	D	Gutierrez, Luis	luisg@hr.house.gov
IL	12	D	Costello, Jerry	jfcil12@hr.house.gov
IL	13	R	Fawell, Harris	hfawell@hr.house.gov
IL	14	R	Hastert, Dennis	dhastert@hr.house.gov
IL	20	D	Durbin, Richard	durbin@hr.house.gov
IN	2	R	McIntosh, David	mcintosh@hr.house.gov
IN	3	D	Roemer, Tim	troemer@hr.house.gov
IN	4	R	Souder, Mark	souder@hr.house.gov
IN	8	R	Hostettler, John	johnhost@hr.house.gov
IN	9	D	Hamilton, Lee	hamilton@hr.house.gov
KS	1	R	Roberts, Pat	emailpat@hr.house.gov
KS	2	R	Brownback, Sam	brownbak@hr.house.gov
KS	4	R	Tiahrt, Todd	tiahrt@hr.house.gov
KY	1	R	Whitfield, Ed	edky01@hr.house.gov
KY	3	D	Ward, Mike	mikemail@hr.house.gov
KY	4	R	Bunning, Jim	bunning4@hr.house.gov
LA	5	R	McCrery, Jim	mccrery@hr.house.gov
MA	5	D	Meehan, Martin	mtmeehan@hr.house.gov
MA	6	R	Torkildsen, Peter	torkma06@hr.house.gov
MA	9	D	Moakley, Joe	jmoakley@hr.house.gov
MD	2	R	Ehrlich, Robert	rallen@lattanze.loyola.edu ehrlich@hr.house.gov
MD	3	D	Cardin, Ben	cardin@hr.house.gov
MD	4	D	Wynn, Albert	alwynn@hr.house.gov
ME	2	D	Baldacci, John	baldacci@hr.house.gov
MI	1	D	Stupak, Bart	stupak@hr.house.gov
MI	2	R	Hoekstra, Peter	tellhoek@hr.house.gov
MI	2	R	Hoekstra, Peter	usavoice@hr.house.gov

State	*District*	*Party*	*Name*	*E-Mail Address*
MI	3	R	Ehlers, Vernon	congehlr@hr.house.gov
MI	4	R	Camp, Dave	davecamp@hr.house.gov
MI	7	R	Smith, Nick	repsmith@hr.house.gov
MI	8	R	Chrysler, Dick	chrysler@hr.house.gov
MI	13	D	Rivers, Lynn	lrivers@hr.house.gov
MI	14	D	Conyers, John	jconyers@hr.house.gov
MN	1	R	Gutknect, Gil	gil@hr.house.gov
MN	2	D	Minge, David	dminge@hr.house.gov
MN	3	R	Ramstad, Jim	mn03@hr.house.gov
MN	4	D	Vento, Bruce	vento@hr.house.gov
MN	5	D	Sabo, Martin	msabo@hr.house.gov
MN	6	D	Luther, Bill	tellbill@hr.house.gov
MN	7	D	Peterson, Collin	tocollin@hr.house.gov
MN	8	D	Oberstar, James	oberstar@hr.house.gov
MO	2	R	Talent, James	talentmo@hr.house.gov
MO	3	D	Gephardt, Richard	gephardt@hr.house.gov
MO	8	R	Emerson, Bill	bemerson@hr.house.gov
MS	2	D	Thompson, Bennie	ms2nd@hr.house.gov
NC	2	R	Funderburk, David	funnc02@hr.house.gov
NC	4	R	Heineman, Frederick	thechief@hr.house.gov
NC	5	R	Burr, Richard	mail2nc5@hr.house.gov
NC	7	D	Rose, Charlie	crose@hr.house.gov
NC	9	R	Myrick, Sue	myrick@hr.house.gov
NC	10	R	Ballenger, Cass	cassmail@hr.house.gov
NC	11	R	Taylor, Charles	chtaylor@hr.house.gov
NC	12	D	Watt, Mel	melmail@hr.house.gov
ND	AL	D	Pomeroy, Earl	epomeroy@hr.house.gov
NE	2	R	Christensen, Jon	talk2jon@hr.house.gov
NH	1	R	Zeliff, Bill	zeliff@hr.house.gov
NH	2	R	Bass, Charlie	cbass@hr.house.gov

State	District	Party	Name	E-Mail Address
NJ	1	D	Andrews, Robert	randrews@hr.house.gov
NJ	7	R	Franks, Bob	franksnj@hr.house.gov
NJ	11	R	Frelinghuysen, Rodney	njeleven@hr.house.gov
NJ	12	R	Zimmer, Dick	dzimmer@hr.house.gov
NM	3	D	Richardson, Bill	billnm03@hr.house.gov
NV	1	R	Ensign, John	ensign@hr.house.gov
NY	1	R	Forbes, Michael	mpforbes@hr.house.gov
NY	2	R	Lazio, Rick	lazio@hr.house.gov
NY	3	R	King, Peter	peteking@hr.house.gov
NY	7	D	Manton, Thomas	tmanton@hr.house.gov
NY	8	D	Nadler, Jerrold	nadler@hr.house.gov
NY	13	R	Molinari, Susan	molinari@hr.house.gov
NY	15	D	Rangel, Charles	rangel@hr.house.gov
NY	16	D	Serrano, Jose	jserrano@hr.house.gov
NY	17	D	Engel, Eliot	engeline@hr.house.gov
NY	18	D	Lowey, Nita	nitamail@hr.house.gov
NY	19	R	Kelly, Sue	dearsue@hr.house.gov
NY	21	D	McNulty, Michael	mmcnulty@hr.house.gov
NY	23	R	Boehlert, Sherwood	boehlert@hr.house.gov
NY	26	D	Hinchey, Maurice	hinchey@hr.house.gov
NY	27	R	Paxon, Bill	bpaxon@hr.house.gov
OH	2	R	Portman, Rob	portmail@hr.house.gov
OH	4	R	Oxley, Michael	oxley@hr.house.gov
OH	10	R	Hoke, Martin	hokemail@hr.house.gov
OH	13	D	Brown, Sherrod	sherrod@hr.house.gov
OH	15	R	Pryce, Deborah	pryce15@hr.house.gov
OH	17	D	Traficant, James	telljim@hr.house.gov
OK	5	R	Istook, Jr. Ernest	istook@hr.house.gov

State	District	Party	Name	E-Mail Address
OR	1	D	Furse, Elizabeth	furseor1@hr.house.gov
OR	4	D	DeFazio, Pete	pdefazio@hr.house.gov
OR	5	R	Bunn, Jim	askbunn@hr.house.gov
PA	7	R	Weldon, Curt	curtpa7@hr.house.gov
PA	11	D	Kanjorski, Paul	kanjo@hr.house.gov
PA	12	D	Murtha, John	murtha@hr.house.gov
PA	13	R	Fox, Jon	jonfox@hr.house.gov
PA	15	D	McHale, Paul	mchale@hr.house.gov
PA	16	R	Walker, Robert	pa16@hr.house.gov
SC	1	R	Sanford, Mark	sanford@hr.house.gov
SC	5	D	Spratt, John	jspratt@hr.house.gov
SC	6	D	Clyburn, James	jclyburn@hr.house.gov
TN	5	D	Clement, Bob	clement@hr.house.gov
TN	9	D	Ford, Harold	hford@hr.house.gov
TX	1	D	Chapman, Jim	jchapman@hr.house.gov
TX	2	D	Wilson, Charles	cwilson@hr.house.gov
TX	3	R	Johnson, Sam	samtx03@hr.house.gov
TX	6	R	Barton, Joe	barton06@hr.house.gov
TX	10	D	Doggett, Lloyd	doggett@hr.house.gov
TX	24	D	Frost, Martin	frost@hr.house.gov
TX	25	D	Bentsen, Ken	bentsen@hr.house.gov
TX	29	D	Green, Gene	ggreen@hr.house.gov
UT	2	R	Waldholtz, Enid	enidutah@hr.house.gov
UT	3	D	Orton, Bill	ortonut3@hr.house.gov
VA	2	D	Pickett, Owen	opickett@hr.house.gov
VA	6	R	Goodlatte, Bob	talk2bob@hr.house.gov
VA	8	D	Moran, Jim	repmoran@hr.house.gov
VA	9	D	Boucher, Rick	ninthnet@hr.house.gov
VA	11	R	Davis, Tom	tomdavis@hr.house.gov

State	District	Party	Name	E-Mail Address
VT	AL	I	Sanders, Bernie	bsanders@igc.apc.org
WA	1	R	White, Rick	repwhite@hr.house.gov
WA	3	R	Smith, Linda	asklinda@hr.house.gov
WA	8	R	Dunn, Jennifer	dunnwa08@hr.house.gov
WA	9	R	Tate, Randy	rtate@hr.house.gov
WI	1	R	Neumann, Mark	mneumann@hr.house.gov
WI	2	R	Klug, Scott	badger02@hr.house.gov
WI	4	D	Kleczka, Gerald	jerry4wi@hr.house.gov
WI	5	D	Barrett, Tom	telltom@hr.house.gov
WI	6	R	Petri, Tom	tompetri@hr.house.gov
WI	8	R	Roth, Toby	roth08@hr.house.gov
WI	9	R	Sensenbrenner, James	sensen09@hr.house.gov
WV	2	D	Wise, Robert	bobwise@hr.house.gov
WV	3	D	Rahall, Nick	nrahall@hr.house.gov

House Committees

House Committee on Commerce
  commerce@hr.house.gov

House Committee on Economic and Educational Opportunities
Subcommittee on Employer-Employee Relations
  slabmgnt@hr.house.gov

House Committee on Resources
  resource@hr.house.gov

House Committee on Science
  science@hr.house.gov

House Commitee on Science (minority)
  scidems@hr.house.gov

House Committee on Small Business
  smbizcom@hr.house.gov

House Republican Policy Committee
  repubpol@hr.house.gov

Congressional Web Sites

Note: Official web sites only. Political campaign and political party web sites are available through CAPWEB's Political Page (http://policy.net/capweb/political.html) or David Morgan's Congress home page (http://www.geopages.com/Capitol-Hill/1007/

United States Senate Web Sites

Generic web pages are available for all Senators by name or state at the Senate web site (http://www.senate.gov)

State	*Party*	*Name*	*Web Site*
AK	R	Murkowski, Frank	http://www.senate.gov/~murkowski/ http://www.state.ak.us/local/akpages/CONGRESS/aksenfm.htm
AK	R	Stevens, Ted	http://www.senate.gov/~stevens/ http://www.state.ak.us/local/akpages/CONGRESS/aksents.htm
AZ	R	Kyl, Jon	http://aspin.asu.edu/~pctp/kyl/kyl.html
AZ	R	McCain, John	http://aspin.asu.edu/~pctp/mccain/mccain.html
CA	D	Boxer, Barbara	http://www.senate.gov/~boxer/
CA	D	Feinstein, Dianne	http://www.senate.gov/~feinstein/
CO	R	Campbell, Ben Nighthorse	http://www.falcontech.com/nighthorse/
CT	D	Dodd, Christopher	http://www.uconn.edu/dodd/dodd.html
CT	D	Lieberman, Joseph	http://www.senate.gov/~lieberman/
DE	D	Biden, Joe	http://www.senate.gov/~biden/
FL	D	Graham, Bob	http://www.senate.gov/~graham/
FL	R	Mack, Connie	http://www.senate.gov/~mack/
IA	D	Harkin, Tom	http://www.senate.gov/~harkin/

State	Party	Name	Web Site
ID	R	Craig, Larry	http://www.senate.gov/~craig/
ID	R	Kempthorne, Dirk	http://www.senate.gov/~kempthorne/
IL	D	Simon, Paul	http://www.senate.gov/~simon/
KY	D	Ford, Wendell	http://www.senate.gov/~ford/
LA	D	Breaux, John	http://www.senate.gov/~breaux/
LA	D	Johnston, Bennett	http://www.senate.gov/~johnston/
MA	D	Kennedy, Ted	http://www.ai.mit.edu/projects/iiip/Kennedy/homepage.html http://www.senate.gov/~kennedy/
MA	D	Kerry, John	http://www.senate.gov/~kerry/
MD	D	Mikulski, Barbara	http://www.senate.gov/~mikulski/
MD	D	Sarbanes, Paul	http://www.senate.gov/~sarbanes/
ME	R	Cohen, William	http://www.senate.gov/~cohen/
MI	D	Levin, Carl	http://www.senate.gov/~levin/
MN	R	Grams, Rod	http://www.senate.gov/~grams/
MN	D	Wellstone, Paul	http://www.senate.gov/~wellstone/
MO	R	Ashcroft, John	http://www.senate.gov/~ashcroft/
MT	D	Baucus, Max	http://www.senate.gov/~baucus/
ND	D	Conrad, Kent	http://www.senate.gov/~conrad/
ND	D	Dorgan, Byron	http://www.bps.k12.nd.us/Dorgan/Dorgan.html
NE	D	Kerrey, Bob	http://www.senate.gov/~kerrey/
NH	R	Smith, Robert	http://www.senate.gov/~smith/
NJ	D	Bradley, Bill	http://www.senate.gov/~bradley/
NM	D	Bingaman, Jeff	http://www.senate.gov/~bingaman/
NV	D	Reid, Harry	http://www.senate.gov/~reid/
NY	D	Moynihan, Daniel Patrick	http://www.senate.gov/~moynihan/
OH	D	Glenn, John	http://little.nhlink.net/john-glenn/

State	Party	Name	Web Site
OH	R	DeWine, Michael	http://www.senate.gov/~dewine/
OK	R	Nickles, Don	http://www.senate.gov/~nickles/
OR	D	Wyden, Ron	http://www.house.gov/wyden/welcome.html
PA	R	Santorum, Rick	http://www.senate.gov/~santorum/
SC	D	Hollings, Ernest	http://www.senate.gov/~hollings/
SD	D	Daschle, Thomas	http://www.senate.gov/~daschle/
TN	R	Frist, Bill	http://www.senate.gov/~frist/ http://www.surgery.mc.vanderbilt.edu/frist/frist.html
TX	R	Hutchison, Kay Bailey	http://www.senate.gov/~hutchison/
UT	R	Bennett, Robert	http://www.senate.gov/~bennett/
UT	R	Hatch, Orrin	http://www.senate.gov/~hatch/
VA	D	Robb, Charles	http://www.senate.gov/~robb/
VA	R	Warner, John	http://www.senate.gov/~warner/
VT	D	Leahy, Patrick	http://www.senate.gov/~leahy/
VT	R	Jeffords, Jim	http://www.senate.gov/~jeffords/
WA	D	Murray, Patty	http://www.senate.gov/~murray/
WI	D	Feingold, Russell	http://www.senate.gov/~feingold/
WI	D	Kohl, Herbert	http://www.senate.gov/~kohl/
WV	D	Rockefeller, Jay	http://www.senate.gov/~rockefeller/
WY	R	Simpson, Alan	http://www.senate.gov/~simpson/

General Senate Sites

Senate:
> http://www.senate.gov

Senate Committee on Energy and Natural Resources:
> http://www.senate.gov/~energy/

Senate Committee on Small Business:
> http://www.senate.gov/~sbc/

Senate Committee on Veterans Affairs:
> http://www.senate.gov/~svac/

Senate Democratic Policy Committee:
    http://www.senate.gov/~dpc/

Senate Republican Conference:
    http://www.senate.gov/~src/

Senate Republican Policy Committee:
    http://www.senate.gov/~rpc/

Senate Office of the Legal Counsel:
    ftp://ftp.senate.gov/committee/legal/general/lchome.html

Senate Special Committee on Aging:
    http://www.senate.gov/~aging/

United States House of Representatives

Generic web sites are also available for House members under:
http://www.house.gov/mbr_dir/membr_dir.html

State	District	Party	Name	Web Site
AK	AL	R	Young, Don	http://www.state.ak.us/local/akpages /CONGRESS/akcondy.htm
AL	1	R	Callahan, Sonny	http://www.house.gov/callahan /welcome.html
AL	3	D	Browder, Glen	http://www.house.gov/browder /welcome.html
AL	5	D	Cramer, Bud	http://www.house.gov/cramer /welcome.html
AZ	1	R	Salmon, Matt	http://aspin.asu.edu/~pctp/salmon /salmon.html
AZ	2	D	Pastor, Ed	http://aspin.asu.edu/~pctp/pastor /pastor.html http://www.house.gov/pastor /welcome.html
AZ	3	R	Stump, Bob	http://aspin.asu.edu/~pctp/stump /stump.html
AZ	4	R	Shadegg, John	http://aspin.asu.edu/~pctp/shadegg /shadegg.html
AZ	5	R	Kolbe, Jim	http://www.house.gov/kolbe/welcome.html http://www.arizona.edu/kolbe/kolbe.html
AZ	6	R	Hayworth, John D.	http://aspin.asu.edu/~pctp/hayworth /hayworth.html

State	District	Party	Name	Web Site
CA	3	D	Fazio, Vic	http://www.house.gov/fazio/welcome.html
CA	7	D	Miller, George	http://www.house.gov/georgemiller/welcome.html
CA	8	R	Pelosi, Nancy	http://www.house.gov/pelosi/welcome.html
CA	9	D	Dellums, Ron	http://www.house.gov/dellums/welcome.html
CA	12	D	Lantos, Tom	http://www.house.gov/lantos/welcome.html
CA	14	D	Eshoo, Anna	http://www-eshoo.house.gov
CA	15	R	Campbell, Tom	http://www.campbell.org/
CA	16	D	Lofgren, Zoe	http://www.house.gov/lofgren/welcome.html
CA	17	D	Farr, Sam	http://www.house.gov/farr/welcome.html
CA	19	R	Radanovich, George	http://www.house.gov/radanovich/welcome.html
CA	40	R	Lewis, Jerry	http://www.house.gov/jerrylewis/
CA	41	R	Kim, Jay	http://www.house.gov/kim/welcome.html
CA	46	R	Dornan, Robert	http://www.umr.edu/~sears/primary/dornan.html
CA	47	R	Cox, Christopher	http://www.house.gov/cox/
CA	48	R	Packard, Ron	http://www.house.gov/packard/welcome.html
CA	49	R	Bilbray, Brian	http://www.house.gov/bilbray/welcome.html
CT	2	D	Gejdenson, Samuel	http://www.house.gov/gejdenson/welcome.html
CT	4	R	Shays, Christopher	http://www.house.gov/shays/welcome.html
DE	AL	R	Castle, Michael	http://www.house.gov/castle/welcome.html
FL	4	R	Fowler, Tillie	http://www.house.gov/fowler/welcome.html
FL	5	D	Thurman, Karen	http://www.house.gov/thurman/welcome.html
FL	6	R	Stearns, Cliff	http://www.house.gov/stearns/welcome.html
FL	9	R	Bilirakis, Michael	http://www.house.gov/bilirakis/welcome.html
FL	23	D	Hastings, Alcee	http://www.house.gov/alceehastings/welcome.html
GA	1	R	Kingston, Jack	http://www.gasou.edu/first_district
GA	8	R	Chambliss, Saxby	http://www.house.gov/chambliss/welcome.html
GU	AL	D	Underwood, Robert	http://www.house.gov/underwood/welcome.html
IA	1	R	Leach, Jim	http://www.house.gov/leach/welcome.html

State	District	Party	Name	Web Site
IL	1	D	Rush, Bobby	http://www.house.gov/rush/welcome.html
IL	15	R	Ewing, Thomas	http://www.house.gov/ewing/welcome.html
IL	20	D	Durbin, Richard	http://www.house.gov/durbin/welcome.html
IN	3	D	Roemer, Tim	http://www.house.gov/roemer/welcome.html
IN	4	R	Souder, Mark	http://www.house.gov/souder/welcome.html
IN	8	R	Hostettler, John johnhost@ hr.house.gov	http://www.house.gov/hostettler /welcome.html
IN	9	D	Hamilton, Lee	http://www.house.gov/hamilton /welcome.html
KS	2	R	Brownback, Sam	http://www.house.gov/brownback /welcome.html
KS	4	R	Tiahrt, Todd	http://www.house.gov/tiahrt/welcome.html
LA	5	R	McCrery, Jim	http://www.house.gov/mccrery/welcome.html
MA	4	D	Frank, Barney	http://www.house.gov/frank/welcome.html
MA	9	D	Moakley, Joe	http://www.house.gov/moakley/welcome.html
MD	2	R	Ehrlich, Robert	http://lattanze.loyola.edu:80/research/Ehrlich /index.html
MD	3	D	Cardin, Benjamin	http://www.house.gov/cardin/welcome.html
MD	4	D	Wynn, Albert	http://www.house.gov/wynn/welcome.html
+MD	7	D	Mfume, Kweisi	http://www.house.gov/mfume/welcome.html
MI	2	R	Hoekstra, Peter	http://www.house.gov/hoekstra /welcome.html
MI	3	R	Ehlers, Vern	http://www.house.gov/ehlers/welcome.html
MI	7	R	Smith, Nick	http://www.house.gov/nicksmith /welcome.html
MI	8	R	Chrysler, Dick	http://www.house.gov/chrysler /welcome.html
MI	14	D	Conyers, John	http://www.house.gov/conyers/welcome.html
MN	4	D	Vento, Bruce	http://www.house.gov/vento/welcome.html
MN	5	D	Sabo, Martin	http://www.house.gov/sabo/welcome.html
MN	6	D	Luther, Bill	http://www.house.gov/luther/welcome.html
MN	7	D	Peterson, Collin	http://www.house.gov/collinpeterson /welcome.html
MN	8	D	Oberstar, James	http://www.house.gov/oberstar/welcome.html
MO	2	R	Talent, James	http://www.house.gov/talent/welcome.html
MO	8	R	Emerson, Bill	http://www.house.gov/emerson/welcome.html
MS	2	D	Thompson, Bennie	http://www.house.gov/thompson/welcome.html

State	District	Party	Name	Web Site
NC	5	R	Burr, Richard	http://www.house.gov/burr/welcome.html
NE	2	R	Christensen, Jon	http://www.house.gov/christensen/welcome.html
NH	1	R	Zeliff, William	http://www.house.gov/zeliff/welcome.html
NJ	7	R	Franks, Bob	http://www.house.gov/bobfranks/welcome.html
NJ	13	D	Menendez, Bob	http://www.house.gov/menendez/welcome.html
NY	1	R	Forbes, Michael	http://www.house.gov/forbes/welcome.html
NY	2	R	Lazio, Rick	http://www.house.gov/lazio/welcome.html
NY	8	D	Nadler, Jerrold	http://www.house.gov/nadler/welcome.html
NY	16	D	Serrano, Jose	http://www.house.gov/serrano/welcome.html
NY	21	D	McNulty, Michael	http://www.house.gov/mcnulty/welcome.html
NY	23	R	Boehlert, Sherwood	http://www.house.gov/boehlert/welcome.html
OH	2	R	Portman, Rob	http://www.house.gov/portman/welcome.html
OH	4	R	Oxley, Michael	http://www.house.gov/oxley/welcome.html
OH	7	R	Hobson, David	http://www.house.gov/hobson/welcome.html
OH	10	R	Hoke, Martin	http://www.house.gov/hoke/welcome.html
OK	1	R	Largent, Steve	http://www.house.gov/largent/welcome.html
*OK	5	R	Istook, Ernest	http://www.house.gov/istook/welcome.html
OR	4	D	DeFazio, Pete	http://darkwing.uoregon.edu/~pdefazio /index.html
PA	12	D	Murtha, John	http://www.house.gov/murtha/welcome.html
PA	15	D	McHale, Paul	http://www.house.gov/mchale/welcome.html
PA	16	R	Walker, Robert	http://www.house.gov/walker/welcome.html
RI	1	D	Kennedy, Patrick	http://www.house.gov/patrickkennedy /welcome.html
SC	5	D	Spratt, John	http://www.house.gov/spratt/welcome.html
TN	3	R	Wamp, Zach	http://www.house.gov/wamp/welcome.html
TN	4	R	Hilleary, Van	http://www.house.gov/hilleary/welcome.html
TN	5	D	Clement, Bob	http://www.house.gov/clement/welcome.html
TN	9	D	Ford, Harold	http://www.house.gov/ford/welcome.html
TX	3	R	Johnson, Same	http://www.house.gov/samjohnson /welcome.html
TX	6	R	Barton, Joe	http://www.house.gov/barton/welcome.html
TX	21	R	Smith, Lamar	http://www.house.gov/lamarsmith /welcome.html
TX	22	R	Delay, Tom	http://www.house.gov/delay/welcome.html
TX	25	D	Bentsen, Ken	http://www.house.gov/bentsen/welcome.html
TX	26	R	Armey, Dick	http://www.house.gov/armey/welcome.html

State	District	Party	Name	Web Site
TX	29	D	Green, Gene	http://www.house.gov/green/welcome.html
VA	1	R	Bateman, Herbert	http://www.house.gov/bateman/welcome.html
VA	9	D	Boucher, Rick	http://www.house.gov/boucher/welcome.html
WA	1	R	White, Rick	http://www.house.gov/white/welcome.html
WA	3	R	Smith, Linda	http://www.house.gov/lindasmith/welcome.html
WA	9	R	Tate, Randy	http://home.worldweb.net/tate
WI	1	R	Neumann, Mark	http://www.house.gov/neumann/welcome.html
WI	3	R	Gunderson, Steve	http://www.house.gov/gunderson/welcome.html
WI	5	D	Barrett, Tom	http://www.house.gov/barrett/welcome.html
WI	8	R	Roth, Toby	http://www.house.gov/roth/welcome.html
WI	9	R	Sensenbrenner, James	http://www.house.gov/sensenbrenner/welcome.html
WV	2	D	Wise, Bob	http://www.house.gov/wise/welcome.html

*Elected to Senate, 1-30-96; web address expected to change

+Resigned 2-18-96; web site still active

House Web Site:
> http://www.house.gov/

House Banking/Subcommittee on Domestic & Intl. Monetary
> http://www.house.gov/castle/banking/welcome.html

House Econ.&Educational Opportunity:
> http://www.house.gov/eeo/welcome.html

House Govt.Reform& Oversight
> http://www.house.gov/reform/welcome.html

House Judiciary:
> http://www.house.gov/judiciary/welcome.html

House Resources:
> http://www.house.gov/resources/welcome.html

House Science:
> http://www.house.gov/science/welcome.html

House Science (Democrats):
> http://www.house.gov/science_democrats/welcome.html

House Standards of Official Conduct:
> http://www.house.gov/ethics/ethics_memos.html

House Transportation:
http://www.house.gov/transportation/welcome.html

House Democratic Caucus:
http://www.house.gov/demcaucus/welcome.html

House Democratic Leadership:
http://www.house.gov/democrats/

House Leadership:
http://www.house.gov/orgs_pub_hse_ldr_www.html

House Majority Whip:
http://www.house.gov/majoritywhip/welcome.html

House Republican Conference:
http://www.house.gov/gop/conference.html

House Republican Policy Committee:
http://www.house.gov/republican-policy/policyhome.htm

Joint Committee Web Sites

Joint Committee on Printing:
http/www.access.gpo.gov/demo/jcp.html

Joint Economic Committee:
http://www.town.hall.org:80/places/jec
http://www.senate.gov/~jec/
http://www.house.gov/jec/welcome.html
(House Republicans on JEC)

Congressional Black Caucus

http://drum.ncsc.org/~carter/CBC.html

The above information was compiled from the Senate and House Gophers, Capweb, David Morgan (http://www.geopages.com/CapitolHill/1007/), and contributions from individual citizens. It is updated on a continuous basis.

The most current version is available on the University of Michigan Library Gopher. Gopher to the University of Michigan Library Gopher. Path: Social Sciences/Government/U.S. Government: Legislative Branch/E-Mail Addresses.

Access is also provided through the Documents Center's web site: http://www.lib.umich.edu/libhome/Documents.center/federal.html and the ULIBRARY Gopher's web interface: gopher://una.hh.lib.umich.edu:70/00/socsci/poliscilaw/uslegi/conemail

Corrections/additions to graceyor@umich.edu

1996 Presidential Campaign Sites

http://www.clinton96.org/
http://www.dole96:com/
http://www.buchanan.org/
http://www.nashville.net/~lamar/
http://www.forbes96.com/

Sites to See

I have described a number of Internet resources in this book, and the following list provides the addresses for many of them.

Senator Ted Kennedy
   http://www.ai.mit.edu/projects/iiip/Kennedy/homepage.html

Open Government—Canada
   http://info.ic.gc.ca/opengov/

CapWeb
   http://policy.net

Senate Democratic Policy Committee
   http://www.senate.gov/~dpc

United States Senate
   http://www.senate.gov

House of Representatives
   http://www.house.gov

House Democratic Leadership
   http://www.house.gov/democrats/welcome.html

House Republican Conference
   http://www.house.gov/gop/conference.html

The Library of Congress
   http://lcweb.loc.gov/homepage/lchp.html

Thomas
   http://thomas.loc.gov/

GPO
   http://www.access.gpo.gov/

The Medicare Page
   http://www.senate.gov/~dpc/medicare.html

Senate Republican Policy Committee
   http://www.senate.gov/~rpc

Govline Congressional Committee Transcript Service
    http://world.std.com/govline/

Office of Senate Legal Counsel
    ftp://ftp.senate.gov/committee/legal/general/lchome.html

Office of the House Chief Administrative Officr
    http://www.house.gov/cao/credo.htm

Washington GOP Balanced Budget Web Site
    http://www.house.gov/white/budget/budget.html

Internet Multicasting Service: U.S. Congress Proceedings
    http://www.town.hall.org/radio/congress.html

Democratic Senatorial Campaign Committee
    http://www.dscc.org/d/dscc.html

Kennedy for Senate —1994
    http://www.dscc.org/d/ma.html

Tom Campbell for Congress
    http://www.campbell.org/

Jerry Estruth for Congress
    http://www.webcom.com/~digitals/states/ca/15/estruth.html

Voters Telecom Watch
    http://www.vtw.org/

Wyden for Senate
    http://www.teleport.com/~wyden/

Sims for Senate WWW Archive
    http://pantheon.cis.yale.edu/~lewison/sims.html

Bogus Dole for President
    http://www.dole96.org/dole96.html

NewtWatch
    http://www.cais.com:80/newtwatch/

Dole Watch
    http://user.aol.com/dolewatch1/private/page1.htm

Gephardt Web Watch
    http://www.crl.com:80/~becnel/dick.html

The Unofficial Dianne Feinstein
    http://www.zpub.com/un/un-df.html

The World According to Helms
    http://www.nando.net/sproject/jesse/helms.html
Hayworth Watch
    http://www.azdem.org/6thcd/jd1.htm
The Newt Gingrich WWW Fan Page
    http://www.clark.net/pub/jeffd/mr_newt.html
Live Multicast Feeds of House and Senate Floor
    http://town.hall.org/radio/congress.html
Congressional Memory Project
    http://town.hall.org/Congress/Memory/index.html
Joint Economic Committee Hearing — 6/12/95
    http://town.hall.org/places/jec/Hearing/
The Federal Election Commission
    http:www.fec.gov
ROLL CALL — The Newspaper of Capitol Hill
    http://www.rollcall.com
C-SPAN
    http://www.c-span.org
ILC Glossary of Internet Terms
    http://www.matisse.net/files/glossary.html
Highway 1
    http://www.highway1.org

Index